Critical Terrorism Studies at Ten

Critical Terrorism Studies emerged around 2007, in the context of the rapidly intensifying War on Terror. It was in this era that "terrorism" became a "growth industry" which generated a huge amount of academic research as well as social and political activity. Yet a yawning gap developed between the actual material threat posed by terrorists, and the level of investment and activity devoted to responding to this threat. Similarly, the quality of terrorism research was noticeably weak and lacking in methodological rigour.

Critical Terrorism Studies set out to explore the exceptional treatment of political violence, to challenge the political manipulation of terrorism fears and increase in draconian anti-terrorism legislation, and to address some of the conceptual and methodological failings of terrorism research.

In the 10 years since the journal *Critical Studies on Terrorism* was launched, that context and mission remains as important as ever. This volume looks back on the achievements and failures of Critical Terrorism Studies in this period, as well as collecting state of the art research into terrorism discourse, queerness and the War on Terror, the Prevent Strategy, epistemology in terrorism studies, state repression, the ambiguous ends of militant campaigns, the epistemology of preventative counterterrorism, and the question of non-violent responses to terror.

The chapters in this book were originally published as a special issue of *Critical Studies on Terrorism*.

Richard Jackson is Professor of Peace and Conflict Studies at the University of Otago, New Zealand. He is one of the founding members of the Critical Terrorism Studies project and the Editor-in-Chief of *Critical Studies on Terrorism*.

Harmonie Toros is Senior Lecturer in International Conflict Analysis at the University of Kent, UK. Her research lies at the crossroad between conflict resolution/conflict transformation, peace studies, and terrorism studies.

Lee Jarvis is Professor of International Politics at the University of East Anglia, UK. His current research explores the proscription of terrorist organisations, and the impact of 'British Values' discourses upon Muslim communities across Eastern England.

Charlotte Heath-Kelly is Associate Professor of Politics and International Studies at the University of Warwick, UK. Her research explores the memorialisation of terrorist attacks, as well as the development of counter-radicalisation policies and practices.

Critical Terrorism Studies at Ten
Contributions, Cases and Future Challenges

Edited by
**Richard Jackson, Harmonie Toros,
Lee Jarvis and Charlotte Heath-Kelly**

LONDON AND NEW YORK

First published 2019
by Routledge
2 Park Square, Milton Park, Abingdon, Oxon, OX14 4RN, UK

and by Routledge
711 Third Avenue, New York, NY 10017, USA

Routledge is an imprint of the Taylor & Francis Group, an informa business

Introduction, Chapters 1-2, 4-5, 7-9 © 2019 Taylor & Francis
Chapter 3 © 2017 Oxford University Press
Chapter 6 © 2017 Charlotte Heath-Kelly

With the exception of Chapter 6, no part of this book may be reprinted or reproduced or utilised in any form or by any electronic, mechanical, or other means, now known or hereafter invented, including photocopying and recording, or in any information storage or retrieval system, without permission in writing from the publishers. For details on the rights for Chapter 6, please see the chapter's Open Access footnote.

Trademark notice: Product or corporate names may be trademarks or registered trademarks, and are used only for identification and explanation without intent to infringe.

British Library Cataloguing in Publication Data
A catalogue record for this book is available from the British Library

ISBN 13: 978-1-138-31808-3

Typeset in Myriad Pro
by RefineCatch Limited, Bungay, Suffolk

Publisher's Note
The publisher accepts responsibility for any inconsistencies that may have arisen during the conversion of this book from journal articles to book chapters, namely the possible inclusion of journal terminology.

Disclaimer
Every effort has been made to contact copyright holders for their permission to reprint material in this book. The publishers would be grateful to hear from any copyright holder who is not here acknowledged and will undertake to rectify any errors or omissions in future editions of this book.

Contents

Citation Information	vii
Notes on Contributors	ix

Introduction: 10 years of *Critical Studies on Terrorism* — 1
Richard Jackson, Harmonie Toros, Lee Jarvis and Charlotte Heath-Kelly

1. "9/11 is alive and well" or how critical terrorism studies has sustained the 9/11 narrative — 7
   Harmonie Toros

2. Interpretation, judgement and dialogue: a hermeneutical recollection of causal analysis in critical terrorism studies — 24
   Lucas Van Milders

3. "The terrorist": the out-of-place and on-the-move "perverse homosexual" in international relations — 44
   Cynthia Weber

4. Beyond binaries: analysing violent state actors in Critical Studies — 57
   Shir Daphna-Tekoah and Ayelet Harel-Shalev

5. "Academics for Peace" in Turkey: a case of criminalising dissent and critical thought via counterterrorism policy — 78
   Bahar Baser, Samim Akgönül and Ahmet Erdi Öztürk

6. The geography of pre-criminal space: epidemiological imaginations of radicalisation risk in the UK Prevent Strategy, 2007–2017 — 101
   Charlotte Heath-Kelly

7. Prevention, knowledge, justice: Robert Nozick and counterterrorism — 124
   Matthias Leese

8. How terrorism ends – and does not end: the Basque case — 142
   Joseba Zulaika and Imanol Murua

9. CTS, counterterrorism and non-violence — 161
   Richard Jackson

Index — 175

Citation Information

The following chapters were originally published in *Critical Studies on Terrorism*, volume 10, issue 2 (August 2017). When citing this material, please use the original page numbering for each article, as follows:

Introduction
Introduction: 10 years of Critical Studies on Terrorism
Richard Jackson, Harmonie Toros, Lee Jarvis and Charlotte Heath-Kelly
Critical Studies on Terrorism, volume 10, issue 2 (August 2017), pp. 197–202

Chapter 1
"9/11 is alive and well" or how critical terrorism studies has sustained the 9/11 narrative
Harmonie Toros
Critical Studies on Terrorism, volume 10, issue 2 (August 2017), pp. 203–219

Chapter 2
Interpretation, judgement and dialogue: a hermeneutical recollection of causal analysis in critical terrorism studies
Lucas Van Milders
Critical Studies on Terrorism, volume 10, issue 2 (August 2017), pp. 220–239

Chapter 3
"The terrorist": the out-of-place and on-the-move "perverse homosexual" in international relations
Cynthia Weber
Critical Studies on Terrorism, volume 10, issue 2 (August 2017), pp. 240–252

Chapter 4
Beyond binaries: analysing violent state actors in Critical Studies
Shir Daphna-Tekoah and Ayelet Harel-Shalev
Critical Studies on Terrorism, volume 10, issue 2 (August 2017), pp. 253–273

Chapter 5
"Academics for Peace" in Turkey: a case of criminalising dissent and critical thought via counterterrorism policy
Bahar Baser, Samim Akgönül and Ahmet Erdi Öztürk
Critical Studies on Terrorism, volume 10, issue 2 (August 2017), pp. 274–296

CITATION INFORMATION

Chapter 6
The geography of pre-criminal space: epidemiological imaginations of radicalisation risk in the UK Prevent Strategy, 2007–2017
Charlotte Heath-Kelly
Critical Studies on Terrorism, volume 10, issue 2 (August 2017), pp. 297–319

Chapter 7
Prevention, knowledge, justice: Robert Nozick and counterterrorism
Matthias Leese
Critical Studies on Terrorism, volume 10, issue 2 (August 2017), pp. 320–337

Chapter 8
How terrorism ends – and does not end: the Basque case
Joseba Zulaika and Imanol Murua
Critical Studies on Terrorism, volume 10, issue 2 (August 2017), pp. 338–356

Chapter 9
CTS, counterterrorism and non-violence
Richard Jackson
Critical Studies on Terrorism, volume 10, issue 2 (August 2017), pp. 357–369

For any permission-related enquiries please visit:
http://www.tandfonline.com/page/help/permissions

Notes on Contributors

Samim Akgönül is a Professor at the Faculty of Law, Social Science and History at the University of Strasbourg, France, and a Researcher at the French National Centre for Scientific Research. He also teaches Political Science at Syracuse University.

Bahar Baser is a Research Fellow at the Centre for Trust, Peace and Social Relations (CTPSR) at Coventry University, UK, and an Associate Research Fellow at the Security Institute for Governance and Leadership in Africa (SIGLA) at Stellenbosch University, South Africa.

Shir Daphna-Tekoah is a Senior Lecturer in the School of Social Work of the Ashkelon Academic College, Ashkelon, Israel, and a Researcher in the Social Work Department, Kaplan Medical Center, Rehovot, Israel. Her academic interests include Gender, Health and Violence, Women Combatants, Child Abuse and Neglect, and Dissociation and Trauma.

Ayelet Harel-Shalev is a Senior Lecturer in the Conflict Management and Resolution Program and the Department of Politics and Government at Ben-Gurion University of the Negev, Beer-Sheva, Israel. Her academic interests include Feminist International Relations, Women Combatants, Ethnic Conflicts and Democracy, Minority Rights, and Women and Politics.

Charlotte Heath-Kelly is Associate Professor of Politics and International Studies at the University of Warwick, UK. Her research explores the memorialisation of terrorist attacks, as well as the development of counter-radicalisation policies and practices.

Richard Jackson is Professor of Peace and Conflict Studies at the University of Otago, New Zealand. He is one of the founding members of the Critical Terrorism Studies project and the Editor-in-Chief of *Critical Studies on Terrorism*.

Lee Jarvis is Professor of International Politics at the University of East Anglia, UK. His current research explores the proscription of terrorist organisations, and the impact of 'British Values' discourses upon Muslim communities across Eastern England.

Matthias Leese is a Senior Researcher at the Center for Security Studies, ETH Zurich, Switzerland. His main research interests are in Critical Security Studies, Surveillance Studies, and STS – specifically, the development and design of security technologies, and the wider societal and normative consequences that emerge from the implementation of technologies in particular contexts.

Imanol Murua is a Lecturer on Journalism at the University of the Basque Country, Spain. He has been a professional journalist with various magazines, newspapers and journals, and he is the author of six books and the co-author of four books.

NOTES ON CONTRIBUTORS

Ahmet Erdi Öztürk is a PhD candidate and Research Assistant at the Faculty of Law, Social Science and History at the University of Strasbourg, France. He is the Turkey correspondent for EUREL (Sociological and Legal Data on Religions in Europe). He mainly focuses on religion-politics and international relations; specifically on the Balkan Peninsula, Turkey, and continental Europe.

Harmonie Toros is a Senior Lecturer in International Conflict Analysis at the University of Kent, UK. Her research lies at the crossroad between conflict resolution/conflict transformation, peace studies, and terrorism studies.

Lucas Van Milders is a PhD candidate and an Assistant Lecturer in International Relations at the University of Kent UK. His research focuses on International Relations Theory and radical hermeneutics. His work lies at the intersection between political and international thought and deals with the notion of epistemicide, the murder of knowledge.

Cynthia Weber is Professor of International Relations at the University of Sussex, UK. She has written extensively on sovereignty, intervention, and US foreign policy, as well as on feminist, gendered, and sexualised understandings, and organisations of international relations.

Joseba Zulaika is a Professor at the Center for Basque Studies at the University of Nevada, USA. He teaches an introductory course to Basque Cultural Studies and two capstone courses – on Basque Culture (online), and on Museums, Architecture and City Renewal: the Bilbao Guggenheim Museum.

INTRODUCTION

Introduction: 10 years of *Critical Studies on Terrorism*

Richard Jackson, Harmonie Toros ⓘ, Lee Jarvis and Charlotte Heath-Kelly ⓘ

When the editors of *Critical Studies on Terrorism* wrote their introduction to the inaugural issue in April 2008, they noted that "terrorism" was a "growth industry" which generated a huge amount of social and political activity, and affected an extensive list of areas of social and cultural life (Breen Smyth et al. 2008, 1). They also noted that there was a yawning gap between the actual material threat posed by terrorists, and the level of investment and activity devoted to responding to it. They suggested that a central analytical task facing critical scholars of terrorism was therefore to explain "how such a small set of behaviours by such small numbers of individuals generates such a pervasive, intrusive and complex series of effects across the world" (ibid). Lastly, they noted that the political, legal, cultural and academic context in which the journal was being launched was characterised by a very violent global war on terror, frequent moral panics and the political manipulation of terrorism fears, increasingly draconian anti-terrorism legislation, and the mass proliferation of academic and cultural terrorism-related texts.

It is clear that little has changed in this regard in the 10 years since *Critical Studies on Terrorism* (CST) was launched; the context in which the journal first began its work remains largely unchanged. In fact, it could be argued that, if anything, the editors underestimated how transformative the terrorism discourse would be of society and culture in the following decade – particularly in the global North – and the extent to which the transformations engendered would stretch and sometimes exceed our theoretical and conceptual capacities to understand, explain and in most cases, resist the transformations. The aim of this Introduction is to briefly reflect on the first 10 years of the journal's successes and failures, particularly in relation to some of the key aspirations and hopes that were laid out by the founding editors and the context in which they have since played out. However, more importantly, we aim to take the opportunity afforded by the 10-year anniversary to reflect on the future of the journal and its erstwhile contributors, and to express our hopes and aspirations for the broader field of critical terrorism studies (CTS) as we go forward into the second decade of this journal.

Looking back, the first point to note is that the journal remains committed to its original self-identification as a "research orientation that is willing to challenge dominant knowledge and understandings of terrorism, is sensitive to the politics of labelling in the terrorism field, is transparent about its own values and political standpoints, adheres to a set of responsible research ethics, and is committed to a broadly defined notion of emancipation" (Breen Smyth et al. 2008, 2). Even the most cursory survey of the journal's 10 volumes provides ample evidence that the editors and contributors have remained loyal to these important commitments, even when they have been criticised for doing so (see Jones and Smith 2009, 2011; Michel and Richards 2009).

More specifically, a survey of the journal supports the assessment that it has been successful in its goal of provoking and encouraging open and rigorous debate on a wide array of important issues, not least on the question of the intrinsic value of critical terrorism studies itself (see Horgan and Boyle 2008; Michel and Richards 2009), and the way in which the CTS field has evolved and developed over the years. In addition to many examples from previous volumes, in this special issue, two of the contributing articles raise questions about the way in which CTS has developed over the past decade that perhaps does not live up to some of its stated aims (see Toros 2017; Van Milders 2017). In our assessment, this speaks to the growing maturity and confidence of a field (and the journal) which can question its most fundamental and treasured assumptions, theories, approaches and values, including questions about emancipation, narrow versus wide conceptions of criticality, the reification of the "terrorism" discourse and the like. Going forward, we remain committed to fostering rather than flattening out or resolving such creative tensions, as it is in the process of grappling with such tensions and conflicts that new ideas and questions emerge. We also remain committed to encouraging further debate and criticism of CTS itself, as we view this as a necessary part of reflexivity and continuing intellectual development.

Related to this, the journal has continued to encourage greater reflexivity among scholars of terrorism about the ethics and consequences of the research process, the ways in which knowledge is used by different actors, and the role of the scholar in relation to their research subjects and to existing power structures in society. A recent issue, for example, includes a debate between two of the current editors about whether CTS scholars ought to engage with policy-makers or instead reject policy relevance and make common cause with resistance groups (see Jackson 2016; Toros 2016). Despite such disagreements on with whom one should engage, CTS has remained committed to an engagement with the world, whether by standing quite literally side by side with protest movements across the world (as advocated by Jackson 2016 and in this issue) or through listening empathetically to Israeli women combatants (as argued in Daphna-Tekoah and Harel-Shalev also in this issue).

More broadly, the journal aimed to draw in new and existing researchers from outside the terrorism studies field, encourage and publish early career scholars, pluralise the theoretical, methodological and disciplinary basis of terrorism-related research, and encourage research on a range of subjects that tended to be ignored in much orthodox terrorism research. Although these aims remain live and ongoing, the journal has done much to realise them to date, not least in the special issue we present here which consists of a collection of articles which employ and engage with queer theory, critical realism, gender studies, memory studies, and political philosophy, among others, and which discuss topics as wide-ranging as the cultural-political construction of 9/11, causality in terrorism research, state terrorism, counter-radicalisation, the queering of IR, state repression, counterterrorism, the history of ETA, and gender and violence. Once again, this plurality and diversity speaks to the maturing of the field and the success of its aim to provide a broad "home" for the "critical" study of terrorism and counterterrorism.

However, at the same time, an honest appraisal of the past 10 years shows that a number of the editors' original aims are yet to be fully realised. For example, it remains the case that the majority of contributors to the journal originate from and/or work in the global north, and the perspectives and concerns of the global south are still rarely heard. And, if we look at the variety of "critical" approaches employed in the journal's articles, it is noticeable that post-colonialism is rarely employed as a framework of analysis. Although there have been concerted efforts in the wider network to begin to address this – the Critical Studies on Terrorism Working Group's annual conference of 2016 was titled *Intersecting Critical Terrorism Studies and (Post)Colonialism: Standards, Subjects And Spectacle* – there is, clearly, a continuing need to take further steps to decolonise CTS and to draw in the voices of the global south through, for example, assisting global south scholars to publish in the journal.

In relation to one of the most publicised calls by CTS and the original journal editors, there continues to be a dearth of research on the many aspects of state terrorism. While research on state counterterrorism has surged in the past 10 years, including research on violent forms of counterterrorism such as torture and war on terror, the total number of articles which examine aspects of state terrorism is disappointingly low – although articles which have been published have made an important contribution (see, for example, Furtado 2015; Jarvis and Lister 2014). Within this broader failure, two questions stand out. The first is the need to investigate the overlap between state terrorism and counterterrorism and the difficulty of distinguishing the two conceptually and empirically. CTS needs to question the term "counterterrorism" in the same way it has questioned the term "terrorism". This, in turn, raises questions about the compatibility of different research agendas within critical terrorism studies, including, for instance, between historical materialist analyses of state terrorism and discursive explorations of the ways in which "(state) terrorism" is constructed. Second, in a research field with its fair share of taboos, the specific taboo on speaking about particular examples or campaigns of state terrorism remains particularly noticeable. In late 2008, for instance, the journal editors debated among themselves whether it was the right time to publish a special issue on the nature, causes and consequences of Israeli state terrorism, but ultimately decided that the professional risks for the journal and the contributors to such an issue would be too high, given the kind of response public discussions of Israeli state terrorism and repression tends to generate.

It could be argued that this decision and a broader failure to interrogate Western state terrorisms in particular speaks to a common characteristic of many "critical" projects: namely, an unconscious desire for acceptance and legitimacy within and beyond the academy, and therefore, a certain hesitation or timidity towards speaking out too loudly on controversial or polarising issues. If this is the case here, going forward, it calls for critical self-examination and a conscious acceptance that remaining "critical" necessarily involves courage, risk, and the willingness to go against the grain – with all that this might entail in relation to academic credibility and legitimacy. This, of course, may be far easier for certain types of researcher, with certain demographic or professional attributes (seniority, employment status, nationality, ethnicity, gender and so on), working in certain types of academic role or institution, than for others.

Lastly, looking back, it is clear that the so-called Atlantic divide between terrorism scholars doing "orthodox" research mostly located in North America, and CTS scholars mostly located in Europe and elsewhere remains as wide as ever. Although there may now be name recognition for the journal and the broader CTS field, the level of dialogue and engagement remains as low as ever. In fact, after an initial, somewhat tentative dialogue in which a number of critiques of CTS from orthodox scholars were published in the journal, too little subsequent dialogue has occurred. Although there are exceptions, scholars working on orthodox research questions or paradigms tend to confine their discussions to forums and venues sympathetic to this work, while CTS scholars tend do the same. It may be the case that the original editors and CTS as a whole were overly optimistic about the possibility that the profound ontological, epistemological and praxealogical differences between the two orientations could be sufficiently bridged for real dialogue to occur. Nonetheless, the current editors remain optimistic and hopeful that such a dialogue might one day occur, and might go beyond adversarial positioning towards a more creative, generative discussion.

In a related reflection, we also note that the CTS field remains tangentially linked to – rather than integrated within – European Critical Security Studies research. These Critical Security Studies research agendas often take counterterrorism practice as their field of exploration, focusing on the deployment of risk calculus, critical infrastructure protection, surveillance of financial transactions and the materiality of counterterrorist technologies (Aradau 2010; Bellanova and Duez 2012; De Goede 2012), but the CTS project has remained somewhat distinct from these wider projects. Why are these topics of critical research on counterterrorism published elsewhere? Does the CTS project appear somehow unwelcoming to these traditions of thought, given its origination in more Anglo-American traditions of research into terrorism? There are both advantages and disadvantages to this parallel positioning alongside European IR. CTS retains a distinct identity as a research brand catering to questions of gender, memory, epistemology and cultural discourse in the field of terrorism studies; however, the alienation of the CTS project from broader research on security praxis and calculation creates a puzzling disconnect from the European IR field. Questions of materiality and technology in counterterrorism practice are of great relevance to the CTS project, but remain underrepresented (with the exception of Hoijtink 2015).

In short, 10 years after the first issue of *Critical Studies on Terrorism* was published, we celebrate its substantive achievements, reflect on its continuing failures and weaknesses, and look to the future with a renewed sense of purpose, courage and optimism. We offer this issue as a kind of exemplar of what rigorous, theoretically pluralistic, creative, "critical" approaches to the study of terrorism and counterterrorism can offer. We hope that it will provoke debate, critical reflection, inspiration and the courage to confront some of the most pressing issues facing our world in an intellectually rigorous, and practically emancipatory manner.

Finally, we take this opportunity to thank a great many people who have contributed to the growth and success of the journal over the years. Without the tireless work of all the editors, editorial assistants and editorial board members who do the day-to-day work, the journal would have failed at the first hurdle. In addition, we are most grateful to all the researchers and scholars who have contributed their work to be published, and to the legion of reviewers who have rigorously assessed the quality of each publication.

Journals cannot exist without all the unpaid intellectual labour and expertise of their contributors and reviewers. We are also grateful to the team at Routledge who took a chance on launching a new journal, and have since then professionally supported and sustained its smooth running. Lastly, we want to thank all of the supporters of the journal and the wider community of CTS scholars, including the BISA Critical Studies on Terrorism Working Group (CSTWG), who have encouraged and promoted the journal and contributed articles, special issues, ideas and general enthusiasm. We hope that this relationship between the journal and the wider community of CTS can continue to grow and mature over the next 10 years.

Disclosure statement

No potential conflict of interest was reported by the authors.

ORCID

Harmonie Toros http://orcid.org/0000-0002-9139-5292
Charlotte Heath-Kelly http://orcid.org/0000-0002-5237-4691

References

Aradau, C. 2010. "Security that Matters: Critical Infrastructure and Objects of Protection." *Security Dialogue* 41 (5): 491–514. doi:10.1177/0967010610382687.
Bellanova, R., and D. Duez. 2012. "A Different View on the Making of European Security: The EU Passenger Name Record System as A Socio-Technical Assemblage." *European Foreign Affairs Review* 17 (Special Issue): 109–124.

Breen Smyth, M., J. Gunning, R. Jackson, G. Kassimeris, and P. Robinson, eds. 2008. "Critical Terrorism Studies – an Introduction". *Critical Studies on Terrorism* 1 (1): 1–4. doi:10.1080/17539150701868538.

De Goede, M. 2012. *Speculative Security: The Politics of Pursuing Terrorist Monies*. Minneapolis: University of Minnesota Press.

Furtado, H. 2015. "Against State Terror: Lessons on Memory, Counterterrorism and Resistance from the Global South." *Critical Studies on Terrorism* 8 (1): 72–89. doi:10.1080/17539153.2015.1005936.

Hoijtink, M. 2015. "Performativity and the Project: Enacting Urban Transport Security in Europe." *Critical Studies on Terrorism* 8 (1): 130–146. doi:10.1080/17539153.2015.1005937.

Horgan, J., and M. J. Boyle. 2008. "A Case against 'Critical Terrorism Studies'." *Critical Studies on Terrorism* 1 (1): 51–64. doi:10.1080/17539150701848225.

Jackson, R. 2016. "To Be or Not to Be Policy Relevant? Power, Emancipation and Resistance in CTS Research." *Critical Studies on Terrorism* 9 (1): 120–125. doi:10.1080/17539153.2016.1147771.

Jarvis, L., and M. Lister. 2014. "State Terrorism Research and Critical Terrorism Studies: An Assessment." *Critical Studies on Terrorism* 7 (1): 43–61. doi:10.1080/17539153.2013.877669.

Jones, M., and M. L. R. Smith. 2009. "We are All Terrorists Now: Critical – or Hypocritical – Studies on Terrorism?" *Studies in Conflict and Terrorism* 32 (4): 292–302. doi:10.1080/10576100902744128.

Jones, M., and M. L. R. Smith. 2011. "Terrorology and Methodology: A Reply to Dixit and Stump." *Studies in Conflict and Terrorism* 34 (6): 512–522. doi:10.1080/1057610X.2011.571196.

Michel, T., and A. Richards. 2009. "False Dawns or New Horizons? Further Issues and Challenges for Critical Terrorism Studies." *Critical Studies on Terrorism* 2 (3): 399–413. doi:10.1080/17539150903306097.

Toros, H. 2016. "Dialogue, Praxis and the State: A Response to Richard Jackson." *Critical Studies on Terrorism* 9 (1): 126–130. doi:10.1080/17539153.2016.1147775.

Toros, H. 2017. "'9/11 Is Alive and Well' or How Critical Terrorism Studies Has Sustained the 9/11 Narrative." *Critical Studies on Terrorism* 10 (2): 203–219. doi:10.1080/17539153.2017.1337326.

Van Milders, L. 2017. "Interpretation, Judgement, and Dialogue: A Hermeneutical Recollection of Causal Analysis in Critical Terrorism Studies." *Critical Studies on Terrorism* 10 (2): 220–239. doi:10.1080/17539153.2017.1335383.

"9/11 is alive and well" or how critical terrorism studies has sustained the 9/11 narrative

Harmonie Toros 🔘

ABSTRACT
This article argues that despite engaging in a powerful critique of the construction of the attacks of 11 September 2001 (or "9/11") as temporal break, critical terrorism scholars have sustained and reproduced this same construction of "9/11". Through a systematic analysis of the research articles published in *Critical Studies on Terrorism*, this article illustrates how critical scholars have overall failed to extricate themselves from this dominant narrative, as they inhabit the same visual, emotional and professional landscape as those they critique. After examining how CTS has reproduced but also renegotiated this narrative, the article concludes with what Michel Foucault would describe as an "effective history" of the attacks – in this case, a personal narrative of how the attacks did not constitute a moment of personal rupture but nonetheless later became a backdrop to justify my scholarship and career. It ends with a renewal of Maya Zeyfuss' call to forget "9/11".

Introduction

... I slept through 9/11 ...

"Pre-9/11", "post 9/11", "since 9/11", "in the wake of 9/11", "prior to 9/11", "following 9/11": No specific day has been quite as ubiquitous in the 21st-century political landscape, and *Critical Studies on Terrorism* has led the way over the past 10 years in offering a powerful critique of the politics behind this temporal construction. From Richard Jackson (2005) to Lee Jarvis (2008) to Holland and Jarvis (2014), many have in this journal and elsewhere engaged in a thorough investigation of the construction of "9/11" as a temporal marker – primarily one of rupture, but as Jarvis (2008, 246) argues, also one of temporal linearity and timelessness. As they have demonstrated, this construction serves to justify a violent counterterrorism response and delegitimise other possible responses such as negotiations and dialogue (Jackson 2005), creates "9/11" as a cause (of the war on terror) that itself is uncaused (Zeyfuss 2003), and silences or attempts to silence any alternative reading of the attacks. "9/11" exemplifies the observation made by Meir Sternberg (1990, 902) that "[t]he and-then form avoids you having to ask the 'why?' question."

This article aims both to further this already rich literature and to challenge it. It aims to further it by drawing on historiographical research on the production of chronologies across the centuries and their political implications, particularly focusing on how chronologies have been used as an extension of hegemonic power – that is, by extending sovereignty over lands that adopt the hegemon's chronology. If, as Rowlandson (2015, 20) argues, definitions are "really a debate about who owns the words", then chronologies are really a debate about who owns time. By successfully spreading a "9/11" timeline or chronology on the world, the US administration then led by President George W. Bush and sustained by western political leaders since has effectively extended western sovereignty over global time.

In part two, the article goes further to examine how, despite CTS' critique of the construction of "9/11" as a temporal marker, many CTS scholars have actually adopted this very same construction. Through a qualitative and quantitative analysis of every research article published by this journal since its inception in 2008 (totaling 219), this article will show how the CTS subfield has sustained and reproduced the narrative of "9/11" as the opening of a new era. I will argue that this has two origins. First, it reflects the fact that CTS scholars are part of the same visual, emotional and professional landscape as mainstream international relations (IR), security and terrorism scholars. They are thus vulnerable to the same perceptive dispositions that Pierre Bourdieu (1977) calls *habitus*. The article thus challenges the construction of CTS as "exceptional" or immune to mainstream *habitus*. Second, I will argue that while internalising this construction, CTS scholars renegotiated its understanding into a different temporal rupture from that put forward by the dominant "9/11" narrative. Indeed, rather than arguing that on "9/11" a relatively peaceful and orderly world was forever changed by this "new threat" called terrorism (particularly of the radical Islamic kind), CTS scholars collectively have constructed a narrative in which the "pre-9/11" world was to be sure violent but was *progressively* inching towards less violence. It has been replaced by a "post-9/11" world in which states have given up the pretense of progress and more openly embraced violent logics and practices. The section will conclude with why such a construction remains problematic.

The final section of this article will offer what Michel Foucault (1984, 89) calls an "effective history", that is, a history that "shortens its vision to those things nearest to it – the body, nervous system, nutrition, digestion, and energies." Through a personal history of "9/11" – from my lived experience in New York City on the day of the attacks to its construction as a temporal marker in my life – this final section aims to offer an illustration of how what was lived as a moment of continuity on a personal level was later constructed, through an internalisation of the dominant narrative, as a marker of temporal rupture. This final section aims to make me "the target of my words" (Inayatullah 2010, 2), but also offers a modest counter-narrative that may become a "kind of dissociating view that is capable of shattering the unity of man's being through which it was thought that he could extend his sovereignty to the events of the past" (Foucault 1984, 87). In the conclusion, the article will renew Maja Zeyfuss' (2003) appeal to forget "9/11", arguing that it will make us better teachers and more coherent critical scholars.

"9/11" as temporal rupture and the extension of sovereign power over time

> A beginning is that which does not itself follow anything by causal necessity, but after which something naturally is or comes to be. (Aristotle 1902, 31)

As Holland and Jarvis (2014, 194–195) effectively argue, "9/11" came to be near universally adopted following a "sustained attempt" by the Bush administration soon after the attacks "to construct the date of 11 September 2001 as a marker of crisis and historical discontinuity."[1] From George W. Bush's assertion that "night fell on a different world" (quoted in Holland and Jarvis 2014, 194) to then-Vice President Dick Cheney's characterisation of that day as "a day like no other we have ever experienced" (quoted in Jarvis 2008, 246), the administration successfully called upon the US public and beyond to mark the memory as a fundamental break not only in the life of the United States as a nation, or in international politics more broadly, but in their own lives. As noted by Maja Zeyfuss (2003, 514), when Bush told his public that "each of us will remember what happened that day", what he was saying was "nothing as it was before" (ibid., 525). Thus, "[b]efore anyone really had time to think about what it all means, about what, if anything, we should do, September 11 had already been turned into a symbol, into a watershed" (ibid.). US administration officials, relayed by other political figures across the world, "inserted a politically driven narrative" into the "void of meaning" (Jackson 2005, 31) that immediately succeeded the attacks so that "9/11" would become "known as a horrible defining date in history" (Baker quoted in Jackson 2005, 33).

This had several functions. Importantly, and in line with Aristotle's understanding of the functions of a beginning in a narrative, "9/11" was turned into "the root, the cause, the origin" (Zeyfuss 2003, 520) – a cause that crucially was uncaused. In this narrative,[2] any relationship between previous US policies and the attacks was eliminated, making "9/11" a simple act of evil whose perpetrators needed to be destroyed:

> It was as if nothing had ever happened before … In other words, the events of September 11 are the 'cause' of its policies today. We may not, however, ask how we got there lest we be disrespectful of the dead. (Zeyfuss 2003, 520)

This construction allowed the US administration to delegitimise any questioning or even reference to the decades of violent US policy in the Middle East and elsewhere. They were irrelevant, as they had not caused the attacks, and mentioning them became an unpatriotic attempt to justify these callous acts (see also Jackson 2005).

Importantly, this watershed narrative was extremely effective in both legitimising the actions of states domestically and internationally, and in delegitimising dissenting voices. Jackson (2005) argues that the "war on terror" was written as the only natural and just response to the attacks: "[o]ne of the purposes of constructing a myth of exceptional grievance is to divest the nation of the moral responsibility for counter-violence" (ibid., 36). On the other hand, alternative non-violent responses were delegitimised. As George W. Bush (quoted in Toros 2012, 163) said in 2003, "the only way to deal with these people is to bring them to justice. You can't talk to them, you can't negotiate with them." Thus, the "9/11" narrative as a moment of temporal rupture sustained policies of violent counter-terrorism the world over and undermined those working toward non-violent responses. Furthermore, this narrative not only dominated political circles but was also adopted by mainstream terrorism and security studies. To quote but a few, Hoffman (2006, 22), one of the most cited terrorism scholars, speaks of the "chain of events that began on 9/11"; Wilkinson (2011, 9), in his later edition of *Terrorism vs Democracy: The Liberal State Response*, writes that "the 9/11 suicide hijacking attacks … had a colossal effect not only on US foreign and security policy and public opinion. They had a major influence on international relations, the US and international economy and on the patterns of conflict in the Middle East."

Many of the arguments on the political implications of the "9/11" narrative as a moment of temporal rupture have thus already been made. Here, however, I wish to argue that the overall effect of the "9/11" temporal narrative and of its near universal adoption was an extension of US hegemony over world time. To support this argument, it is useful to draw on historiographical work on how the establishment of eras and chronologies has historically been a means to extend sovereign power over other territories. Masayuki Sato's (1991, 290) analysis of East Asian chronologies and the establishment of eras linked to new dynasties stresses how the adoption by other states of the new era name represented the extension of sovereign power:

> It became normal practice in international relations that a country under the suzerainty of another country should use the era name of the suzerain country. This shows that an era name was a mirror reflecting the realities themselves, going beyond the sphere of symbol. (Sato 1991, 290)

In another example, the near universal adoption of the Christian Gregorian calendar with the fundamental rupture built around the birth of Jesus Christ can be seen as part of Christian and Western hegemonic extension (Sato 1991; Mazrui 2001). For Ali Mazrui (2001, 15), it is a sign that "an informal cultural empire is born, hegemony triumphant":

> Many countries in Africa and Asia have adopted wholesale the Western Christian calendar as their own. They celebrate their independence day according to the Christian calendar, and write their own history according to Gregorian years, using distinctions such as before or after Christ. Some Muslim countries even recognize Sunday as the day of rest instead of Friday. In some cultures, the entire Islamic historiography has been reperiodized according to the Christian calendar instead of the Hijjra.

Indeed, very few countries have not adopted the BC/AD or BCE/CE time frame, such as Iran and Saudi Arabia, which can be seen as much as an insistence in maintaining their cultural and religious heritage as a rejection of Western hegemony over their time.

Similarly, one can argue that the establishment and spread of the "9/11" era – best represented by the common use of "pre-" and "post-9/11" – is a discursively hegemonic move that extends US sovereignty over time frames outside the United States. Thus, "9/11" was not only a turning point for the United States, but a global one. Examples of this can be found in government statements the world over. Manuel Valls, then French interior minister, noted in a key speech on the reform of the French intelligence services that they had to keep their focus on the terrorism threat, beginning a list of attacks that "remain in the collective memory" with the 11 September 2001 attacks,[3] disregarding attacks by al Qaeda in Paris in 1996. The key UK counterterrorism CONTEST (2011, 15) strategy document concludes its Executive Summary by stating that "[i]nternational counter-terrorism work since 9/11 has made considerable progress in reducing the threats we face" – forgetting the decades of British counterterrorism work in Northern Ireland. From 2001 to 2006, 14 African countries passed counterterrorism legislation in what is seen as a "largely externally-driven" (Knudsen 2015) push by the United Nations Counter-Terrorism Committee and donor governments following "United Nations Security Council adopted Resolution 1373 calling on member states to become party to all relevant international conventions on terrorism and to enact the necessary domestic legislation to enforce these agreements" (Whitaker 2007, 1018). Even the prime minister of the small island state of Barbados, with an extremely low terrorism threat, spoke of the need to devise a growth strategy in the "post 9/11" world.[4]

Thus, I argue that the narrative of "9/11" as a moment of temporal rupture does more than legitimise violent counterterrorism policies and legislation, delegitimise non-violent responses such as negotiation and dialogue, and silence dissenting voices. It extends US hegemony over world time, establishing the new "post 9/11" era much like the imposition of eras linked to Chinese dynasties in East Asia. Despite different worlds being marked by different moments of temporal rupture – the fall of the Berlin Wall for some, the Rwandan genocide for others, the 2004 Tsunami for others still – "9/11" came to be nearly universally adopted as a moment of temporal rupture, which did not completely replace these other moments but took its own place as a moment of *universal* temporal rupture.

Critical terrorism studies: reproducing the "9/11" narrative

This sovereignty also extended to the sub-field of critical terrorism studies (CTS). Indeed, the main contention of this article is that although CTS has spearheaded the rejection of the "9/11" chronology, it has nonetheless succumbed to its sovereignty by internalising and adopting "9/11" as a marker of temporal rupture. This may be inevitable. Sternberg (1990, 901) indeed argues in his analysis of power of chronologies that "the straining against the 'tyranny of time' throughout the ages … only reaffirms and redefines the tyrant's power with each abortive rebellion." By rejecting the "9/11" chronology, CTS is forced to restate it.

However, beyond this somewhat facile argument, an analysis of the CTS engagement with "9/11" demonstrates that the CTS scholars have actually taken on "9/11" as a marker of temporal rupture. After presenting data based on a qualitative and quantitative analysis of all research articles published in this journal since its inception, I will argue that this journal demonstrates both a process of internalisation of "9/11" as a moment of temporal rupture – the result of a powerful *habitus* in the social and professional fields inhabited by CTS scholars – and an adoption of this construction in a widespread narrative in CTS that distinguishes between a "pre-9/11 world" in which states engaged in counter-emancipatory violence but were slowly progressing towards a reduction of these counter-emancipatory practices, and a "post-9/11 world" in which states unashamedly increased these counter-emancipatory violent practices, now sustained by overt counter-emancipatory narratives.

A simple descriptive statistical analysis shows that of the 219 research articles published by this journal since its first volume in 2008 (excluding interviews, review articles, book reviews, and forums), 210 articles (96 percent) made referenced to the 9/11 attacks. In total, 131 articles (60 percent) used the attacks as a moment of temporal rupture (62 percent of those referring to the attacks). "9/11" was far more used than "September 11th" or "11 September" or simply "the September" attacks with the former garnering 955 references compared to 301 for all three latter labels. Of the 955 references to "9/11", 633 used the term as a marker of temporal rupture (66 percent) using any of the following expressions: "since 9/11", "before 9/11", "post-9/11", "pre-9/11", "after 9/11", "prior to 9/11", "following 9/11", and "in the wake of 9/11". In a search using the same language constructions for temporal rupture, any of the three labels using the word "September" represented 48 percent of the total references. Some articles were particularly prone to this construction. Excluding the Holland and Jarvis article (2014) that specifically deals with the question of "9/11" as a moment of temporal rupture, five articles (Aning 2010; Lynch 2013; Pokalova 2013; Clini 2015; Feigenbaum and Weissman 2016) referred to "9/11" as a moment of temporal rupture more than 20 times, with Clini (2015) having the highest number of references at 26 in an article entitled "International Terrorism? Indian Popular Cinema and the Politics of Terror." Another 14 articles used this construction more than 10 times. On average, counting all the 219 research articles published by *Critical Studies on Terrorism*, "9/11" was referred to as moment of temporal rupture three times per article published and the three "September" labels figured as temporal rupture 0.7 times per article.

Although this simple statistical analysis gives a sense of the extent of this construction in CTS, a qualitative analysis of each article offers a fuller picture of how "9/11" and the "(11) September (11th)" attacks have been constructed. To begin with, "9/11" becomes a moment of temporal rupture much beyond the question of terrorism and counterterrorism. There are thus references to a "post-9/11 culture" (Wild 2014, 434), the description of an artist as a "post-9/11 cartoonist" (Martin 2012, 475), and a reference to the "post-9/11 animal liberation" movement (Recarte 2016, 247). Although the "pre-9/11" construction is overall less used, Youngs (2009, 97) speaks of "pre-9/11 multiculturalism", for example. Some present this rupture as all-encompassing. For Rykkya, Laegreid, and Fimreite (2011, 220), "[s]ince the 9/11 attacks and the subsequent 'war on terror', the world has come to be perceived as increasingly insecure and dangerous", while for this journal's founding and chief editor, Jackson (2015, 50), the "epistemological crisis of terrorism is now an inherently expansionary, self-replicating and increasingly structurally embedded feature of the post-9/11 world." There is thus a "post-9/11 world" in CTS. In this world, little things have changed so that we are told that "after 9/11, Osama became a fashionable name in Pakistan (and throughout the Muslim world)" (Nazir 2010, 74). More important things have changed too, as Oriola (2009, 261) tells us that "national security has taken on a heightened urgency since 9/11."

Even when CTS scholars are trying to tell readers that "9/11" does not represent a temporal rupture, they still refer to "9/11". In some cases, this may be inevitable, such as for Mac Ginty (2010, 213), when he writes that the "post-9/11 adoption of social science methodologies by Western military forces is not novel", although one wonders why there is a need to mention "9/11" at all. For others, it leads to very awkward syntax in which "9/11" as a moment of temporal rupture is forced into a sentence aimed at stating temporal continuity. Thus, Milton-Edwards (2012, 219) says "far from leading the revolutionary wave and jihadi vanguard, as Islamists were characterised to be doing throughout the 1980s and 1990s and the post-9/11 era, there is already evidence to suggest that today's jihadi Islamists are struggling with the challenge of the democracy movement."

Thus, the "2000s" become "post-9/11". Interestingly, only one article (Gentry and Whitworth 2011) rejects 9/11 as a "temporal marker" entirely and many of those arguing that "9/11" did not affect change in their subject of analysis at the same time reinstate "9/11" as a temporal marker. So Jeffrey Sluka (2008, 179) writes that

> Amnesty International has extensively documented the fact that global human rights suffered serious setbacks and state terrorism massively escalated during the 1970s and 1980s, and that this trend continued through the 1990s and into the new century after the '9/11' terrorist attacks, which stimulated a major new global surge in state human rights abuses justified as 'counterterrorism' measures.

Thus, "9/11" witnessed a continuation of a trend, but also a rupture through its accentuation of this trend. Indeed, 19 articles presented this double approach to "9/11" both rejecting and accepting it as temporal marker.

A simple statistical analysis followed by an in-depth qualitative investigation thus show that CTS has as a sub-field overall confirmed "9/11" as a moment of temporal rupture. I argue that there are two reasons for this: one is linked to an internalisation of the social and professional landscape in which CTS scholars – more or less willingly – inhabit; the other is the result of the explicit or implicit renegotiation of this narrative so that "9/11" comes to be understood as a temporal rupture, but one that is characterised by a qualitative change in state violence rather than in non-state violence. Each argument will be dealt with in turn.

Bourdieu's (1977) practical theory, and particularly his understanding of *habitus*, are particularly helpful to understand how CTS scholars have internalised the dominant "9/11" narrative. *Habitus*, for Bourdieu (1977, 18), is "a system of schemes of perception and thought", those "perceptive dispositions" which bring actors, "even the most disadvantaged ones", to "perceive the world as natural and to accept it much more readily than one might imagine" (Bourdieu 1989, 18). In the case of CTS scholars, these perceptive dispositions are drawn from their sharing the very same visual, political, emotional, and professional landscape as that of policy-makers and traditional scholars after the attacks. Thus, when Bush said that "everyone" would remember what happened that day – when he exhorted, as paraphrased by Zeyfuss (2003, 514) to "Remember. You saw it. Thousands dead" – this included CTS scholars and not only those we study or critique. CTS scholars were also "under the influence of a strong visual memory and the horror of a tragedy" (ibid., 522). Thus, in the "*dialectic of the internalization of externality and the externalization of internality*" (Bourdieu 1977, 72 emphasis in original), I argue that CTS scholars internalised the powerful construction of "9/11" as an exceptional moment, a moment of transformation.

This is not only an individual internalisation due to a personal response to the attacks, but also arguably a collective one. Indeed, CTS scholars are part of the same professional environment as the far more numerous traditional terrorism and security scholars. We attend the same conferences (the International Studies Association Annual Convention, the British International Studies Association Conference, Political Studies Association (PSA) among others), sometimes publish in the same journals, and most importantly, have positioned our work *in opposition to* traditional terrorism scholarship. This positioning required – at least to some degree – a reproduction of the dominant narratives in order for them to be countered. As Michel Foucault (1984) argues, the "weapons of reason" are forged by "the passion of scholars, their reciprocal hatred, their fanatical and unending discussions, and their spirit of competition." It can also be argued that "9/11" as a weapon of reason has been forged by our fanatical and unending discussions and our spirit of competition with traditional security and terrorism scholars. Writing "since 9/11", "post-9/11", "pre-9/11", etc., was a means to challenge traditional terrorism scholars on their own turf and using their own language. I would argue that we thus collectively internalised the narrative of "9/11" as temporal rupture to be able to insert ourselves in the professional field of security and terrorism studies.

Individuals do not however simply reproduce dominant narratives or practices. According to Bourdieu, individuals are continuously renegotiating and transforming – sometimes in a barely noticeable fashion – social relations. Therefore, "rather than merely enacting an already established system of exchange by the following of rules, individuals renegotiate their relations with other individuals by manipulating common understandings" (King 2000, 421). CTS scholars have not simply adopted "9/11" as temporal rupture but rather have renegotiated it and adapted it for greater coherence with the other perceptive dispositions that dominate our subfield. Indeed, an analysis of the temporal rupture narrative shows that CTS scholars do not present this rupture as one between a safe world made insecure by terrorism, but rather as one of an already violent world that was made more violent by states' use of "9/11" as moral and political justification for violent counterterrorism practices.

This is visible in many of the arguments published in this journal. Out of the 131 articles using the attacks as temporal rupture, 58 (44 percent) present it as a moment of increase in state violence, making the latter the single most referred to issue in the temporal rupture constructions. A qualitative analysis further reveals the extent of this: For McGowan (2016, 14), for example, "the scale of victimisation as a result of state led counterterrorism policies at home and abroad since '9/11' far exceeds that of officially recognised terrorist violence." This was largely also true prior to "9/11" as is demonstrated by studies of state violence (see Blakeley 2009), but nevertheless state violence is seen as having qualitatively and quantitatively changed with "9/11". From discourses ("post-9/11 counter-terrorism discourse has fulfilled our worst fears" (Zulaika and Douglass 2008, 29)) to legislation ("Since 9/11, the frenetic proliferation of anti-terror laws in Australia is in a class of its own" (Oriola 2009, 260)) to practices (the attacks "stimulated a major new global surge in state human rights abuses justified as 'counter-terrorism' measures" (Sluka 2008, 179)), CTS has placed a particular focus on this change.

In particular, human and civil rights and liberties are presented as under greater threat in the "post-9/11" environment. So, for Hidek (2011, 254), "[s]ince 9/11, the geography of Manhattan has been saturated with surveillance technologies that serve as a living laboratory for the establishment of a ubiquitous security apparatus in domestic territory." This threat to the rights and liberties of individuals is particularly true for Muslims living in Western countries. Cherney and Murphy (2016, 159) state that "[s]ince 9/11, there is a general feeling among Muslims living in the West that their communities are 'under siege'", due to what Oriola (2009, 261) describes as "a moral panic about Muslims post-9/11." The situation is presented as so dire that Grossman (2014, 321) feels the need to reiterate that "'solidarity and diversity' can coexist in a post-9/11 world." It is important to note that the aim of this list is not to contest that many of the elements have indeed changed in the "post-9/11" period, but rather to highlight how our subfield has reproduced and sustained, but importantly also renegotiated, the construction of "9/11" as a moment of temporal rupture.

There are several important conclusions to be drawn from this analysis. First, we CTS scholars are not as exceptional as we may think we are, and this can be seen by our internalisation of the same construction of "9/11" that is visible in traditional terrorism, security, and IR scholars. We too saw the towers crumble, we too were told to remember that moment for its exceptionality, its extreme violence, the fear it spread in Westerners, us included. When Butler (cited in Wibben 2011, 107) says "most Americans have probably experienced something like the loss of their First-Worldism as a result of September 11 and its aftermath", she is also speaking about CTS scholars. To this personal response to the attacks, one can add a powerful professional one. Our work is in part relevant because of "9/11". If terrorism were not seen and presented as "the most important threat" facing the contemporary world, our work would be less important. There would be fewer panels in conferences, fewer publications, maybe no *Critical Studies on Terrorism*, and overall fewer jobs. This article would not be published. We are, to a certain degree, professionally relevant because of "9/11" and states' discourses and practices since the attacks.

This reliance on "9/11" to justify our relevance, however, has a cost. First, this makes some of our research ahistorical – possibly one of the worst crimes from a CTS perspective. Indeed, although numerous social and political practices may have changed in the "post-9/11" period – such as the representation of Muslim minorities, or the proliferation of counterterrorism legislation – by universalising "9/11" as a moment of temporal rupture and spreading it far beyond counterterrorism practice, we are imposing an alien and essentially hegemonic chronology on other fields. Feminism, culture, cartoons, names in Pakistan, and elsewhere may not have all changed drastically on "9/11". If they did, we need to support this with evidence to justify starting our chronology on that day. I must stress that am not arguing here that any scholars cited in this article are examples of bad practice or bad research, and I myself have written and spoken statements such as these (see part three of this article). The argument here is rather that CTS collectively has – largely unknowingly – fallen into the "9/11" chronology-trap, and that by adopting this starting point for chronologies by default and (at times) without supporting evidence, we are guilty of the same ahistoricism we regularly accuse traditional terrorism scholars and others of.

Second, we run the risk of partially depoliticising – and indeed exonerating – the very state violence that we are trying to expose. By turning the "War on Terror" into "post-9/11" state violence, we are at least semantically accepting that these are "responses" to "9/11". Much of this is part of the critique already put forward by CTS of the traditional terrorism approach to "9/11" and its aftermath (as discussed in part one). The "post-9/11" construction – even if it focused on state violence – assumes that the violent response *chosen* by state actors was the only course of action. It is presented as a natural knee-jerk reaction to "9/11". Thus, whether acting excessively or not, states are exonerated from firing the first shot in this narrative. "9/11" remains the cause that was uncaused (Zeyfuss 2003). Furthermore, it turns "9/11" into the cause of some cases of state violence that CTS and others have demonstrated to be unrelated to the attacks themselves, the 2003 invasion of Iraq being a prime example of this. From the extraordinary manipulation of intelligence findings to the military-industrial agenda pursued by the George W. Bush administration, there are few left arguing that the Iraq war was a "response" to "9/11" (Kauffman 2004), and incorporating the war in Iraq and its aftermath into a "post-9/11" narrative maintains this exonerating smokescreen we have worked so hard to remove.

Indeed, pushing this argument further, it can be argued that much of today's "War on Terror" – from domestic counter-radicalisation strategies, to western and non-western alliances to defeat the so-called Islamic State, to state policies towards refugees and migrants – are more connected to the war in Iraq and its subsequent ramifications than they are to the al Qaeda which carried out the 11 September 2001 attacks. Thus, the terrorism/counterterrorism landscape that we are in today is arguably far more of a "post-2003 world", including the near-15 years of insurgency experience for both state and non-state actors and the recent question of returnees, than a "post-9/11 world". Such an internalisation of the "9/11" narrative as temporal rupture – however renegotiated – arguably undermines some of the key principles and goals of CTS: It risks making our research ahistorical and risks at least partially exonerating the very state violence we have spent 10 years exposing.

The Stoics and reflexive narratives

How can this internalisation and adoption of the dominant "9/11" construction be undone? One means may be a reflexive analysis of how this construction has crept into each of our lives. Reflexive analysis is what allows human beings to be not only the result of "internalization of externality", but also of the "externalization of internality". Through moments of reflection, we can transform *habitus*. Indeed, drawing on the Stoics, Bourdieu invites us to judge a human being by their second reaction to an event, rather than their first:

> The Stoics used to say that what depends upon us is not the first move but only the second one. It is difficult to control the first inclination of habitus, but reflexive analysis, which teaches that we are the ones who endow the situation with part of the potency it has over us, allows us to alter our perception of the situation and thereby our reaction to it. It enables us to monitor, up to a certain point, some of the determinisms that operate through the relation of immediate complicity between position and dispositions. (Bourdieu in Bourdieu and Wacquant 1992, 133)

In this final section, I thus aim to engage in a reflexive analysis of how "9/11" went from being a moment that did not shake my inner self to a moment that marked the start of a clear chronology in my professional life as a CTS scholar.

Inserting itself in the broader move towards autoethnographic work in international relations and security studies (see, e.g., the work of Inayatullah 2010; Dauphinee 2013; and powerful work published in the *Journal of Narrative Politics*), this section stands as an "owning up" to the very behaviour critiqued in this article and illustrates how such a transformation can occur in its minutiae. It comes from the need to "make myself the target of my words" (Inayatullah 2010, 2). It is also the result of the adoption of a methodology that is driven by the desire "to show rather than tell", to "exhibit a process of discovery, rather than steer towards a conclusion" (ibid.). Thus, this personal narrative or Foucauldian "effective history" hopes to illustrate intimately how the "9/11" narrative came to be internalised and negotiated over time in one CTS scholar.

It also offers an alternative story. Carol Cohn (2000, 146) argues that "stories circulate like paper currency, passed on from hand to hand, without anyone ever seeing, or asking to see, the gold that backs it up." She goes on to say that "[a]s in any other institution, the power of the stories comes not from their evidentiary value (even though they are often offered as evidence), but from their ability to condense and symbolise something that people believe and think important." We have all been told endless times the story of how "9/11" changed the life of the young (white) American man who saw the towers falling on TV and realised he needs to fight to defend his people. The aim of the final section is thus also to offer another story in which "9/11" itself did not represent a temporal rupture, but rather a story of continuity that can be passed on as a counter-narrative.

For me, "9/11" was not born on 11 September 2001. In fact, I slept through the attacks. I was less than three miles away in a flat in Brooklyn, barely asleep after an overnight shift at The Associated Press where I worked as an editor on the International Desk. My 90-something landlady sent her West Indies carer to knock on my door, "Mrs. Rosy thinks you should see this." I don't remember if both towers had already fallen, one I think had and I may have seen the second one fall live on TV. I can't be sure. I thought of my friend Amy, who had left the AP to work for the Wall Street Journal, the offices of which were in the World Financial Center, across the street from the World Trade Center. She lived nearby in Brooklyn and I walked to her house and rang her doorbell over and over again. I remember screaming her name. It was completely useless as she clearly was not there. I walked further up towards the Brooklyn Bridge, woke up my cousin and aunt (night owls). By midday, I stood on the Brooklyn promenade – one of my favourite places in the entire world – and watched the fire, the ashes, the paper blow across the East River into Brooklyn. The only thing I remember clearly was a man selling throwaway cameras, saying something along the lines of, "Don't miss your chance! Take a picture of history as it happens!". I remember being both disgusted by his callousness and in awe of his quick thinking: "The World Trade Centre has collapsed? Time to make a buck!". That is maybe the only feeling I remember of that day, being impressed by how life went on. By 6 pm, I took the subway: The F Train that usually passes under Lower Manhattan had been diverted but it took me right into work at Rockefeller Center. I was not even late to work that day. I was not afraid or shaken. I felt for the people who died and their families, but my heart did not break that day.

My heart had broken on March 29 of that year and in the week that followed the death of my friend, Kerem Lawton. My "First-Worldism", as Butler calls it, had been lost six months prior, when a young man who resembled me in personal history, education, profession, and cheek – someone just like me – had been killed reporting on the shelling of a village in Kosovo, part of the spillover from the conflict in neighbouring Macedonia. By September 11, I knew already that violence could rip even nice middleclass professional families, shatter our misplaced sense of security. I had already seen the pain but also the void and incomprehension left by sudden death, particularly the sudden death of young professionals, so "full of life" as so many of those killed in the towers were. Kerem's death and the pain it caused in those who loved him had shaken me to the core, undermined my trust in the world, shattered the arrogant belief that things (for us) "would be okay". My body had already been inhabited by pain and occupied by fear months before the attacks.

My eyes had also already seen massive destruction – destruction far greater than that of the Twin Towers. In August 1999, I had covered the earthquake that had destroyed thousands of homes across 200 kilometers and killed more than 17,000 people in Western Turkey. I had already seen building after building flattened like stacks of pancakes. So many buildings had collapsed that many of them did not see any rescue operation for days. So I remember – much more vividly than any visual memory of the September 11 attacks – sitting with a woman at the bottom of a pile of rubble as she screamed the names of her two children. They were trapped or dead underneath the building and no one was looking for them. Proper rescue teams had not yet arrived in her town and the few surviving local firemen were working to extract people from another building further down the road where other parents pleaded with them. So we sat there on that warm morning of 17 August 1999, surrounded by death.

Over the years, however, people have found far more interesting the fact that I was in New York for "9/11" than in Turkey for the earthquake. They either ask "How was it?" or more politely wait for me to tell them "how it was". I usually tell my story of how I slept through it – it leads to some surprise, some laughter. Then I quickly go on to say that what I do remember vividly is Bush's speech to the joint houses on 20 September 2001. This is where *my* "9/11" narrative begins, contributing in its own small way to the CTS narrative of "9/11" as temporal rupture, one in which states increased their direct, structural, and cultural violence under the banner of counterterrorism. I tell of how tears rolled down my face as I saw New Yorkers in a hip bar of Hell's Kitchen cheer on Bush as we watched him on a giant screen promise war onto the world. Then I remember the feeling of discomfort, even offence, when I found a framed picture of the still-standing Twin Towers with a hand-written note saying "America, love it or get out!" in a hole-in-the-wall coffee place where I'd get my breakfast on my way to work every morning. Countless times I have told the story of how I "remember" thinking, "I just want my coffee, not a lecture on patriotism!". I recount the discomfort of being a foreigner, even in New York where everyone is a "New Yorker", how I eventually left the United States, gave up journalism, and went back to university to study conflict resolution and focus on terrorism.

"9/11" thus came into my life as a temporal rupture that changes the character of New York from a welcoming cosmopolitan city to a culturally violent nationalistic environment in which I did not feel welcome. The attacks that I lived through without going through profound shock or pain – possibly because I had been jolted by both shock and pain just a few months earlier – and that did not come to represent a sharp moment of rupture in my life *became* such a moment months and then years after the attacks. Indeed, this narrative strengthened the more I studied global counterterrorism practices, dialogued with other CTS scholars, and challenged mainstream security and terrorism studies in *their* construction of "9/11". This invariably entered my own writing. So my book (Toros 2012) makes seven references to the attacks, six of them as temporal rupture. The references are also all-encompassing as I speak of a "pre-September 11 landscape" (19). In my teaching, although I argue that terrorism has is many aspects not changed "since 9/11", I then point at the differences that do exist in "pre-9/11" and "post-9/11" terrorism, particularly in state violent responses. I may have slept through the attacks and later been struck by the continuity of life, but in the months and years that followed them, "9/11" became a part of my personal and professional narratives as a moment of temporal rupture.

Conclusion

If the aim of this article was only to point an accusatory finger at my colleagues and myself in CTS, it would be of minimal utility. The article has indeed illustrated through a quantitative and qualitative analysis of all research articles published in this journal that CTS has also been guilty of constructing "9/11" as a moment of temporal rupture. It has argued that this can be traced to an internalisation of the *habitus* by CTS scholars both personally as human beings emotionally affected by the attacks and professionally as scholars inserting themselves in the narrative dominating security and terrorism studies. This internalisation, however, has come with a renegotiation of this narrative that has transformed "9/11" from a moment of rupture that separates the safe pre-"9/11" world to one threatened by terrorism, to a moment of rupture from a violent but slowly improving world to one now driven by the increasingly violent logics of counterterrorism and state repression. The article argued that this CTS narrative puts us at risk of being guilty of the very ahistoricism we accuse traditional terrorism scholars of and more importantly of depoliticising state "responses" to "9/11". The final section of the article offers an example – a story – of how a relatively untraumatic experience of the attacks became a "9/11" narrative that strengthened over time and became part of the collective CTS narrative.

This article though aims to do more than point an accusatory finger or indulge in a public mea culpa. It is an appeal to heed Zeyfuss's call (2003) nearly 15 years ago to critical scholars to "Forget September 11". Such a collective act of forgetting no doubt has costs. "9/11", as argued in this article, has helped CTS be relevant, be listened to, even by those simply intent on dismissing or denigrating our arguments. Ten years into CTS, however, I believe we have the professional and institutional strength to abandon this problematic platform: taking a step down at this point is not as costly as it may seem. But if we forget "9/11", what do we replace it with? A coherent CTS answer is that we replace "9/11" with whichever starting date is most relevant to the subject at hand. Thus, Indian or American cinema may have indeed transformed after the 11 September 2001 attacks, but they may not have, and an investigation into their endogenous chronology is essential. The same thing is true for cartooning, culture, and the first names preferred in Muslim-majority countries. Each of these areas of research – many of them only tangentially related to terrorist and counterterrorist violence – are likely to have very different chronologies from the dominant "9/11" one. We could go further and focus on the repetitive everyday nature of political violence, moving altogether away from an understanding of time "as project, teleology, linear and prospective unfolding; time as departure, progression, and arrival – in other words, the time of history" (Kristeva, Jardine, and Blake 1981, 17), in favour of a cyclical understanding of time that one can find in feminist methodologies (Felski 2000; 2002). Whichever avenue we choose, we should finally liberate research from the hegemonic "9/11" chronology. We can start by ensuring that each time we use "9/11" as a temporal marker, we have carried out a thorough investigation (via whichever methodology one may choose) and can provide the supporting evidence that demonstrates that "9/11" was indeed a temporal rupture.

In this move away from the hegemonic chronology, we will be aided by the increasing realisation that "9/11" may have finally past its sell-by date. Anecdotally, in the past few years, several of my students have had difficulty placing "9/11" accurately in a timeline, referring to the attacks that took place on 9 September 2001 or in September 2011. Indeed, to someone born in 1999, the attacks make as much sense in a timeline beginning 6 years ago as in one beginning 16 years ago. And, such forgetting may go beyond the younger generations. In 2016, then US presidential hopeful Donald Trump spoke of "7/11" (the convenience store) instead of "9/11",[5] and according to a poll carried out by the Pew Research Centre the same year, only 68 percent of American adults can correctly identify 2001 as the year of the attacks.[6] This is not ignorance as much as a natural passage of time in which the visual and emotional memory of an event slowly dissipates.

In the case of our students, we are therefore not only sustaining the "9/11" narrative, we are actually instilling it by asking them to adopt intellectually a collective memory that, in their case, is not individual. As argued by several authors in critical studies of memory, "the 'past' is a production of the present" and "sensory experiences cannot be processed into memories without reliance upon social frameworks of language and political understanding" (Heath-Kelly 2012, 1; 2013). In this case, we are imposing social frameworks of language and political understanding on students who do not have the sensory experiences of the attacks. We are actually imposing hegemonic memories on them, rather than simply sustaining them. Thus, for them and for us, this article concludes with an appeal to return to one of the founding principles of CTS: embedding our analysis in the socio-historical context of violence. For some analyses, "9/11" may still be relevant, but for most, we may do ourselves, our students, and everyone else a favour and finally forget "9/11".

Notes

1. Jarvis (2008) points out that "9/11" was not only one of temporal discontinuity but also one of temporal linearity (since America was once again being called up to defend world order) and timelessness (in the endless battle of good versus evil). However, as he illustrates, the presentation of "9/11" as a temporal break was and remains the dominant narrative.
2. Narrative here is understood as "the primary way by which human experience it made meaningful" (Polkinghorne in Wibben 2011, 43). Importantly, as Wibben (2011, 43) argues, "[n]arratives both enable and limit representation – and representation shapes our world and what is possible within it. Narratives, therefore, are profoundly political."
3. http://www.interieur.gouv.fr/Archives/Archives-ministre-de-l-interieur/Archives-Manuel-Valls-mai-2012-avril-2014/Interventions-du-Ministre/Reforme-du-renseignement.
4. http://www.barbadosparliament.com/uploads/document/ddfd976f0200ee092a9ad8149798f134.pdf .
5. http://edition.cnn.com/2016/04/18/politics/donald-trump-9-11-7-11-mix-buffalo/.
6. http://www.people-press.org/2016/09/07/15-years-after-911-a-sharp-partisan-divide-on-ability-of-terrorists-to-strike-u-s/.

Acknowledgments

I wish to thank Lee Jarvis, William Rowlandson, Luca Mavelli, and the two anonymous reviewers for their insightful comments on earlier versions of this article.

Disclosure statement

No potential conflict of interest was reported by the author.

ORCID

Harmonie Toros http://orcid.org/0000-0002-9139-5292

References

Aning, K. 2010. "Security, the War on Terror, and Official Development Assistance." *Critical Studies on Terrorism* 3 (1): 726. doi:10.1080/17539151003594178.

Aristotle. 1902. *The Poetics of Aristotle*. London: MacMillan.

Blakeley, R. 2009. *State Terrorism and Neoliberalism: The North in the South*. Abingdon: Routledge.

Bourdieu, P. 1977. *Outline of a Theory of Practice*. Cambridge: Cambridge University Press.

Bourdieu, P. 1989. "Social Space and Symbolic Power." *Sociological Theory* 7 (1): 14–25. doi:10.2307/202060.

Bourdieu, P., and L. J. D. Wacquant. 1992. *An Invitation to Reflexive Sociology*. Chicago: University of Chicago Press.

Cherney, A., and K. Murphy. 2016. "What Does It Mean to Be a Moderate Muslim in the War on Terror? Muslim Interpretations and Reactions." *Critical Studies on Terrorism* 9 (2): 159–181. doi:10.1080/17539153.2015.1120105.

Clini, C. 2015. "International Terrorism? Indian Popular Cinema and the Politics of Terror." *Critical Studies on Terrorism* 8 (3): 337–357. doi:10.1080/17539153.2015.1070531.

Cohn, C. 2000. "'How Can She Claim Equal Rights When She Doesn't Have to Do as Many Push-Ups as I Do?' the Framing of Men's Opposition to Women's Equality in the Military." *Men and Masculinities* 3 (2): 131–151. doi:10.1177/1097184X00003002001.

CONTEST. 2011. *The United Kingdom's Strategy for Countering Terrorism*. Cm. 8123. London: The Stationary Office.

Dauphinee, E. 2013. *The Politics of Exile*. Abingdon: Routledge.

Feigenbaum, A., and D. Weissman. 2016. "Vulnerable Warriors: The Atmospheric Marketing of Military and Policing Equipment before and after 9/11." *Critical Studies on Terrorism* 9 (3): 481–498. doi:10.1080/17539153.2016.1197642.

Felski, R. 2000. *Doing Time: Feminist Theory and Postmodern Culture*. New York: New York University Press.

Felski, R. 2002. "Telling Time in Feminist Theory." *Tulsa Studies in Women's Literature* 21 (1): 21–28. doi:10.2307/4149213.

Foucault, M. 1984. "Neitzsche, Genealogy, History." In *The Foucault Reader*, edited by M. Foucault and P. Rabinow, 76–100. New York: Pantheon Books.

Gentry, D., and K. Whitworth. 2011. "The Discourse of Desperation: The Intersections of Neo-Orientalism, Gender and Islam in the Chechen Struggle." *Critical Studies on Terrorism* 4 (2): 145–161. doi:10.1080/17539153.2011.586202.

Grossman, M. 2014. "Disenchantments: Counterterror Narratives and Conviviality." *Critical Studies on Terrorism* 7 (3): 319–335. doi:10.1080/17539153.2014.937097.

Heath-Kelly, C. 2012. "Do You Remember Revolution? Interrogating Political Representations of Counter-Memory and Trauma." Paper presented at the International Studies Association Annual Conference, San Diego.

Heath-Kelly, C. 2013. *Politics of Violence: Militancy, International Politics, Killing in the Name.* Abingdon: Routledge.

Hidek, M. 2011. "Military Doctrine and Intelligence Fusion in the American Homeland." *Critical Studies on Terrorism* 4 (2): 239–261. doi:10.1080/17539153.2011.586207.

Hoffman, B. 2006. *Inside Terrorism.* New York: Columbia University Press.

Holland, J., and L. Jarvis. 2014. "'Night Fell on a Different World': Experiencing, Constructing and Remembering 9/11." *Critical Studie s on Terrorism* 7 (2): 187–204. doi:10.1080/17539153.2014.886396.

Inayatullah, N., ed. 2010. *Autobiographical International Relations: I, IR.* Abingdon: Routledge.

Jackson, R. 2005. *Writing the War on Terrorism: Language, Politics and Counter-Terrorism.* Manchester: Manchester University Press.

Jackson, R. 2015. "The Epistemological Crisis of Counterterrorism." *Critical Studies on Terrorism* 8 (1): 33–54. doi:10.1080/17539153.2015.1009762.

Jarvis, L. 2008. "Times of Terror: Writing Temporality into the War on Terror." *Critical Studies on Terrorism* 1 (2): 245–262. doi:10.1080/17539150802184637.

Kauffman, C. 2004. "Threat Inflation and the Failure of the Marketplace of Ideas: The Selling of the Iraq War." *International Security* 29 (1): 5–48.

King, A. 2000. "Thinking With Bourdieu Against Bourdieu: A 'Practical' Critique of the Habitus." *Sociological Theory* 18 (3): 417–433.

Knudsen, D. 2015. "A New Wave of African Counterterrorism Legislation: Contextualizing the Kenyan Security Laws." *Georgetown Journal of International Affairs.* Accessed February 14 2017 http://journal.georgetown.edu/a-new-wave-of-african-counterterrorism-legislation-contextualizing-the-kenyan-security-laws/Last

Kristeva, J., A. Jardine, and H. Blake. 1981. "Women's Time." *Signs: Journal of Women in Culture and Society* 7 (1): 13–35. doi:10.1086/493855.

Lynch, O. 2013. "British Muslim Youth: Radicalisation, Terrorism and the Construction of the 'Other'." *Critical Studies on Terrorism* 6 (2): 241–261. doi:10.1080/17539153.2013.788863.

Mac Ginty, R. 2010. "Social Network Analysis and Counterinsurgency: A Counterproductive Strategy?" *Critical Studies on Terrorism* 3 (2): 209–226. doi:10.1080/17539153.2010.491319.

Martin, E. 2012. "'I' for Iconoclasm: Graphic Novels and the (Re)Presentation of Terrorism." *Critical Studies on Terrorism* 5 (3): 469–481. doi:10.1080/17539153.2012.723521.

Mazrui, A. 2001. "Pretender to Universalism: Western Culture in a Globalizing Age." *Journal of Muslim Minority Affairs* 21 (1): 11–24. doi:10.1080/13602000120050523.

McGowan, W. 2016. "Critical Terrorism Studies, Victimisation, and Policy Relevance: Compromising Politics and Challenging Hegemony?" *Critical Studies on Terrorism* 9 (1): 12–32. doi:10.1080/17539153.2016.1147772.

Milton-Edwards, B. 2012. "Revolt and Revolution: The Place of Islamism." *Critical Studies on Terrorism* 5 (2): 219–236. doi:10.1080/17539153.2012.686658.

Nazir, P. 2010. "War on Terror in Pakistan and Afghanistan: Discursive and Political Contestations." *Critical Studies on Terrorism* 3 (1): 63–81. doi:10.1080/17539151003594236.

Oriola, T. 2009. "Counter-Terrorism and Alien Justice: The Case of Security Certificates in Canada." *Critical Studies on Terrorism* 2 (2): 257–274. doi:10.1080/17539150903010764.

Pokalova, E. 2013. "Authoritarian Regimes against Terrorism: Lessons from China." *Critical Studies on Terrorism* 6 (2): 279–298. doi:10.1080/17539153.2012.753202.

Recarte, C. A. 2016. "Animal Liberation, American Anti-Terrorist Cultura and Denis Hennelly's." *Bold Native. Critical Studies on Terrorism* 9 (2): 247–268. doi:10.1080/17539153.2016.1163864.

Rowlandson, W. 2015. *Imaginal Landscapes: Reflections on the Mystical Visions of Jorge Luis Borges and Emanuel Swedenborg.* London: Swedenborg Society.

Rykkya, L., P. Laegreid, and A. Fimrite. 2011. "Attitudes Towards Anti-Terror Measures: The Role of Trust, Political Orientation and Civil Liberties Support." *Critical Studies on Terrorism* 4 (2): 219–237. doi:10.1080/17539153.2011.586206.

Sato, M. 1991. "Comparative Ideas of Chronology"." *History and Theory* 30 (3): 275–301. doi:10.2307/2505559.

Sluka, J. 2008. "Terrorism and Taboo: An Anthropological Perspective on Political Violence against Civilians." *Critical Studies on Terrorism* 1 (2): 167–183. doi:10.1080/17539150802184579.

Sternberg, M. 1990. "Telling in Time (1): Chronologoy and Narrative Theory." *Poetics Today* 11 (4): 901–948. doi:10.2307/1773082.

Toros, H. 2012. *Terrorism, Talking, and Transformation: A Critical Approach*. Abingdon: Routledge.

Whitaker, B. E. 2007. "Exporting the Patriot Act? Democracy and the "War on Terror" in the Third World." *Third World Quarterly* 28 (5): 1017–1032. doi:10.1080/01436590701371751.

Wibben, A. 2011. *Feminist Security Studies: A Narrative Approach*. Abingdon: Routledge.

Wild, P. 2014. "Sam Fisher and the "War on Terror': An Analysis of Splinter Cell in a Post-9/11 Context." *Critical Studies on Terrorism* 7 (3): 434–445. doi:10.1080/17539153.2014.953309.

Wilkinson, P. 2011. *Terrorism versus Democracy: The Liberal State Response*. Abingdon: Routledge.

Youngs, G. 2009. "Media and Mediation in the 'War on Terror': Issues and Challenges." *Critical Studies on Terrorism* 2 (1): 95–102. doi:10.1080/17539150902752846.

Zeyfuss, M. 2003. "Forget September 11." *Third World Quarterly* 24 (3): 513–528. doi:10.1080/0143659032000084447.

Zulaika, J., and W. Douglass. 2008. "The Terrorist Subject: Terrorism Studies and the Absent Subjectivity." *Critical Studies on Terrorism* 1 (1): 27–36. doi:10.1080/17539150701844794.

Interpretation, judgement and dialogue: a hermeneutical recollection of causal analysis in critical terrorism studies

Lucas Van Milders

ABSTRACT
This article problematises Critical Terrorism Studies's (CTS) seeming reluctance to engage in causal explanation. An analysis of the meta-theoretical assumptions on causation in both orthodox and critical terrorism studies reveals that the latter's refusal to incorporate causal analysis in its broader research agenda reproduces – despite its commitment to epistemological pluralism – the former's understanding of causation as the only sustainable one. Elemental to this understanding is the idea that causation refers to the regular observation of constant conjunction. Due to the positivist leanings of such a conception, CTS is quick to dismiss it as consolidating Orthodox Terrorism Studies's lack of critical self-reflexivity, responsibility of the researcher, and dedication towards informing state-led policies of counterterrorism. Drawing on recent work in the philosophy of science and International Relations, this article advances an alternative understanding of causation that emphasises its interpretative, normative and dialogical fabric. It is therefore argued that CTS should reclaim causal analysis as an essential element of its research agenda. This not only facilitates a more robust challenge against Orthodox Terrorism Studies' conventional understanding of causation but also consolidates CTS's endeavour of deepening and broadening our understanding that (re) embeds terrorist violence in its historical and social context.

Introduction

Examining causation in relation to the turn to political violence has always been a central, though often implicit, concern in the study of terrorism and political violence. Frequently, this has boiled down to asking: "what leads a person to turn to political violence?" (Sageman 2014, 565). Whereas many academic disciplines have sought to examine this question in differing ways, it can be seen as constituting the very *raison d'être* of terrorism studies, in its both orthodox and critical manifestations. Indeed, whether engagement with the causes of terrorism is driven by an agenda to provide more efficacy to policies of prevention (Kydd and Walter 2006) or whether it concerns a more fundamental disposition for alleviating human suffering (Jackson 2012a), teasing out the causes of political violence or terrorism seems to be insurmountable for both the orthodox and critical strand of terrorism studies. Although causation might at first not appear to be an essential concept in the study of terrorism and political violence, substantial reflection on causation is indispensable, since every theoretical engagement in this field, both orthodox and critical, is bound to make explicit or implicit assumptions on the causes or conditions of terrorism. Indeed, the very fact that one is to critically interrogate the notion of terrorism as an event and/or process is in itself entangled within causal assumptions.

It goes without saying then that orthodox and critical terrorism studies greatly differ in their conceptualisation of causation. Despite the fact that Critical Terrorism Studies (CTS) has successfully exposed the fundamental shortcomings of its orthodox sibling whilst offering a substantiated and effective alternative to it, the main argument of this article will be that CTS has been rather reluctant to explicitly engage causation when it comes to studying terrorism. The effect of this is that CTS risks being ignored by those interested in and committed to critically probing the causes of terrorism. The reasons for CTS's reluctance to explicitly engage causation can arguably be attributed to the fact that the orthodox understanding of causation, which involves the notion of so-called "root" causes behind terrorism (Bjørgo 2005; Richardson 2006; Campana and Lapointe 2012), is taken to be subscribing to an agenda that involves the very reified conception of terrorism that CTS so fiercely opposes. This concerns the fact that orthodox research tends to decontextualise and dehistoricise the notion of terrorism in an attempt to inform state-led policies of counterterrorism (Jackson 2012b). For CTS, the engagement with causation in Orthodox Terrorism Studies (OTS) is therefore taken to be grounded in the very critique it has raised against the orthodox study of terrorism (Jackson et al. 2009b, 214–221).

The purpose of this article is to assess the costs of CTS's seeming reluctance to examine causation more explicitly, as this entails an unwanted reproduction of the deeply problematic understanding of the concept in OTS. This will involve the contention that the latter in fact propels the dehistoricised and decontextualised notion of terrorism that underpins OTS. Yet, this is far from the only conception of causation out there. In the philosophy of science and the field of International Relations (IR) for instance, causation has undergone considerable critical scrutiny that seeks to move beyond the unhelpful stalemate between either the conventional understanding of causation (as it is produced in OTS) or a reluctance to engage it more critically (as in CTS) (Harré and Madden 1975; Bhaskar [1978] 2008; Kurki 2008; Suganami 2013). Drawing on this more nuanced and philosophically grounded understanding of causation, the argument will tease out a conceptualisation of causation that further extends the insights that Critical Realism (CR) brings to the table, while further developing the interpretative, normative, and dialogical fabric of causation (Herring and Stokes 2011; Porpora 2011). Accordingly, the argument will essentially contend that CTS can benefit a great deal from reclaiming causation as a more central and explicit element of both its argument and agenda. This involves a historicised and contextualised conception of the causes of terrorism that transforms CTS's rejection of the problematic understanding of causation in OTS into an effective alternative that is instrumental to CTS's fundamental commitment to a more critical understanding of terrorism.

The argument will proceed in three steps. First, a brief overview will be provided of causation in OTS and the way causal explanation is conceptualised in reference to the philosophy of Hume ([1777] 1962). Second, a contrast will be drawn with CTS and flesh out the reasons why the latter has been reluctant to engage causation more explicitly.

Most importantly, it will indicate how CTS, despite its profound commitment to episte-mological and methodological pluralism, unknowingly reproduces the hegemony of the conventional understanding of causation that was analysed in the first section. The final section will then bring in a number of insightful contributions to causation that have proliferated in IR over recent years. Drawing on a CR notion of causation that disavows the Humean conception without discarding the ontological quality of causal laws, the contention will be made that the conventional understanding of causes of terrorism – produced in OTS and "reproduced" by CTS – requires an urgent overhaul by highlighting the interpretative, normative, and dialogical fabric of explaining causes. This also requires moving beyond CR's conception of causation as it risks reproducing the sub-ject/object distinction. More so, by emphasising the interpretive and normative char-acter of causation, the elemental claim will be made that the causes of terrorism cannot be divorced from both the historicity and context within which (socially constructed) acts of terrorism occur as well as the normative and ethical concerns that it invokes. This hermeneutical understanding of causation will then be presented as *the* substantial and necessary contribution that CTS can make to the debate on the causes of terrorism.

Causation in Orthodox Terrorism Studies

Similar to other event-driven disciplines, OTS emerged and developed as an attempt to causally explain events that were depicted as acts of terrorism or political violence. As it emerged out of the broader field of counter-insurgency studies (Suganami 2013), one of the first volumes to systematically engage the causes of political violence was Ted Gurr's *Why Men Rebel* (1970) in which the issue of causal explanation was approached as follows: "What are the psychological and social sources of the potential for collective violence? [...] And what societal conditions affect the magnitude and form, and hence the consequences, of violence?" (7–8). Although Gurr does not refer to the notion of terrorism explicitly or even accounts for the political nature of the violence he seeks to explain, it is nonetheless important to understand how he immediately situated one of the main causal conditions in the psychological realm. As such, his argument reflects a strong emphasis on the psychological processes that individuals and collectives undergo as they resort to political violence.

This explanation is, following Charles Tilly, not a very novel argument as it concerns the simple idea that when people psychologically perceive a gap between what they have and what they deserve, they will resort to violence when the opportunity presents itself (1971, 417). This emphasis on psychological factors was soon challenged when scholars started to relate political violence to what were described as acts of terrorism. In order to replace Gurr's focus on violence amidst rebellions with an emphasis on the resort to violence itself, David Rapoport, for instance, argued that terrorism should be understood as an entirely new concept (1971). Subsequently, adopting the nomencla-ture of terrorism pushed the causal explanation into a more strategy-driven under-standing of the concept – something that was further elaborated by Martha Crenshaw who codified some of the key elements in terrorism research. Although she still acknowl-edged terrorism's roots in civil wars and revolutionary insurgencies, Crenshaw under-stood that the causes of terrorism have to be found in its strategic efficacy as the "weapon of the weak" (1981, 387).

Accordingly, both these elements (psychological and strategic) were combined in the assumption that the causes for terrorism were to be found in an attempt to install fear in order to produce a political effect (Reich 1990).[1] This remained the dominant understanding of terrorism's causes until the period around the turn of the millennium introduced a supposedly new form of terrorism that was seemingly driven by religious motivations. Tellingly, this new form of terrorism was quickly defined as the "new terrorism" and was held to be distinguished from previous acts of terrorism or political violence by its small number of members, higher degree of radicalisation, lack of a rational agenda (which gave rise to the assumption of fanaticism), and deeper infiltration into society (Laqueur 1999). Even though the term itself would be widely debated in the field (Kurtulus 2011; Lynch and Ryder 2012), the succession of so-called terrorist attacks in Western cities in the twenty-first century were depicted as supporting some of the key assumptions of "new terrorism" that make it still a noteworthy concept in OTS today (Jäckle and Baumann 2015).

Before we unearth the causal mechanisms that underpin these various causal explanations, it is worth emphasising the catalysing effect that the aforementioned attacks had on the field of OTS. A number of key works that were published in the first decade of the new century would namely consolidate the popular idea that "9/11 changed everything" (Dunmire 2009). Although it is commonly agreed that these attacks also induced a professionalisation of the field (Jackson 2012b), the canonical texts of OTS that appeared around this time subordinated causal explanation to an agenda that was ultimately geared towards policy information, implementation, and improvement (Sageman 2004; Hoffman 2006). No work reflects this catering towards the so-called War on Terror more unambiguously than Robert Pape's *Dying to Win: The Strategic Logic of Suicide Terrorism* (2005), which boldly states that "[o]ur enemies have been studying suicide terrorism for over twenty years. Now is the time to level the playing field" (12). It is this automatic deployment of causal explanation in the service of state-led policies of counterterrorism that constitutes a central point of critique for CTS.

The question then is how this taxonomy of causal explanations (psychological, strategic, religious) can be translated into effective causal mechanisms. In other words, how does OTS conceptualise causation? A more elaborate and direct engagement with the causes behind terrorism is given by Louise Richardson (2006), who argues that causes are to be located at the level of the individual (which are willing to join an organisation), the level of the organisation itself (which is willing to resort to violence), and the level of the sponsoring state (which is willing to sponsor organisations that enhance their strategic and political interests). Additionally, Richardson also refers to societal factors such as degrees of poverty, inequality, and the idea of relative deprivation, yet she designates these as risk factors that may improve the likelihood of terrorism but are not explicit causes (57). Most importantly, however, Richardson highlights that these causes work together, claiming that both individual and organisational motivations as well as external sponsorship are required to induce the occurrence of terrorist violence.

A similar concession to multi-causal explanation is provided in Tore Bjørgo's volume *Root Causes of Terrorism* (2005), which differentiates the following types of causes (3–4): structural (macro-level indicators such as demographic imbalances, globalisation, rapid modernisation), facilitating (causal instruments such as evolution of modern and social media, advanced weapons technology), motivational (people's experiences of grievances and trigger motivations to act), and triggering (direct triggers such as political calamity or an outrageous act committed by a political adversary). Regarding the causal mechanisms that orchestrate the workings of these causes, Bjørgo admits that it is unclear to what extent the concept of "root" cause itself is actually effective terminology, as this suggests a process of generalising particularities beyond an immediate efficacy for research.

The main point to draw from this brief overview is that OTS has never produced a substantial and detailed account of how it understands causation in relation to terrorism.[2] This is problematic since it nonetheless makes a number of implicit yet strong assumptions about the causes of terrorism that are incessantly reproduced throughout its theorising. Indeed, due to OTS's fundamental disposition towards counterterrorist policy information, discriminatory attention is paid to particular factors (i.e. so-called "root" causes such as individuals, groups, and states) while subjugating other factors that are "merely" facilitating (i.e. societal or communal conditions, the historical context, the effects of counterterrorist policies, etc.). This hierarchy then creates an epistemological crisis whereby critical elements are systematically ignored by the epistemic community of OTS in favour of those factors that support prevailing counterterrorist policies (Jackson 2015). An important criterium that determines how a causal relationship can effectively be established is then the extent to which they can be measured and/or observed.

It is for these reasons that OTS's account of causation comfortably falls under a conception of causal analysis that is informed by the philosophy of David Hume. Describing cause as "an object, followed by another, and where all the object similar to the first are followed by objects similar to the second" ([1777] 1962, 76), Hume's understanding of causation largely ascribes to the idea that causal relations can be established by regular occurrence of a correlation between what is simultaneously established as cause and effect. Referring to this understanding as "Humeanism", causes are understood as the efficient agent of change, i.e. that which "pulls or pushes" something. This is, for instance, why Richardson does not consider issues like poverty, inequality, or deprivation as causal factors since they cannot be established as actively "pushing or pulling" terrorism in a regular and observable way. What is interesting then is that, since the aforementioned issues are indeed equally measurable and observable, OTS tends to apply the Humean conception of causation arbitrarily. As such, it actively subjugates factors that are not observed as directly "pushing and pulling" acts of terrorism, which then further exacerbates its epistemological crisis.

In summary, OTS makes an implicit yet fundamental assumption about causation that is steeped in empiricism, as it solely focusses on causes that can be observed regularly through sensory experience. Whether this can be attributed to broader positivist or behaviourist assumptions is not at stake here (Kurki 2008, 97–105). The important issue is to understand that even though there is no explicit engagement with causation as such, OTS directly mirrors other disciplines in what can be referred to as the rationalist mainstream of social sciences, which articulates causes as levers that regularly produce a particular outcome in a given context and can be observed consistently (King, Keohane, and Verba 1994, 75). Important in this regard is that this conception has a discriminatory dynamic which subjugates historical and contextual factors that are not taken to be actively "pushing and pulling" acts of terrorism, and entrenches its epistemic community into an epistemological crisis. I will return to the consequences of these assumptions in the last section; yet, before this is done, an important contrast needs to be drawn with the way CTS understands causation.

Causation in Critical Terrorism Studies

Ten years ago, a subfield emerged in terrorism studies that sought to achieve two things: highlight the pitfalls and shortcomings of orthodox research on terrorism on the one hand, and provide a full-fledged alternative that could successfully move beyond these, on the other. In the form of a new academic journal and an edited volume (Jackson et al. 2009a), CTS is a broad academic endeavour that presents an alternative study of terrorism and critically probes some of the fundamental assumptions that guide OTS. The quintessential question for the present inquiry then is: to what extent did CTS present an alternative account of causation in relation to studying terrorism? In line with CTS's twofold agenda, this would imply conceptualising the dissatisfaction with the conventional understanding of causation in OTS on the one hand, and providing an alternative account that moves beyond these shortcomings, on the other. Yet, before this question can be addressed directly, a little more needs to be said about CTS's history and its elemental lines of inquiry.

Broadly speaking, CTS's general dissatisfaction with OTS stems from four persistent issues (Jackson et al. 2009b, 217–221): an incoherent and depoliticised definition of the term terrorism itself that reflects an intrinsic state-bias and thereby excludes state-led terrorism; an artificial separation of terrorist attacks and the broader social, political, and economic context within which they occur; the absence of an ethical disposition that dogmatically adheres to state-led practices of counterterrorism and fails to account for the responsibility the researcher has in this context; and, most importantly, a fundamental lack of a critical reflective attitude that fails to account for the discursive nature within which acts or events are depicted as corresponding to the label "terrorism". As mentioned in the previous section, this critique amounts to the fact that OTS subjugates particular knowledges, which entrenches its epistemological crisis and makes its conception of causation deeply problematic.

The theoretical pillars upon which CTS's critique is predicated can be defined as a "Frankfurt School-inspired critical theory approach" (Toros and Gunning 2009, 87). Although the notion of Critical Theory as such has not received a codified definition, the general assumption is that CTS – much like the other Critical Theory-inspired subfield of Critical Security Studies (Wyn Jones 1999) – took its conceptual inspiration from two well-known understandings of Critical Theory: on the one hand, there is Max Horkheimer's seminal dichotomy between traditional and critical theory (1982), and on the other hand, there is Robert Cox's differentiation between problem-solving and critical theory in IR (1981). Whereas the way CTS receives and deploys this conceptual heritage has been put under critical scrutiny elsewhere (Heath-Kelly 2010), the central assumption is that Critical Theory stands apart from conventional modes of theorising that are impeded by a lack of critical self-reflectivity. In Horkheimer's case, this involves a conception of traditional theory as incorporating an untenable subject-object divide (and the corresponding fact-value distinction) that does not account for the way it continuously reproduces the existing order or status quo. With Cox, there is a similar treatment of the relationship between reality and the researcher, as he conceptualises problem-solving theory as a form of theorising that obfuscates its performative character since theory is "always for someone, and for some purpose" (Cox 1981, 128). In short, Critical Theory operates out of a fundamental concern with the political (and subsequently ethical) dynamics through which theory is produced and operates. This involves a process of continuously deconstructing the artificial separation of object/subject, reality/researcher, fact/value, etc.

It should be immediately clear that the broader framework of Critical Theory proved to be exceptionally useful for an endeavour that sought to criticise the way OTS has treated its subject matter. Advocating the importance of a critical reflective disposition, Toros and Gunning, for instance, argue that in CTS, critical means "to stand apart from the prevailing order of the world and asking how that order came to be" (Cox 1986, 208). This practice of questioning how a prevailing order came to be essentially points towards the shallowness of the orthodox conception of terrorism (see earlier discussion). CTS therefore emphasises the importance of both deepening and broadening this conception (Toros and Gunning 2009, 89–99). Regarding the former, this involves a process of unearthing the wider power structures within which the orthodox conception of terrorism has emerged. Regarding the later, this involves the inclusion of state responses to violence and other forms of structural violence into a more holistic approach to the notion of terrorism. As such, CTS seeks to de-exceptionalise events depicted as terrorism – which constitute OTS as an event-driven discipline – by embedding them in a broader context of political protest and other forms of contentious politics. As such, CTS is a project of (re)contextualising and (re)historicising the notion of terrorism.

It appears then that CTS's agenda of deepening and broadening the orthodox conception of terrorism has a direct relevance to the concept of causation. If terrorism is to be regarded as a discursive label that is produced through a particular nexus of power relations (e.g. conventional assumption that only non-state actors can engage in terrorist attacks, or that negotiations necessarily encourage terrorism, or that counterterrorist policies necessarily increase citizen's security), the question arises to what extent terrorism as a notion corresponds to a reality "out there". In other words, the emphasis on the discursive and social construction of terrorism risks obfuscating the so-called material reality "out there" (i.e. the *event* that is discursively depicted as an *act* of terrorism) into an entangled web of social interactions that tend to obscure the objective existence of that reality. This would then make it virtually impossible to even consider the existence of conditions for causation (i.e. something *causing* something else).

The broader debate within which this can be categorised is a long-running one in the social sciences that concerns the relationship between discourse and reality (Bergen and Luckmann 1966). In IR, this debate has lead to different positions on our assumptions about reality: from a rationalist affirmation of an objective reality (Keohane 1988), to the fundamental questioning of this seeming objectivity (Ashley 1989), and a middle ground that assumes the existence of a reality that is prone to different interpretations (Kratochwil 1989). Circumventing this unhelpful debate, Toros and Gunning are quick to indicate that the category of violence needs to be retained as a minimal foundation upon which the discourse of terrorism operates (2009, 92). Accordingly, it is the extent to which this category can be defined as "terrorism" that CTS seeks to problematise. So it is not a matter of denying the existence of political violence as such, but of interrogating how and why this violence is or can be framed as terrorism. This also prevents CTS from becoming a rigidly codified enterprise, since it is predicated on a pluralist "commitment to encouraging epistemological and methodological diversity" (Jackson 2012b, 6). As such, it is geared towards interrogating the notion of terrorism from a multiplicity of critical angles. The fundamental question then is, what role does causation play in this interrogation?

It goes without saying that CTS strongly objects to the understanding of causation that is enhanced in OTS. This is, for instance, evident in questioning whether focussing on causation itself actually "has a causal impact on reducing terrorism" (Raphael 2009, 61). The general idea seems to be that terrorism itself "is not a causally coherent, free-standing phenomenon which can be identified in terms of characteristics inherent to the violence itself" (Jackson 2009a, 75). CTS therefore takes aim with the so-called epistemic community of OTS as one of "specialists with a common world view about cause and effect relationships which relate to their domain of expertise, and common political values about the type of policies to which they should be applied" (Stone 1996, 86). What is interesting about this objection is that it is directed towards so-called "mono-causal explanations of terrorism" (Jackson 2009a, 7). As such, critiques have been raised against such mono-causal explanations that involve poverty (Huesmann and Huesmann 2012), religion (Goodwin 2012), or democracy (Al-Sumait, Lingle, and Domke 2009).

However, CTS's aversion towards the so-called "covering law" conception of "root" causes of terrorism does not imply that theorists have not engaged with the broader, contextual conditions that facilitate it. In fact, it is precisely the tendency towards decontextualisation in OTS that has urged CTS to bring the sociocultural context within which terrorism emerges back in. Discussing the social construction of organised political violence, Jackson and Dexter have, for instance, indicated that there are enabling structures and conditions that facilitate political violence or terrorism (Jackson and Dexter 2014, 2–3). In arguing that these structures always operate in interplay with agents and processes, they almost echo OTS's earlier mentioned conception of causation that, despite its ultimate subjugation of structural conditions in favour of agential causes, nonetheless sees conditions and causes operating together. Yet for Jackson and Dexter, this interplay is less hierarchical, with both structure and agency considered to be interdependent and co-constitutive: "structures are the product of social actions; social actions are shaped and made possible by structures" (4). Yet, this emphasis on contextual conditions does not make CTS resort to causal discourse. Toros and Gunning, for instance, do "not reject the notion of 'regularities' (what positivists would call laws)" (2009, 92). Jackson goes even further, arguing that CTS explicitly refuses to abide by the conceptualisation of causation in OTS:

> Importantly, CTS refuses to privilege materialist, rationalist, and positivist approaches to social science over interpretive and reflectivist approaches, and seeks to avoid an exclusionary commitment to the narrow logic of traditional social scientific explanation based on linear notions of cause and effect. (Jackson et al. 2009b, 225–226)

CTS thereby takes aim at OTS's positivist conception of causation that is taken to have discursively produced the decontextualised and dehistoricised conception of terrorism. By (re)contextualising and (re)historicising terrorism back into broader socio-contextual processes – such as, for instance, democratisation, modernisation, globalisation, and the widening North-South divide – CTS seeks to challenge the idea that there is such a thing as a solid or "root" cause of terrorism.

Even though omitting causation could be potentially defended as a logical element in CTS's research agenda, the implications of this omission are nonetheless detrimental. By refusing to conceptualise the interplay between agents and structure in causal terms on the one hand, and valorising socio-contextual processes and discursive mechanisms over individual and organisational agency on the other, CTS not only allows OTS to monopolise its conception of the causes of terrorism as the only game in town, but it also risks of undermining its own critique of the latter's subjugation of knowledge. This is unfortunate as the interplay between different levels of analysis is arguably an element where CTS anticipates or implicates a conception of causation that allows for a more multifaceted and sophisticated interrogation of the causes of terrorism. It seems then that CTS's emphasis on epistemological plurality also comes at a cost:

> Critical approaches to terrorism do not have a unified stance on the causes of terrorism. While some critical scholars are sceptical of the entire notion of causation, regarding it as too embedded in positivist, problem-solving perspectives, others accept it but are wary of mono-causal explanations. (Jackson et al. 2011, 199)

Even though this critique of mono-causal explanations could be developed as an effective platform to conceptualise causation more critically, an inherent tendency to depict causal analysis as the very dynamic that has produced a decontextualised and dehistoricised conception of terrorism effectively inhibits such an alternative. Accordingly, this has garnered some criticism in recent years where CTS's constructivist/discursive ontology is seen as undermining its overall efficacy as a theory. Following Jonathan Joseph, the most substantial problem with CTS is, namely, that the social and discursive practices, which are emphasised as determining the orthodox conception of terrorism, only have meaning through the material interests and socio-economic relations it tends to ignore (Joseph 2011, 33).

In other words, even though Toros and Gunning were right to retain a minimal foundationalism when it comes to the material reality of political violence, CTS conceptualisation of terrorism as a social fact tends to obscure this material residue. Joseph therefore criticises CTS for being too quick in discarding material reality "out there" by interpreting it in rather crude and physicalist terms. As such, he regards as unhelpful the binary between social intersubjectivity (terrorism is a label given to a particular *event* through discursive practices and contextual conditions) and brute materiality (terrorism refers to specific *acts* of terrorism such as the attacks on 11 September 2001). A way out of this stalemate would be to highlight that even though terrorism might indeed not constitute a solid and positivist objectivity, there is still something "out there" upon which these discursive practices are constructed without necessitating the assumptions of solid positivism. Joseph considers CTS to be moving too far in the constructivist direction, as he argues that terrorism "is a social relation that is overdetermined by both material and discursive practices" (2011, 34).

A number of arguments have therefore contended that what CTS requires is "a philosophy of science that stands in between positivism and postmodernism" (Porpora 2011, 40).[3] As such, it concerns a meta-theoretical orientation that strongly opposes the ultimately flawed positivist conception of causation without relapsing into a radically discursive argument that indirectly accepts or at least reproduces this conception. This orientation has been presented as a Critical Realist (CR) one (Herring and Stokes 2011). As a so-called "underlabouring meta-theory" "that informs the construction of specific theories in the course of empirical research" (Cruickshank 2002, 50), CR assumes the existence of structures and causal mechanisms as "real" ontological entities which cannot be directly accessed or known in epistemological terms (Archer et al. 1998, 5). It therefore concerns, in the words of Roy Bhaskar, "a non-anthropocentric ontology of structures, generative mechanisms, and active things" ([1978] 2008, 35). Although the scope of the present analysis does not permit a more substantial engagement with CR, what should be taken from Bhaskar's position is a recognition that causation is ontologically real, but that we are limited in our capacity to access these causal mechanisms.

Not only has this sparked immense interest and debate in philosophy of science (Collier 1994) and IR (Kurki 2008; Joseph and Wright 2010), CR has also found its way into CTS as a potential candidate for reclaiming causal analysis. This concerns an endeavour that understands causal analysis as "identifying and describing the mechanisms through which things work" (Porpora 2011, 42). As such, there is no inherent justification for an "aversion to causal language" (Kurki 2008, 130) if the latter can be reconceptualised along anti-positivist lines. Applied to the present analysis, the question then is whether CR's conception of causation can provide an alternative understanding of the causes of terrorism that recollects CTS's multiplicity of interplaying conditions on the one hand yet consolidates this into an explicitly causal analysis that constitutes a substantial alternative to OTS on the other. This will be explored in the next and final section, which will indicate that it is specifically a hermeneutical conceptualisation of causation that can introduce the potential of causal analysis to CTS.

A hermeneutical recollection of causation

In an attempt to move beyond the singular and problematic conception of causation that is (re)produced in both positivist and post-positivist philosophies of science, theories of IR, and terrorism studies, CR theorists have argued that this Humean theory is far from the only way of understanding causation. Kurki, for instance, understands this "pulling and pushing" depiction of causes as merely one of the four Aristotelian causes. These include *material* causes (the matter of an object), *formal* causes (the form of an object), *efficient* causes (the primary source of change, i.e. the agential mover), and *final* causes (that "for the sake of which" something comes to be, i.e. the intention) (Kurki 2008, 25–30). Efficient causes are then the conception of causation that are reproduced by both positivists and post-positivists. What is striking about Kurki's conceptualisation is that, in typical CR fashion, she deploys Aristotle's causal taxonomy in a way that advances an understanding of them as "ontologically grounded" (26). Material causes are, for instance, ontologically prior to all other causes since nothing in the world (natural and social) can exist without materiality, according to Aristotle. As such, Kurki emphasises the insurmountable role material causes play in order to clarify why post-positivists are wrong to dismiss the role of materiality: material causes remind us that there is a material world "out there" that enables and constrains our actions. So it is possible to retain a minimal foundation in causal analysis.

Yet there is more. As the same ontological quality applies to formal and final causes, the *entire* ontological status of causation is reclaimed as something that exists in the world "out there". This is exactly what Bhaskar had argued earlier: causation has an ontological quality as opposed to being merely a construction of the mind. The latter can be understood as the essential assumption on causation that underpins Hume's theory. As mentioned in the first section, the latter understands causation to be the effect of observing regular conjunction. Yet this conception does not ascribe an ontological status to causation as such, since it does not account for causal necessity. It merely provides a psychological explanation of causation as something we perceive through impressions. This, however, presented a fundamental problem for Hume himself, since he believed that "all our ideas [...] are copies of our impressions" ([1777] 1962, 19). Yet if this is the case, then how can we have an idea of causal necessity if there is no perceptual impression that can account for it. This obviously implies that Hume himself would not agree with the deterministic interpretation that his work has been subjected to in the positivist, "pushing and pulling" conception of causation that has been discussed throughout this article. A way out of the dichotomy between causation as objective "pushing and pulling" levers or merely an idea in the mind therefore, involves the deepening of the concept of causation (with broadening being the inclusion of the other Aristotelian causes). Providing causation with a deep ontology thereby consists of grasping "the nature of objects through making existential claims about their constituting structures and causal powers, thereby enabling explanations of various 'actual' or empirical processes and tendencies" (Kurki 2008, 198).

However, before one assumes that this conception of causation can be automatically applied to questions on the causes of terrorism, it is worth pointing to Kurki's contention at the end of her analysis that "the question of causation is not a problem that can be solved: it is merely a problem that can be solved in various different ways" (2008, 307). Not only does this pluralism directly resonate with CTS's commitment to epistemological and methodological diversity, it also reflects an understanding of causal analysis as identifying and describing how things work. Interestingly, Porpora has alternatively referred to this as a "historical narrative" (2011, 42) that binds together agent and structure in a historical context and process. He argues that this involves the development of interpretations that can be assessed in their correspondence to the way the world is. This then strikes a subtle balance between discursive interpretation (causation relates to our historical narration of events) and objective reality (the world "out there" operates as a criterion for falsifying these interpretations). The only problem with it, however, is that it covertly reintroduces the subject/object distinction that CTS and other critical theories so fiercely criticised for facilitating the decontextualised and dehistoricised understanding of causation in positivist philosophy of science.

Although much can be said about the way CR has been applied to IR and CTS (Brown 2007; Chernoff 2007), it seems that rather than finding a third way between positivism and postmodernism – whose arguments are more nuanced and prone to internal debate than CR theorists imply (Jackson et al. 2011) – this unhelpful binary needs to be dismantled entirely. Indeed, it is the interpretive conception of causation that moves beyond the subject/object distinction by developing the notion of historical narrative as a perspectivism that does not deny the existence of a reality "out there" but merely suggests that there are different interpretations of it. This retains the insightful contributions of CR while nonetheless bridging the subject/object divide by depicting causation as effectively the interpretation of events. Not only does this facilitate CTS's pluralist epistemology, it also allows for a profoundly causal analysis of terrorism that further strengthens CTS's core commitments. This will be developed in the remainder of this section.

Causation as interpretation

Understanding causation as interpretation effectively moves beyond the dichotomy between the aforementioned positions of Hume and Bhaskar (and their relative school's of thought). Following Hidemi Suganami, it can be argued that both thinkers saw "the world as an open system, where, by definition, antecedents of causal laws are not followed prevalently by their consequents" (2016, 13). What this means is that the world is by no means a closed system where causal powers can be known in isolation, but an open system where these powers are entangled in a rhizomatic complexity. Yet this complexity does not imply the mere relativity of causation. Richard Feynman has, for instance, stated that "the most important things in the real world appear to be a kind of complicated accidental result of a lot of laws" (1992, 122). Indeed, the open-systemic quality of the world implies that it hosts a great number of laws that can be shown but never known in isolation.

Causal analysis then becomes a practice of fleshing out a causal pattern in the midst of an open system that is not as much directed towards predicting the future as it is about explaining the past. In doing so, causation becomes a matter of interpretive historiography: "*IR theorists*, when attempting to explain the occurrence of a particular event, should do what *historians* commonly try to do" (Suganami 2016, 15). Causation is then the establishing of a historical narrative that seeks to explain a particular event by pointing towards a particular causal dynamic or mechanism. Embracing the open-systemic nature of the social world provides causal analysis with a hermeneutic quality whereby a causal pattern is a matter establishing the most effective and probable interpretation of a particular event. What is at stake here then is to account for the complexity and diversity of the social world without relapsing into an anything goes story where *any* causal pattern can be established.

As such, causal interpretation is grounded in historical explanation that is not fabricated out of thin air. To understand this, it is important to comprehend that asking a question on the cause of something is nothing but the presentation of a narrative that seeks to explain that particular event (Suganami 1996, 150). When we ask "what caused this particular act of political violence?" we do not ask what causes political violence in *general* but what causes this *particular* act; i.e. we try to make sense of this event by historically explaining how it came to be. The reason why history is so important for causal analysis, Suganami argues, is that it does not conflate theorising with generalising (2013, 640). When we understand what caused a particular historical event like an act of political violence, it does not imply that this causal explanation will capacitate us to explain *all* instances of political violence accordingly.

It is within this conceptualisation of causation as historical interpretation that an effective critique against causation as observed regularity can be found, as it undermines the assumptions OTS has made about causation. As we saw in the first section,

OTS's attempt to valorise particular "root" causes over "mere" conditions (i.e. what in Aristotelian terms implies valorising efficient and final causes over material and formal causes), is not grounded in an endeavour to explain a particular event, but to generalise its causes in order to predict other events in the future. Not only does this lead to an epistemological crisis where a particular event is not even adequately explained, it also further deprives the causes of terrorism of their historical context. As Bjørgo himself noted, the assumption of generalising particularity in causal analysis has a tendency of undermining its own efficacy.

Explaining a particular event in terrorism studies will therefore need to cease looking for patterns of regularity and start engaging in the historical interpretation of this event. This stems from the fact that there is no singular cause but a plethora of potential causes that need to be subjected to critical interpretation: "causal powers are *everywhere* – exercised but not always realised" (Suganami 2013, 641; emphasis in original). There is in itself nothing wrong with the emphasis on the multi-causal nature of terrorism, yet this does not necessitate that all causes are always realised in every case. It is therefore a matter of discriminating among these causes depending on the particular case-at-hand – which is different from OTS's hierarchical discrimination between "root" causes and conditions. This chimes well with CTS's agenda of deepening and broadening our understanding of terrorism, as it exhausts the limited causal explanation of OTS.

Moreover, embedding causal explanation in this broader web of historical and contextual analysis addresses CTS's concern that OTS is impeded by an "absence of social theory in terrorism studies, rigid disciplinary boundaries and the lack of theoretical cross-fertilisation, and the tendency to exceptionalise terrorist violence in relation to other forms of violence and political action" (Jackson et al. 2009b, 219). Understanding terrorism as entangled in this broader social web that interconnects agents, structures, and processes therefore requires causal interpretation of how this web produced the events that are analysed. In addition, it also firmly embeds the researcher within as opposed to outside the social world: causal interpretation not only involves a discursive practice in which a particular interpretation is critically presented and assessed, it also directly reflects an orientation of self-reflectivity and auto-ethnography on behalf of the researcher (Jackson 2012b, 3).

Causation as moral judgement

It appears then that CTS's reluctance to engage in causal analysis has overlooked an interpretative conceptualisation of causation that chimes in well with its critical thematic. Indeed, for Suganami, "causal explanations have to do with the workings of the world *as understood by us*" (2011, 720; emphasis in original). This implies that questions of causation bear an intrinsic vernacular quality that seeks to understand the world from a particular perspective. Further debunking the positivist myth of the fact/value distinction, this entails that the particular questions we ask in causal inquiry are by no means neutral statements about an objective world but stem from a phenomenological disposition that seeks to make sense of the world around us. As Suganami writes, "it is not possible to have direct access to the world to ascertain what 'really' goes on there and decide whether or not a given scientific representation of it is 'true' in the sense of 'corresponding to it'" (732). What is meant here is that, when we seek to understand what caused a particular event, we literally attempt to make sense of it. Indeed, interpretation is always tied to a perspective from which the interpreting is done.

Yet what Suganami adds to this is that, in our very questioning of a particular act, we make "a judgement on the moral quality of the particular act" (2011, 728). He clarifies this by arguing that when we ask a question about the causes of an event, we often ask a fundamental question concerning moral responsibility. If we, for instance, ask what caused a particular act of political violence, we are fundamentally interested in isolating the moral responsibility related to the occurrence of this particular act of political violence. In social sciences, the empirical and the moral are often divorced yet the notion of causation clearly exposes the untenability of this separation: "the values to which we subscribe and the kinds of knowledge claim we produce about the world are interrelated" (732).

Causation as moral judgement then directly resonates within CTS's core commitments of dismantling the fact/value distinction but also self-reflexivity and ethics (Breen Smyth 2009). Yet it also puts extra emphasis on CTS's refusal "to define terrorism either in ways that de-legitimise some actors while simultaneously according the mantle of legitimate violence to others" (Jackson 2007, 247). More so, it can take a more forceful stance against the accusation that CTS's emphasis on discourse effectively legitimates violence (Jones and Smith 2010). By adopting a normative conception of causation, CTS is also better positioned to expose the seemingly neutral questions on causation that constitute OTS as obfuscating both the moral values and judgements that inherently underpin them on the one hand and the unreflective catering towards counterterrorist policies, on the other. Moral responsibility therefore resides, among other, within the particular way the researcher has framed the question of research. It goes without saying that this deeply interconnects with CTS's research agenda in its attempt to demand from the researcher a more critical self-reflexive attitude.

Causation ultimately amounts to a type of questioning that seeks to make a particular point about the case at hand and "this is largely an issue of politics and ethics" (2008, 342). Asking causal questions therefore brings both the ethical and the political back in, an endeavour that is central to CTS's agenda of (re)politicisation (Jackson 2009a). What this all entails then is that CTS's commitment to a "'do no harm' approach to research [and] taking responsibility for the anticipated impact of [this] research" (Jackson et al. 2009b, 226) should no longer be understood as mere critique of OTS. By advancing historically and contextually grounded understandings that explain socially constructed acts of terrorism in causal terms, CTS can potentially provide a substantial account of these acts that outperforms the orthodox conception of causation in both its efficacy and its critical disposition.

Causation as dialogue

A final element of CTS's critical orientation that can be developed as elemental to a causal analysis of terrorism concerns the notion of dialogue. This not only stems from the fundamental role that dialogue plays in the transformation of terrorist violence itself (Toros 2012; Jackson and Hall 2016), it also involves bridging the gap between the OTS and CTS epistemic communities (Horgan and Boyle 2008; Ranstorp 2006; Jackson 2012a). Yet the necessity of dialogue also stems from the intrinsically contested character of causal interpretation that undermines the possibility of reified, "root" causes. Causal explanation operates under the assumptions that there can be no "super-criterion, acceptable to all" (Suganami 2008, 343), which can transform a particular causal interpretation into an objective regularity that allows for future prediction. In other words, the problem of multi-interpretability is intrinsic to causal analysis. Yet, as argued earlier, this should not imply a relapse into causal relativism, but rather an open dialogue in which different causal explanations are assessed, something that directly resonates within CTS's commitment to interdisciplinarity and epistemological pluralism.

More so, Suganami has argued that causal explanation should involve this intrinsic openness to conflicting interpretations:

> IR theorists should keep their minds open to a wide range of evidence and possible causal scenarios; they should construct an explanatory narrative and appreciate that any explanation of a historical social process involves a balance of judgement; and any claim to have arrived at a balanced account will remain contested by other interpretations. (Suganami 2016, 15)

Although it is not in the interest of this article to codify how dialogue between causal explanations or interpretations of terrorism can be operationalised, this does not discard the necessity of substantiating what a dialogical conception of causation could potentially look like. As mentioned, dialogue is elemental to practically addressing and transforming terrorism, as well as bridging the gap between the different epistemic communities that are engaged in the study of terrorism. More so, CTS as a research agenda is explicitly predicated on the goal "to generate real dialogue and debate, open up new questions and areas of research, and re-energise, revitalise, and improve the contemporary study of political terrorism" (Jackson et al. 2009a, 4). Accordingly, this has fostered a number of relevant articles in the field (Gad 2012; Mac Ginty 2013; Toros 2016). It therefore does not require much elaboration on why dialogical inquiry is important if not essential to the study of terrorism.

Yet the fact remains that this systematic focus on dialogue between causal explanations has not been picked up in CTS's lines of inquiry. Incorporating such a dialogical conception of causation would not only embolden CTS to further expose OTS's flawed and problematic understanding of causation, but also advance a more inclusive engagement that takes seriously the contextual and historical fabric of the particular case in question without neglecting the agential role. In addition, this would also provide CTS with a full-fledged alternative understanding of causation that provides a platform for the interpretation of and dialogue about the causes of terrorism.

Conclusion

This article has revealed how a problematic conception of causation is haunting both orthodox and critical studies of terrorism. The central concern consisted of highlighting how the latter, despite its commitment to epistemological pluralism, has predominantly refused to engage causal analysis on grounds that are increasingly hard to justify. Indeed, CTS unknowingly reproduces a conventional understanding of causation and thereby excludes the possibility of advancing an alternative conceptualisation of the concept. There is a rather simple explanation for this paradox that is to do with the way post-positivist theories more broadly have been affected by an anti-causal agenda. As such, it is not an internal problem to CTS but one related to a lack of critical yet sustained engagement with causation in other social scientific disciplines such as IR (Kurki 2008). It thereby concerns a persistent conflation of the concept of causation with the advancement of a positivist philosophy of science. More so, even though Hume's understanding of causation as grounded in regular observation of constant conjunction does in no discernible way necessitate such an advancement, post-positivist theories have grounded their rejection on the implicit acceptance of this understanding as the only game in town.

If CTS is serious about its commitment to deepening and broadening our understanding of terrorist violence, an engagement with causation is unavoidable. Understanding and explaining terrorism by engaging in causal analysis does not require compromising one's critical orientation. On the contrary, it has been a repeated contention of this article that incorporating causal analysis within the CTS research agenda offers a more effective and forceful way of criticising the implicit reproduction of the conventional understanding of causation in OTS. Indeed, the latter's problematic understanding of causation tends to confirm some of CTS's primal concerns that have to do with a tendency towards dehistorisation and decontextualisation. Especially in its critique of state-centrism, CTS has made the unfortunate error of taking indiscriminate aim at "discourses concerning the causes of terrorism" (Heath-Kelly 2010, 236). More importantly then, as long as this pattern is reproduced and no viable alternative is offered, OTS will remain emboldened in its quest for "root" causes in the service of counterterrorism policies that decontextualise and dehistoricise structural and contextual conditions.

The essential contribution of this article has therefore consisted of conceptualising a different way of understanding causation that draws on a CR philosophy of science, yet also moves beyond it to advance a hermeneutical alternative that resonates well within CTS's research agenda. Although CR has made a number of important interventions in CTS's meta-theoretical debates, its unfortunate reproduction of the subject/object divide is incompatible with an understanding of terrorism that is predicated on a discursive and reflective orientation (which emphasises the diversity of epistemological perspectives). The argument provided here therefore recollects the interpretative, normative, and dialogical fabric of causation. Accordingly, causal explanation takes on the form of establishing historical narratives through an interpretation of the open-systemic, social world that allows us to make moral judgements and engage in a more profound dialogue about both the particular context in which debates on terrorism occur on the one hand and between different, historically and contextually grounded interpretations of the causes of terrorism on the other. This seamlessly resonates with CTS's commitment to the integration of terrorism studies in a broader context of social theory, as well as issues related to emphasising the responsibility this research has to its subject matter. More so, it allows for causal explanation to bring the historical and contextual back into the core of the research framework.

In the end, the argument inevitably points towards the necessity of advancing a causal analysis that operates from within the CTS research agenda. Although providing such an analysis exhausts the scope of this inquiry, it is nonetheless worthwhile to explore some of the possible directions this could take. The critical space that is opened by causal analysis would first of all bring an end to the uncontested reproduction of the conventional understanding of causation in OTS. Not only would this expose the problematic of subjugating causal analysis to informing state-led policies of counter-terrorism, it would also challenge the hegemonic position that both this understanding of causation in particular and OTS more generally have acquired. Of greater importance, however, would be the more grounded and sustained understanding of terrorist violence that the alternative conceptualisation of causation would foster. Indeed, it would provide the important work that CTS has amassed over the last ten years with the strength and efficacy of causal analysis.

Notes

1. This arguably involved a reinterpretation of the psychological element since it no longer concerned the psychology of the perpetrator but of the psychology of those whom it is perpetrated upon.
2. Porpora also considers interpretivism to be part of post-modern relativism. As this tends to contradict the interpretive and historical conceptualisation of causation that stems from his broader argument, it is not entirely sure what interpretivism exactly stands for in this context.
3. There is of course a tendency to approach OTS as a reified category that no longer corresponds to the heterogenous body of scholarship that it is. Horgan and Boyle, for instance, argue that such a conception is "not representative of the existing breadth of research activity" (2008, 51) in the field. The present analysis therefore engages the way that causation has been conceptualised (or not) in this body of scholarship rather than indicating that it represents a homogenous and codified body of scholarship.

Acknowledgments

I would like to thank Lee Jarvis for his editorial assistance. I would also like to thank Harmonie Toros for involving me in a research project on political violence that provided the original impetus for this article. Finally, also thanks to Charles Devellennes and two anonymous reviewers whose suggestions and comments strengthened the presentation. Needless to say that any errors are mine alone.

Disclosure statement

No potential conflict of interest was reported by the author.

References

Al-Sumait, F., C. Lingle, and D. Domke. 2009. "Terrorism's Cause and Cure: The Rhetorical Regime of Democracy in the US and UK." *Critical Studies on Terrorism* 2 (1): 7–25. doi:10.1080/17539150902752432.

Archer, M., R. Bhaskar, A. Collier, T. Lawson, and A. Norrie. 1998. *Critical Realism: Essential Readings*. London: Routledge.

Ashley, R. K. 1989. "Living on Border Lines: Man, Poststructuralism and War." In *International/ Intertextual Relations: Postmodern Readings of World*, edited by J. Der Derian and M. J. Shapiro, 259–321. Lexington: Lexington Books.

Bergen, P. L., and T. Luckmann. 1966. *The Social Construction of Reality: A Treatise in the Sociology of Knowledge*. New York: Anchor Books.

Bhaskar, R. 1978/2008. *A Realist Theory of Science*. 2nd ed. Brighton: Harvester.

Bjørgo, T. 2005. "Introduction." In *Root Causes of Terrorism: Myths, Reality and Ways Forward*, edited by T. Bjørgo, 1–15. Abingdon, Oxon: Routledge.

Breen Smyth, M. 2009. "Subjectivities, 'Suspect Communities', Governments, and the Ethics of Research on 'Terrorism'." In *Critical Terrorism Studies: A New Research Agenda*, edited by R. Jackson, M. Breen Smyth, and J. Gunning, 194–215. Abingdon, Oxon: Routledge.

Brown, C. 2007. "Situating Critical Realism." *Millennium: Journal of International Studies* 35 (2): 409–416. doi:10.1177/03058298070350020201.

Campana, A., and L. Lapointe. 2012. "The Structural "Root" Causes of Non-Suicide Terrorism: A Systematic Scoping Review." *Terrorism and Political Violence* 24 (1): 79–104. doi:10.1080/09546553.2011.611547.

Chernoff, F. 2007. "Critical Realism, Scientific Realism, and International Relations Theory." *Millennium: Journal of International Studies* 35 (2): 399–407. doi:10.1177/03058298070350021701.

Collier, A. 1994. *Critical Realism: An Introduction to Roy Bhaskar's Philosophy*. London: Verso.

Cox, R. 1986. "Social Forces, States and World Orders: Beyond International Relations Theory." In *. Neorealism and Its Critic*, edited by R. Keohane. New York: Columbia University Press.

Cox, R. W. 1981. "Social Forces, States, and World Orders: Beyond International Relations Theory." *Millennium: Journal of International Studies* 10 (2): 126–155. doi:10.1177/03058298810100020501.

Crenshaw, M. 1981. "The Causes of Terrorism." *Comparative Politics* 13 (4): 379–399. doi:10.2307/421717.

Cruickshank, J. 2002. "Critical Realism and Critical Philosophy: On the Usefulness of Philosophical Problems." *Journal of Critical Realism* 1 (1): 49–66. doi:10.1558/jocr.v1i1.49.

Dunmire, P. L. 2009. "'9/11 Changed Everything': An Intertextual Analysis of the Bush Doctrine." *Discourse & Society* 20 (2): 195–222. doi:10.1177/0957926508099002.

Feynman, R. P. 1992. *The Character of Physical Law*. London: Penguin.

Gad, U. P. 2012. "Concepts of Dialogue as Counterterrorism: Narrating the Self-Reform of the Muslim Other." *Critical Studies on Terrorism* 5 (2): 159–178. doi:10.1080/17539153.2012.677250.

Goodwin, J. 2012. "Religious Terrorism as Ideology." In *Contemporary Debates on Terrorism*, edited by R. Jackson and S. J. Sinclair, 127–133. London: Routledge.

Gurr, T. 1970. *Why Men Rebel*. London: Paradigm.

Harré, R., and E. H. Madden. 1975. *Causal Powers: A Theory of Natural Necessity*. Oxford: Basil Blackwell.

Heath-Kelly, C. 2010. "Critical Terrorism Studies, Critical Theory and the 'Naturalistic Fallacy'." *Security Dialogue* 41 (3): 235–254. doi:10.1177/0967010610370227.

Herring, E., and D. Stokes. 2011. "Critical Realism and Historical Materialism as Resources for Critical Terrorism Studies." *Critical Studies on Terrorism* 4 (1): 5–21. doi:10.1080/17539153.2011.553384.

Hoffman, B. 2006. *Inside Terrorism*. New York: Columbia University Press.

Horgan, J., and M. J. Boyle. 2008. "A Case against 'Critical Terrorism Studies'." *Critical Studies on Terrorism* 1 (1): 51–64. doi:10.1080/17539150701848225.

Horkheimer, M. 1982. *Critical Theory: Selected Essays*. New York: Continuum.

Huesmann, L. R., and G. R. Huesmann. 2012. "Poverty and And Exclusion are Not the Root Cause of Terrorism." In *Contemporary Debates on Terrorism*, edited by R. Jackson and S. J. Sinclair, 113–117. London: Routledge.

Hume, D. 1777/1962. *Enquiries Concerning Human Understanding and Concerning the Principles of Morals*. 2nd ed. Oxford: Clarendon Press.

Jäckle, S., and M. Baumann. 2015. ""New Terrorism" = Higher Brutality? an Empirical Test of the "brutalization Thesis"." *Terrorism and Political Violence*: 1–27. Online publication. doi:10.1080/09546553.2015.1087399.

Jackson, R. 2007. "The Core Commitments of Critical Terrorism Studies." *European Political Science* 6: 244–251. doi:10.1057/palgrave.eps.2210141.

Jackson, R. 2012a. "Unknown Knowns: The Subjugated Knowledge of Terrorism Studies." *Critical Studies on Terrorism* 5 (1): 11–29. doi:10.1080/17539153.2012.659907.

Jackson, R. 2012b. "The Study of Terrorism 10 Years after 9/11: Successes, Issues, Challenges." *Uluslararası İlişKiler* 8 (32): 1–16.

Jackson, R. 2015. "The Epistemological Crisis of Counterterrorism." *Critical Studies on Terrorism* 8 (1): 33–54. doi:10.1080/17539153.2015.1009762.

Jackson, R., and G. Hall. 2016. "Talking about Terrorism: A Study of Vernacular Discourse." *Politics* 1–16.

Jackson, R., and H. Dexter. 2014. "The Social Construction of Organised Political Violence: An Analytical Framework." *Civil Wars* 16 (1): 1–23. doi:10.1080/13698249.2014.904982.

Jackson, R., L. Jarvis, J. Gunning, and M. Breen-Smyth. 2011. *Terrorism: A Critical Introduction*. New York: Palgrave Macmillan.

Jackson, R., M. Breen Smyth, and J. Gunning, eds. 2009a. *Critical Terrorism Studies: A New Research Agenda*. Abingdon, Oxon: Routledge.

Jackson, R., M. Breen Smyth, and J. Gunning. 2009b. "Critical Terrorism Studies: Framing a New Research Agenda." In *Critical Terrorism Studies: A New Research Agenda*, edited by R. Jackson, M. B. Smyth, and J. Gunning, 216–236. Abingdon, Oxon: Routledge.

Jackson, R. 2009. "Knowledge, Power and Politics in the Study of Political Terrorism." In *Critical Terrorism Studies: A New Research Agenda*, edited by R. Jackson, M. B. Smyth, and J. Gunning, 49–65. Abingdon, Oxon: Routledge.

Jones, D. M., and M. L. R. Smith. 2010. "Beyond Belief: Islamist Strategic Thinking and International Relations Theory." *Terrorism and Political Violence* 22 (2): 242–266. doi:10.1080/09546550903472286.

Joseph, J. 2011. "Terrorism as a Social Relation within Capitalism: Theoretical and Emancipatory Implications." *Critical Studies on Terrorism* 4 (1): 23–37. doi:10.1080/17539153.2011.553385.

Joseph, J., and C. Wright. 2010. *Scientific Realism and International Relations*. New York: Palgrave Macmillan.

Keohane, R. O. 1988. "International Institutions: Two Approaches." *International Studies Quarterly* 32 (4): 379–396. doi:10.2307/2600589.

King, G., R. O. Keohane, and S. Verba. 1994. *Designing Social Inquiry: Scientific Inference in Qualitative Research*. Princeton: Princeton University Press.

Kratochwil, F. 1989. *Rules, Norms and Decisions: On the Conditions of Practical and Legal Reasoning in International Relations and Domestic Affairs*. Cambridge: Cambridge University Press.

Kurki, M. 2008. *Causation in International Relations: Reclaiming Causal Analysis*. Cambridge: Cambridge University Press.

Kurtulus, E. N. 2011. "The "New Terrorism" and Its Critics." *Studies in Conflict & Terrorism* 34 (6): 476–500. doi:10.1080/1057610X.2011.571194.

Kydd, A. H., and B. F. Walter. 2006. "The Strategies of Terrorism." *International Security* 31 (1): 49–80. doi:10.1162/isec.2006.31.1.49.

Laqueur, W. 1999. *The New Terrorism: Fanaticism and the Arms of Mass Destruction*. Oxford: Oxford University Press.

Lynch, O., and C. Ryder. 2012. "Deadliness, Organisational Change and Suicide Attacks: Understanding the Assumptions Inherent in the Use of the Term 'New Terrorism'." *Critical Studies on Terrorism* 5 (2): 257–275. doi:10.1080/17539153.2012.692512.

Mac Ginty, R. 2013. "Look Who's Talking: Terrorism, Dialogue and Conflict Transformation." *Critical Studies on Terrorism* 6 (1): 216–223. doi:10.1080/17539153.2013.765708.

Pape, R. A. 2005. *Dying to Win: The Strategic Logic of Suicide Terrorism*. New York: Random House.

Porpora, D. V. 2011. "Critical Terrorism Studies: A Political Economic Approach Grounded in Critical Realism." *Critical Studies on Terrorism* 4 (1): 39–55. doi:10.1080/17539153.2011.553386.

Ranstorp, M., ed. 2006. *Mapping Terrorism Research: State of the Art, Gaps and Future Direction*. London: Routledge.

Raphael, S. 2009. "In the Service of Power: Terrorism Studies and US Intervention in the Global South." In *Critical Terrorism Studies: A New Research Agenda*, edited by R. Jackson, M. Breen Smyth, and J. Gunning, 49–65. Abingdon, Oxon: Routledge.

Rapport, D. 1971. *Assassination and Terrorism*. Toronto: Canadian Broadcasting Corp.

Reich, W., ed. 1990. *Origins of Terrorism: Psychologies, Ideologies, Theologies, States of Mind*. Cambridge: Cambridge University Press.

Richardson, L. 2006. *What Terrorists Want*. New York: Random House.

Sageman, M. 2004. *Understanding Terror Networks*. Philadelphia: University of Pennsylvania Press.

Sageman, M. 2014. "The Stagnation in Terrorism Research." *Terrorism and Political Violence* 26 (4): 565–580. doi:10.1080/09546553.2014.895649.

Stone, D. 1996. *Capturing the Political Imagination: Think Tanks and the Policy Process*. London: Frank Cass.

Suganami, H. 1996. *On the Causes of War*. Oxford: Oxford University Press.

Suganami, H. 2008. "Narrative Explanation and International Relations: Back to Basics." *Millennium: Journal of International Studies* 37 (2): 327–356. doi:10.1177/0305829808097643.

Suganami, H. 2011. "Causal Explanation and Moral Judgement: Undividing a Division." *Millennium: Journal of International Studies* 39 (3): 717–734. doi:10.1177/0305829811402809.

Suganami, H. 2013. "Causation-In-The-World: A Contribution to Meta-Theory of IR." *Millennium: Journal of International Studies* 41 (3): 623–643. doi:10.1177/0305829813484185.

Suganami, H. 2016. "On the Hume/Bhaskar Contrast in Philosophical metatheory of International Relations." *Journal of International Relations and Development*. Advance online publication. doi:10.1057/jird.2016.9.

Tilly, C. 1971. "Review: Why Men Rebel." *Journal of Social History* 4 (4): 416–420. doi:10.1353/jsh/4.4.416.

Toros, H. 2012. *Terrorism, Talking and Transformation: A Critical Approach*. Abingdon, Oxon: Routledge.

Toros, H. 2016. "Dialogue, Praxis and the State: A Response to Richard Jackson." *Critical Studies on Terrorism* 9 (1): 126–130. doi:10.1080/17539153.2016.1147775.

Toros, H., and J. Gunning. 2009. "Exploring a Critical Theory Approach to Terrorism Studies." In *Critical Terrorism Studies: A New Research Agenda*, edited by R. Jackson, M. Breen Smyth, and J. Gunning, 87–108. Abingdon, Oxon: Routledge.

Wyn Jones, R. 1999. *Security, Strategy, and Critical Theory*. London: Lynne Ripener.

"The terrorist": the out-of-place and on-the-move "perverse homosexual" in international relations*

Cynthia Weber

Preface

This piece is an excerpt from my book *Queer International Relations* (Weber 2016a). Harmonie Toros astutely edited this piece to focus in on my arguments about terrorism and the figure of "the terrorist". Many thanks to Harmonie for her excellent work.

The core argument I make in *Queer International Relations* is that international relations (IR) literatures on sovereignty and queer studies literatures on sexuality must be read together. This is because IR scholars undertheorise sexuality, and queer studies scholars undertheorise sovereignty. The story I tell in the book is about how the crafting of sovereign and sexualised figures is a tool in domestic and international games of power that confirms as well as contests traditional logics of what Richard Ashley calls "modern statecraft as modern mancraft" (1989).

By performing a close reading of modern Western theories and foreign policies on development, immigration, terrorism, human rights, and regional and international integration, I demonstrate how answers to the question "Who is 'sovereign man'?" are intricately bound up with answers to the question "Who is 'the homosexual'?". Following in the footsteps of feminist and gender theorists, critical race scholars, post-colonial, decolonial and native studies scholars who evidenced how "sovereign man" is sexed, gendered and racialised often in/through colonial and/or settler colonial practices, I evidence how "sovereign man" is also *sexualised* (something that some but not all of these scholars do). And because "sovereign man" is a figure who is used to authorise political authority within a political community and also to project that authority beyond the boundaries of that political community, this means that it is not only *sovereign man* who is sexualised; formal and informal ways IR are arranged through what IR scholars discuss as order vs. anarchy are also sexualised. I refer to these international arrangements (and additional combinations of order and/or anarchy) as *sexualised organisations of IR*.

The argument in this abridged piece is indicative of how queer migrations and queer terrorism literatures can be read with IR literatures on statecraft as mancraft to complicate IR and queer studies' readings of terrorism and "the terrorist". Yet it is far from comprehensive. For example, apart from a brief mention in a footnote, it does not deal with the figure of "the ISIS terrorist", as it is focused instead on the related but differently figured "al-Qaeda terrorist". I made the decision to focus on "the al-Qaeda terrorist" for two

---

*Extracts from Ch.3 'The Out-of-Place and On-the-Move "Perverse Homosexual" in International Relations: "The Unwanted Im/migrant" and "The Terrorist"' from "Queer International Relations: Sovereignty, Sexuality and the Will to Knowledge" by Weber, Cynthia (2016)
Free permission Author reusing own work by permission of Oxford University Press.

reasons. First, at the time I wrote *Queer International Relations*, "the al-Qaeda terrorist" was the dominant figuration of "the terrorist" found in IR and in queer studies literatures. But second and more importantly, "the al-Qaeda terrorist's" *movements* in relation to the home and the homeland defy and unravel traditional Western logics of statecraft as mancraft in ways that "the ISIS terrorist" does not. How "the al-Qaeda terrorist" puts into motion what Western discourses cast as "civilisational barbarism" and "sexual barbarism" both defies the *either/or* logics of traditional statecraft as mancraft and demands a queer analytical lens that can read "the terrorist" through *and/or* logics. This is precisely what a queer logics of statecraft offers (see Weber 2016a, 2016b, 2016c).

This abridged piece assumes a thorough understanding of queer critiques of modernisation and development theory and (to a lesser extent) queer critiques of migration. For those readers who require this background, it can be found in the longer book.

Introduction

Sexual development and sexual barbarism on the move are rarely discussed in IR. This is because IR tends to see sexuality as the domain of the "home" (the family) rather than as the domain of the "homeland" (the state). Yet the home and the family are as essential to IR as is homeland; indeed, they cannot be dissociated from one another, as IR scholar V. Spike Peterson has long argued (1999, 2010, 2013, 2014a, 2014b). For example, Margaret Mead's claim that there is something called "national character" hinges upon her ability to link activities in the family home with the identity of the nation. This is clear in how she defines "national character" as "an abstraction, a way of talking about the results in human personality, *of having been reared by and among human beings whose behavior was culturally regular*" (Mead 1942, 21, my italics; also see Mead 1928 on "sexual mores"). Similarly, Samuel Huntington's civilisational discourse links activities in the home with the security of the homeland. For example, Huntington stokes US fears of the "Latin American civilizational Hispanic" not just based upon this figure's geopolitical movements but also based upon this figure's sexual activities. Huntington writes that "[t]he most immediate and most serious challenge to Americans" traditional identity comes from the immense and continuing immigration from Latin America, especially from Mexico, *and the fertility rates of these immigrants*" (Huntington 2004, 32, my italics). This, for Huntington, is among the ways in which the "Hispanic" "adhere(s) to and propagates the values, customs, and cultures of their home society" (1996, 304).

It is this strange *emphasis and neglect* of home and its connection to homeland that typifies much of IR scholarship and accounts for its undertheorisation of sexuality on the move. In contrast to most IR literatures, queer migrations literatures make sexual movements in the home and (in)between homelands their primary foci (e.g. Eng 1997; Ahmed 2000; Luibhéid and Cantú 2005; Luibhéid 2008, 2013; Fortier 2000, 2001, 2002, 2003; Gopinath 2005). In so doing, they offer a corrective lens through which to reconsider figures who are presumably on the move and out of place geopolitically, developmentally *and* sexually.

Here I reconsider the "the 'terrorist'"[1] from both an IR and a queer migrations perspective. I argue that complex connections among civilising/civilisational movements and sexual movements in the home/land together do two things. First, they figure the "terrorist" as the out-of-place "underdeveloped" or "undevelopable", whose movements in relation to space, time and desire mark him as an civilisationally and sexually out-of-place global Southerner who holds developmental and/or security risks for the "developed" Western /global Northern home/land. Second, as an instance of statecraft as mancraft, they give rise to sexualised orders of IR that securitise the "terrorist" so that white, Christian, bourgeois, heterosexual, cisgendered, ableized, "developed" Westerners/ Northerners can feel more at ease (Bigo 2002) and at home in their home/lands.

In order to this bring civilisational and sexual figuration *and its movements* into greater relief, I attempt to disentangle the impossibly entangled narratives of civilising/civilisational movement and sexual movement in my analysis of the "terrorist". This leads me to first read the "terrorist" in general terms and then specifically the "al-Qaeda terrorist" as civilisation barbarism on the move before rereading him as sexual barbarism on the move. I conclude by reflecting on how a queer migrations lens exposes the "anxious labor" (Luibhéid 2008, 174) that Western discourses of statecraft as mancraft expend to attempt to create binary sexual figurations of and in the home and homeland that might sustain heteronormative sexualised orders of IR.

The "al-Qaeda terrorist" as civilisational barbarism on the move

How is the "terrorist" – and more specifically the "al-Qaeda terrorist" – known in Western discourses of statecraft as mancraft as the civilisationally barbaric out-of-place "undevelopable"? And how does he put the "Western /global Northern homeland" at risk as civilisational barbarism on the move?

Civilisational barbarism is, by its very definition, out of place in any civilisational discourse, Western or otherwise. This is because civilisational barbarism is the dangerous opposite to the civilisational homeland (Huntington 1996, 321), which is understood as the universal space in which a desire for one or another type of civilisation is formed in populations that either matches or clashes with that of another civilisation. Because it is a perversion of any type of desire for civilisation, civilisational barbarism has no proper place. In this sense, civilisational barbarism is home(land)less. This does not mean that Western /global Northern discourses do not assign civilisational barbarism a place or that Western policies do not try to keep civilisationally barbaric figures in their place. They do – spatially, temporally and in relation to desire. In this section, I analyse the predominant contemporary figuration of the "terrorist" in IR – the "al-Qaeda terrorist". I explain how the "al-Qaeda terrorist" is assigned to specific places in Western discourses and how his movements complicate Western understandings of where the "undevelopable" ought to be placed, in ways that figure the "al-Qaeda terrorist" as a known risk to the "Western /global Northern homeland".

Spatially, even though the "al-Qaeda terrorist" has no proper place in any civilisation, he is assigned two points of origin in Western discourse. The first of these is religious, which understands the "al-Qaeda terrorist" as originating from within a radical, indeed fanatical, pathological Islam. According to this narrative, it is the religious radicalisation of the "al-Qaeda terrorist" that displaces his proper desire as the "underdeveloped" to become "developed" and replaces it with a psychopathologised desire to become "the fanatical Islamic jihadist".[2] As a jihadist, the "al-Qaeda terrorist" becomes civilisationally barbaric by embracing a violent incivility that he expresses through acts of cruelty against communities of nonbelievers, especially populations in or adhering to the values of "Western civilisation".

In this religious narrative, part of what accounts for the misplaced desire of the "al-Qaeda terrorist" is his relationship to time. Temporally, the "al-Qaeda terrorist" acts in historical, earthly time in order to preserve God's laws on earth. This situates him in the eschatological temporality of religious devotion, where his earthly life is a fleeting moment on his path towards his eternal reward in the afterlife. As a primarily eschatological temporal figure whose pathological devotion to God's laws makes him impervious to the implantation of a modern, Western desire for earthly development, the "al-Qaeda terrorist" eschews the progressive temporality of civilising development that promises to deliver him into one or another form of more advanced civilisation. What he desires, instead, is to enforce God's righteous traditions on earth by illuminating (through religious conversion where possible) or eliminating (through terrorism where necessary) nonbelievers who pervert God's laws through their commitments to modernisation and development. This makes the "al-Qaeda terrorist" not just nonfunctional and undevelopmental in any civilisational schema of historical development, but also the pure enemy of modernity itself, figured in Western discourses as "diabolical", as a "henchman", a "dirtbag", a "monster", "a shadow of evil" who is "the opposite of all that is just, human, and good" (Puar and Rai 2002, 118; also see Rutenberg 2001). It is his pathological piety that puts his civilisational barbarism on the move, as a religious crusader against all nonbelievers and against "Western civilization" itself (see Carroll 2004).

In Western discourse, the point from which the "al-Qaeda terrorist" stages his crusade is necessarily geopolitical. This is because every religion and every so-called civilisation in every part of the globe has religious fundamentalists, some of whom are violent. This is why Western discourses spatialise the "al-Qaeda terrorist" a second time, locating this figure who is racialised as non-white in the "global South". Huntington's division of the world into seven or eight civilisations that place each civilisation in a distinct global territory offers one illustration of this move (Huntington 1996, 26).

By freezing this non-white, fanatical "civilisational other" in its place in the postcolonial world, the "West" to some degree succeeds in its own terms in demarcating dangerous "Islamic fundamentalists" from innocuous, white "Western" ones. But it nevertheless fails to keep the "al-Qaeda terrorist" in his civilisation of origin – rhetorically or practically. This is because the "al-Qaeda terrorist" does not (primarily) put his civilisational barbarism on the move at what Huntington calls "the bloody [territorial] borders" between the West and the rest (1996, 254–259). The "al-Qaeda terrorist" puts his civilisational barbarism on the move through a network of terrorist cells. In so doing, he utterly unravels Western attempts to contain him spatially or temporally.

Spatially, the "al-Qaeda terrorist" is postnational in ways Huntington's "Western civilization" never was. As I have argued elsewhere (Weber 2002), this is because al-Qaeda operates more like an international firm in the contemporary neoliberal global order than like a territorial state. For example,

> Just as a KFC franchise succeeds by enticing customers through efficient service and with products that their competitors have yet to think of, so too does al-Qaeda seem to function by providing a product (an Islamic fundamentalist ideology turned terrorist) to meet customer demand through technological efficiency (training programs that enable 'employees' to perform one or more specific tasks in the 'production process') and forward thinking (transforming Hollywood-like scripts [like flying planes into buildings] into actual events).

Like other global corporations, when circumstances sour on the ground, making operations from one locale unattractive (e.g. unfavourable terms from host governments), al-Qaeda just moves its ground operations to more welcoming sites. These places include not only Afghanistan and parts of the [so-called] Arab world, but Germany, Britain, Canada and [the United States of] America. And these are just the ground operations. Not only is al-Qaeda, this time like a 'dot.com' business, located everywhere; it is also located nowhere. It exists as a mobile network of connections of cash and carriers accessible from just about anywhere but locatable almost exclusively as mere network nodal points. (Weber 2002, 142–143)

While this does not stop Western leaders from associating the "al-Qaeda terrorist network" with a sovereign nation state – as President George W. Bush equated Osama bin Laden and his al-Qaeda network with Afghanistan's Taliban government (Bush 2001) – such correlations inevitably fail. The al-Qaeda network of cells cannot be pinned down within a territorial nation state because it is elliptical, fluid and changeable. Today, it is one thing, like a free-flowing dot.com company. Tomorrow it is something else, with its terrorist cells as neoliberal global franchises springing into action as "civilizational (anti)heroes" on US domestic airliners (Weber 2002, 143).

As al-Qaeda cells multiply and divide, appear and disappear, their geographical and "civilisational" origins shift. The end result is figures that were previously unimaginable in Western fantasies about the "al-Qaeda terrorist" – like the civilisational outsider ("the al-Qaeda terrorist") who was the civilisational insider ("the Western civilisational citizen") who is now inside Western civilisation as "irreducible foreignness" (Palumbo-Lui 2002, 122). It was as this confused figuration of the "al-Qaeda terrorist" that British-born Muslims fighting US and British coalition forces in Afghanistan were reported to have become the first "foreign" casualties in the War on Terror.[3] What this means, then, is that the "al-Qaeda terrorist" has no civilisational homefront because he does not reside in nor can he be placed, much less kept in place, within a civilisational homeland. This makes him all the more anarchical, unruly and illusive as the pure enemy of "Western civilisation" and "civilised, developed sovereign man".

Temporally, the "al-Qaeda terrorist" is just as confounding of Western narratives as he is spatially. He is an actor who understands himself to be located in God's eschatological time that is for the moment being played out in man's historical time. But his civilisational barbarism is enacted by mixing so-called traditional and modern temporalities in ways that make a mockery of the Great Dichotomy's developmental temporality designating more primitive versus more advanced. For the "al-Qaeda terrorist" is a presumably primitive, traditional eschatological subject whose actions are made possible because he is plugged into a savvy high-tech network as an anonymous nodal point. And these actions themselves are understood as undevelopable civilisational barbarism that have developed future fictions (like novelist Tom Clancy's idea of flying planes into US government buildings as suicidal terrorist acts; Clancy 1994) into contemporary historical actions.

Taken together, all of this explains how the "al-Qaeda terrorist" puts the Western / global Northern homeland at risk as civilisationally barbaric "antisovereign man" on the move. The "al-Qaeda terrorist" is such a risk to Western civilisation's "civilized, developed sovereign man" that the "al-Qaeda terrorist's" dangerous mobility must be stopped. The "West" tries to immobilise his civilisational barbarism on the move in three ways – by keeping him outside of Western civilisation (Bigo 2002), by keeping him inside containment facilities like those in Guantánamo Bay, Cuba, and finally by making him a necropolitical target of state policies who must be killed (preferably outside the Western homeland/culture/civilisation) before he kills (inside) the Western homeland/culture/civilisation (see Puar 2007; Kuntsman 2009; Haritaworn, Kuntsman, and Posocco 2013).

The "al-Qaeda terrorist" as sexual barbarism on the move

How is the "al-Qaeda terrorist" known in Western discourses of statecraft as mancraft as the sexually barbaric out-of-place "undevelopable"? And how does he put the "Western / global Northern home/land" at risk as sexual barbarism on the move?

Like civilisational barbarism, sexual barbarism is definitionally out of place in any narrative of normalised sexuality. This is because sexual barbarism is the dangerous opposite of civilisational sexuality. Sexually barbaric figures will not naturally mature into sexually civilised beings. Nor can they be successfully implanted with a desire for civilised mature sexuality through social, psychological or political processes. For sexual barbarism describes a modality of sexual conduct that is so violently uncivilised and cruel that it cannot be recuperated by any moral narrative of civilising or civilised sexual development. This makes the sexual barbarian a freak of both nature and culture, the monstrous sexualised "half-human, half-animal" that Foucault (1997) writes about, whose monstrosity, as Jasbir Puar and Amit Rai (2002, 119) explain, is as racialised and culturalised as it is sexualised. As such, it has no proper place in the nuclear family (Parsons 1966), understood as the civilising site of sexual development for the nation (Peterson 1999, 2010, 2013, 2014a, 2014b) and/or for the civilisation (Huntington 1996, 2004). Sexual barbarism, then, is a form of civilisational barbarism that is presumptively homeless.[4]

This does not mean that Western discourses do not assign sexual barbarism a place or that Western policies do not try to keep those they figure as sexually barbaric in their place. Just as they do in discourses on civilisational barbarism in general, these discourses use specific codings of space, time and desire in their attempts to contain civilisationally and sexually barbaric figures.

Spatially, Western discourses assign the civilisationally and sexually barbaric "al-Qaeda terrorist" a home of origin – "the Islamic civilizational home" (Said 1978; also see Razack 2004; Lewis 2006; Fortier 2008). Understood as the home in which the "al-Qaeda terrorist" is reared, this home lies at the heart of civilisational barbarism itself, which (as we saw in the previous section) the Great Dichotomy locates in psychopathological, fanatical Islam and in a primitive Islamic homeland in the global South. The "Islamic civilisational home" is not that of the white Christian bourgeois nuclear family that Talcott Parsons describes (1966), in which reproductive cisgendered heterosexuality is modelled by the able-bodied, matured, white Christian bourgeois figure and harnessed on behalf of society (Parsons 1966) and the nation state (Almond and Powell 1966; Peterson 1999, 2010, 2013, 2014a, 2014b). It is instead a specific perversion of this home, in which a racialised, religiously sanctioned patriarchal polygamy is modelled, matured and harnessed on behalf of "Islamic civilization" (Huntington 1996). It is this "Islamic civilizational home" that is known in Western discourses to be the universal space for sexual development within "Islamic civilization".

49

As measured against the white Western, Christian, bourgeois nuclear familial home, this "Islamic civilisational home" is perverse because it folds a selfish male desire for sexual pleasure with multiple partners into the family home. As it is understood in Western discourse, this selfish sexuality is a specifically Islamic modality of primitive male heterosexual promiscuity that bears traces of primitive male homosexual promiscuity (see Hoad 2000). As such, it legitimises a deviant form of private male hyperheterosexuality that oppresses women and girls in the home, which reflects public forms of male hyperhomosociality that oppress women and girls in the wider "Islamic civilisation". While not always scripted as sexually barbaric in Western discourses, the "Islamic civilisational home" was regimented as such in Western discourses on the War on Terror, in part to justify the US-led war in Afghanistan on the purported grounds of rescuing women and girls from civilisationally and sexually barbaric Islam (e.g. see CLoud 2004; Weber 2005, 2006). This fermented the idea that the "Islamic civilisational home" was dangerously over(re)productive in two senses – as the private sexual site of the public perversion of social relations in "Islamic civilisation" and as the illiberal breading ground of the "al-Qaeda terrorist's" private sexual perversions.

Reared in this always primitive civilisational home, the "al-Qaeda terrorist" in Western discourse is a figure into whom male licence for selfish sexual satisfaction has been implanted. At the same time, he is a figure who has failed to mature into the normative (in Western descriptions of "Islamic" terms/perverse in Western terms) sexuality required to reproduce the "Islamic civilisational home". Western discourse explains the "al-Qaeda terrorist's" (failed) uptake of "Islamic civilisational sexuality" temporally. On the one hand, the "al-Qaeda terrorist's" embrace of a fanatical form of Islamic homosociality is rooted in his temporal failure to develop sexually. This makes him the decadent homosexual found in Freudian psychoanalysis (see Hoad 2000), albeit one with no prospect of ever becoming sexually developed. As such, the "al-Qaeda terrorist" is the frozen countenance of perversion Foucault describes as the "perverse homosexual" (1980, 48). On the other hand, because he is a civilisational barbaric who lives more in God's time than in man's time, the "al-Qaeda terrorist" is described as being less interested in harnessing his perverse sexual desire on behalf of reproducing the earthly Islamic family romance than he is in claiming his heavenly reward for martyring himself in jihad – some sixty to seventy virgins (Puar and Rai 2002, 124). This confirms his undevelopable, nonfunctional status in the family home, making him a sexual outsider, inside the "Islamic civilisational home".

All of this figures the "al-Qaeda terrorist" as a civilisational and sexual barbaric who is hyperheterosexualised while also being hyperhomosexualised and hyperhomosocialised. In Puar and Rai's terms, this is why the "al-Qaeda terrorist" appears in Western (and especially post-9/11 US terrorist) discourses as a psychologised monstrous creature who – marked in part by his failed heterosexuality – is a "monster-terrorist-fag" (2002, 124, 139). For he is an abomination of normality (monster), an undevelopable and uncivilisable threat to the Western home/land and to Western civilisation (terrorist), and a figural "homosexual" (fag). In rendering him sexually barbaric, Western discourses posit the "al-Qaeda terrorist's" perverse desires – which they decree to be religiously inspired and politically irrelevant (Khalil 2001; cited in Puar and Rai 2002) – as the motivation for his movements. How he moves as a civilisational barbaric (as we saw in the previous section) is as a civilisational outsider who eschews any civilisational homeland. How he moves as a sexual barbaric is as a sexual outsider who eschews any civilisational home. In combination, these movements further complicate Western encodings of the "al-Qaeda terrorist" spatially and temporally, while proliferating his threats to the Western /global Northern home and homeland.

Spatially, the "al-Qaeda terrorist" remains more attached to the terrorist cell than to the "Islamic civilisational family". Because this attachment is both civilisationally barbaric and sexually barbaric, this attachment does not just denote a violent entrepreneurial *productivity* (modelled on one or another type of international firm in the contemporary neoliberal global order; Weber 2002). It connotes a dangerous *reproductivity*, in relation to both "the (already dangerously reproductive) Islamic civilisational family" and to civilisation itself. Making sense of this dangerous reproductivity requires looking again at how Western discourses position the "al-Qaeda terrorist" temporally and what this positioning does.

As a figure whose earthly activities are eschatologically directed (towards the non-reproductive afterlife) rather than historically directed (towards reproducing life), the "al-Qaeda terrorist" breaks the link between familial/social reproduction and civilisational reproduction when God's laws demand it, making him a sexually nonfunctional decadent in relation to the civilisational family. Yet I would suggest that the "al-Qaeda terrorist's" designation in Western discourses as sexually decadent is not primarily based upon his decision to (sometimes) opt out of sexual reproductive time, which Western discourses never actually allow him to do (Puar and Rai 2002; Puar 2007). Rather, the "al-Qaeda terrorist's" sexual decadence results because his eschatological existence as a devout, fanatical Islamic jihadist causes him to move "aslant, sideways" (Warner, back cover of Patton and Benigno Sánches-Eppler 2000), by being out of step and out of line with the civilisational family and with familial/social/civilisational reproduction. This queer movement leads him to substitute one kind of reproduction (the homosocial reproduction of the terrorist cell) for another (the heterosexual reproduction of the family) as the privileged site of reproductive activity and to substitute one figure (the monster-terrorist-fag) for another (the child) as the privileged result of his homosocial reproduction.

This makes the primary brand of reproduction belonging to "al-Qaeda terrorist" *asexual*, even though it is characterised in Western discourse as being sexually motivated. More than a hyperheterosexual or hyperhomosexual figure, then, the "al-Qaeda terrorist" is both beyond sex and driven by sex at the same time. As such, he is a kind of sanctified turned zealous Islamic neuter, who functions in civilisational discourses on family, home and homeland as a deliberate static (Barthes 1976, 9) that plays havoc with norms, normativities and antinormativities (Wiegman and Wilson 2015) of the kind expressed in heteronormativities (Berlant and Warner 1998) and in homonationalisms (Puar 2007) on all sides of supposed civilisational divides. For like his civilisational barbarism, the sexual barbarism of the "al-Qaeda terrorist" is all over the sexual and civilisational map. This proliferates his figurations in Western discourses and the risks his civilisational and sexual barbarism on the move create in/for the "Western /global Northern home/land".

For example, the "al-Qaeda terrorist" remains the "monster-terrorist-fag" when his movements violently assault the "West". But he is also any racially darkened "cultural" figure whose "irredeemable foreignness" (Palumbo-Liu 2002, 112) might be seen by the

"West" as emanating from the "Islamic civilisational home". These cultural turned civilisational others – including but not limited to so-called Arabs, Muslims and Sikhs (Puar and Rai 2002; Puar 2007) – might have settled in the "West" generations ago and taken a Western citizenship. Or they might be newly settling im/migrants to the "West". Either way, their misassociation with how Western discourses describe the "Islamic civilisational home" transforms them into "unwanted im/migrants", with all that conveys in terms of their civilisational development and sexual development on the move *and* with all that conveys in terms of their association with the "al-Qaeda terrorist".

Read through this Western lens, these "unwanted im/migrants" are forever those "diasporic ethics" (Palumbo-Liu 2002, 120–121) in whom the "American Creed" (Huntington 2004, 41) or some more generalised Western creed of modernisation and development has not and cannot be implanted. This is because they model the wrong type of civilisational family in the geopolitical West/North and harness this civilisational family for the wrong types of reproduction. By this reading, they are not "Westerners" or "Northerners", nor can they become "Westerners" or "Northerners". They are infiltrators of the "Western/global Northern home/land" who deprive the "West" of the cultural and civilisational purity it understands itself to require in order to survive (Palumbo-Liu 2002, 119–120). More than anything else, then, these "unwanted im/migrants" as modellers, breeders or conductors of al-Qaeda terrorism bring "the violence of the world we live in *at the heart of the home*, the heart of the national self" (Fortier 2008, 60; emphasis in original). These are among the ways the "al-Qaeda terrorist" – as a mobile figure or as the "unwanted im/migrant" settled in the "West" – is figured as a known threat to the "Western /global Northern home/land" because of how he puts sexual barbarism on the move.[5]

The extreme uneasiness the "al-Qaeda terrorist" causes Westerners is used in Western discourses to justify a Huntingtonian revival of a Western wartime footing of the sort Mead's cultural defence of the "American national character" justified during World War II. In this War on Terror discourse, the "al-Qaeda terrorist" as "civilisationally barbaric, undevelopable, antisovereign man" is such a risk to "Western civilisation" that his dangerous mobility must be stopped. The "West" tries to immobilise his civilisational barbarism on the move in three ways – by keeping him outside of Western civilisation (Bigo 2002), by keeping him inside containment facilities like those in Guantánamo Bay, Cuba, and finally by making him a necropolitical target of state policies who must be killed (preferably outside the Western homeland/culture/civilisation) before he kills (inside) the Western homeland/culture/civilisation (see Puar 2007; Kuntsman 2009; Haritaworn, Kuntsman, and Posocco 2013).

Conclusion

In their analyses of queer migration and queer diaspora, queer migrations scholars demonstrate how any attempt to posit home and homeland as secure ontological places is confounded by encounters with movement *and queerness* inside the home/land (Eng 1997; Ahmed 2000; Fortier 2001, 2003; Luibhéid 2002, 2008, 2013; Luibhéid and Cantú 2005; Luibhéid, Buffington, and Guy 2014). As is demonstrated here, their conclusion is as true in IR as it is in queer migration studies. For the (sometimes) queer movements of the "unwanted im/migrant" and the "al-Qaeda terrorist" – as civilisational and sexual development on the move and as civilisational and sexual barbarism on the move – occur across, between and within heteronormatively understood homes, home-lands and sexualities in ways that expose these foundational sites of national/civilisational reproduction as irregular, indeterminate and transposable.

Western responses to these irregularities – to these intricately produced anarchies – are rooted as much in the desires of Western populations for ease in the homeland as they are in their desires for ease in the home. This is why Western (post)developmental (Bigo 2002) and security narratives reoppose to the "Islamic civilisational family" their figuration of the "Western civilisational family" as the foundation of national/civilisational sovereignties. This is why these discourses contrast the properly patriotic and cultural attachments to nation, culture and home/land of the "Western civilisational family" with the improper attachments of the "Islamic family" to nation, culture, and home/land (Puar and Rai 2002; Puar 2007). And this is how these discourses fix the "unwanted im/migrant" and the "al-Qaeda terrorist" as the necessary civilisationally and sexually perverse figures who are called upon to normalise Western individual, familial, and national/civilisational figures and attachments to "civilised, developed sovereign man" and the sovereign orders he authorises as rational, reasonable, and just.

These "homing desires" (Brah 1996, 187) – these desires "to feel at home achieved by physically or symbolically (re)constituting spaces which provide some kind of ontological security in the context of migration" (Fortier 2000, 163) – are usually understood to be the desires of im/migrating or diasporic subjects. What this analysis suggests is that the civilisational and sexual movements of figures like the "unwanted im/migrant" and the "al-Qaeda terrorist" implant homing desires in Western subjects. These homing desires take practical form in Western (post)developmental and security discourses that attempt and fail to "manage unease" in the homeland (Bigo 2002) *and also in the home* by figuring a Western "civilized, developed sovereign man" as the manager of their unease by being the manager of their security. In so doing, they expose the "anxious labor" (Luibhéid 2008, 174) Western discourses expend to create binary sexual figurations of and in the home and homeland that might sustain heteronormative sexualised orders of IR (also see Peterson 1999).

I suggest that these "homing desires" have long been a feature of how Western heteronormativities put sex into discourse in intimate, national and IR. The tropes of home and homeland participate in creating these four figurations of the "perverse homosexual" as the primary performativities that (post)colonial subjects can inhabit. These tropes tie the "underdeveloped", the "undevelopable", the "unwanted im/migrant", and the "terrorist" to specific places, times and desires that establish specific figures – the normal sovereign versus the perverse antisovereign – who guarantee various *either/or* anarchy-versus-order binaries as perverse-versus-normal binaries. And these tropes mobilise these binaries to create specific (albeit unreliable) mappings of the world to contain the movements of these "dangerous figures" in that world, which no amount of determined work can contain geopolitically or sexually. In all of these ways, then, heteronormative Western discourses script the "underdeveloped", the "undevelopable", the "unwanted im/migrant" and the "terrorist" as "perverse homosexuals" who are foundational to traditional *either/or* Western logics of statecraft as mancraft and Western sexual organisations of IR.

Notes

1. There are innumerable figurations of the "terrorist," many of which share the general genealogy of the "al-Qaeda terrorist" that I outline here, while others do not (e.g. white men in the US militia movements like Timothy McVeigh who drove a car bomb into an Oklahoma federal building in 1995 or white men embracing US white supremacist ideologies like Dylann Roof who shot and killed unarmed, mainly female, black worshippers in a historic black church in South Carolina in 2015). This is why I sometimes write about the "terrorist" in general terms (who in IR discourses is generally known to be "undevelopable" or "barbaric" or "uncivilisable", which is why those racialised as white are so rarely marked as the "terrorist") and other times write about a very specific figuration of the "terrorist" as the "al-Qaeda terrorist", who is a figure arising out of the histories I sketch out here as well as additional historical and contemporary constructions of race and religion, for example. It is also important to note that the "al-Qaeda terrorist" is not the only contemporary figuration of the "Islamic terrorist", as emerging figurations of the "Islamic State (ISIS) terrorist" demonstrate. These figurations need to be distinguished analytically because distinct Western discursive mobilisations of space, time, and desire give rise to them. For example, in the register of space, the "ISIS terrorist" is connected in geopolitical territory and the "Islamic family" differently than is the "al-Qaeda terrorist". This has consequences for how home and homeland are cast in relation to the "ISIS terrorist", geopolitically and in terms of how sexuality and "sexuality on the move" function in relation to this figure.
2. On how terrorism studies takes "the psyche as its privileged site of investigation", see Puar and Rai (2002, 122).
3. These reports circulated in the British press in late October 2001. By late November 2001, they were retracted when the missing fighters were spotted in Afghanistan. Since then, however, numerous such figures have appeared in the press.
4. Although for feminist analyses of violence in the home, see, for example, Sjoberg and Gentry (2007), Gentry and Sjoberg (2015) and Sjoberg (2015).
5. For additional ways in which the "al-Qaeda terrorist" is queerly sexed, gendered and sexualised, see Weber (2002) and Puar (2007).

Disclosure statement

No potential conflict of interest was reported by the author.

References

Ahmed, S. 2000. *Strange Encounters: Embodied Others in Post-Coloniality*. London: Routledge.
Almond, G. A., and B. Powell. 1966. *Comparative Politics: A Developmental Approach*. Boston, MA: Little, Brown.

Ashley, R. K. 1989. "Living on Borderlines." In *International/Intertextual Relations*, edited by J. Der Derian and M. J. Shapiro, 259–321. Lexington, MA: Lexington.

Barthes, R. 1976. *Sade, Fourier, Loyola*. (Richard Miller, trans.). New York, NY: Hill and Wang.

Berlant, L., and M. Warner. 1998. "Sex in Public." *Critical Inquiry* 24 (2): 547–566. doi:10.1086/448884.

Bigo, D. 2002. "Security and Immigration: Toward a Critique of the Governmentality of Unease." *Alternatives: Global, Local, Political* 27 (1 suppl): 63–92. doi:10.1177/03043754020270S105.

Brah, A. 1996. *Cartographies of Diaspora: Contesting Identities*. London: Routledge.

Bush, G. W. 2001. "Speech to Congress." September 20. https://georgewbush-whitehouse.archives. gov/news/releases/2001/09/20010920-8.html

Carroll, J. 2004. "The Bush Crusade." *Nation*, September 20. Accessed 21 October 2014. http://www. thenation.com/article/bush-crusade.

Clancy, T. 1994. *Debt of Honor*. New York, NY: HarperCollins.

Eng, D. 1997. "Out Here and over There: Queerness and Diaspora in Asian American Studies." *Social Text* 15 (52/53): 31–52. doi:10.2307/466733.

Fortier, A. 2000. *Migrant Belongings: Memory, Space, Identity*. Oxford: Berg.

Fortier, A. 2001. ""Coming Home": Queer Migrations and Multiple Evocations of Home." *European Journal of Cultural Studies* 4 (4): 405–424. doi:10.1177/136754940100400403.

Fortier, A. 2002. "Queer Diasporas." In *Handbook of Lesbian and Gay Studies*, edited by D. Richardson and S. Seidman, 183–197. Thousand Oaks, CA: Sage.

Fortier, A. 2003. "Making Home: Queer Migrations and Motions of Attachment." In *Uprootings/ Regroundings: Questions of Home and Migration*, edited by S. Ahmed, C. Castañeda, and A. Fortier, 115–135. Oxford: Berg.

Fortier, A. 2008. *Multicultural Horizons: Diversity and the Limits of the Civil Nation*. London: Routledge.

Foucault, M. 1980. *Power/Knowledge: Selected Interviews and Other Writings, 1972–1977*. (C. Gordon, L. Marshall, J. Mepham, and K. Soper, trans., C. Gordon, ed.). New York, NY: Pantheon.

Foucault, M. 1997. "The Abnormals". In *Ethics: Subjectivity and Truth*, Translated by Robert Hurley. edited by P. Rabinow, 51–52. New York, NY: New Press.

Gentry, C., and L. Sjoberg. 2015. *Beyond Mothers, Monsters, Whores*. London: Zed Books.

Gopinath, G. 2005. *Impossible Desires: Queer Diasporas and South Asian Public Cultures*. Durham, NC: Duke University Press.

Haritaworn, J., A. Kuntsman, and S. Posocco, eds 2013. "Murderous Inclusions: Queer Politics, Citizenship and the "Wars without End"". *Special Issue of International Feminist Journal of Politics* 15 (4): 445–452. doi:10.1080/14616742.2013.841568.

Hoad, N. 2000. "Arrested Development or the Queerness of Savages: Resisting Evolutionary Narratives of Difference." *Postcolonial Studies* 3 (2): 133–158. doi:10.1080/13688790050115277.

Huntington, S. P. 1996. *The Clash of Civilizations and the Remaking of World Order*. New York, NY: Penguin.

Huntington, S. P. 2004. "The Hispanic Challenge." *Foreign Policy* 141 (141): 30–45. doi:10.2307/ 4147547.

Khalil, A. 2001. "Sex and the Suicide Bomber." *Salon*, November 7. Accessed 21 October 2014. http://www.salon.com/2001/11/07/islam_2/.

Kuntsman, A. 2009. *Figurations of Violence and Belonging: Queerness, Migranthood, and Nationalism in Cyberspace and Beyond*. Bern: Peter Lang.

Lewis, G. 2006. "Imaginaries of Europe: Technologies of Gender, Economies of Power." *European Journal of Women's Studies* 13: 87–102. doi:10.1177/1350506806062749.

Loud, D. L. 2004. "'To Veil the Threat of Terror': Afghan Women and the Clash of Civilizations in the Imagery of the US War on Terrorism." *Quarterly Journal of Speech* 90 (3): 285–306. doi:10.1080/ 0033563042000270726.

Luibhéid, E. 2002. *Entry Denied: Controlling Sexuality at the Border*. Minneapolis: University of Minnesota.

Luibhéid, E., ed 2008. "Queer/Migrations: An Unruly Body of Scholarship." *Special Issue of GLQ: A Journal of Lesbian and Gay Studies* 14: 2–3.

Luibhéid, E. 2013. *Pregnant on Arrival: Making the 'Illegal' Immigrant*. Minneapolis: University of Minnesota Press.

Luibhéid, E., R. Buffington, and D. Guy, eds. 2014. *A Global History of Sexuality*. Malden, MA: Wiley-Blackwell.

Luibhéid, E., and L. Cantú Jr. 2005. *Queer Migrations: Sexuality, U.S. Citizenship, and Border Crossings*. Minneapolis: University of Minnesota Press.

Mead, M. 1928. *Coming of Age in Samoa*. New York, NY: Blue Ribbon Books.

Mead, M. 1942. *And Keep Your Powder Dry: An Anthropologist Looks at America*. New York, NY: William Morrow.

Palumbo-Liu, D. 2002. "Multiculturalism Now: Civilization, National Identity, and Difference before and after September 11th." *Boundary 2* 29 (2): 109–127. doi:10.1215/01903659-29-2-109.

Parsons, T. 1966. *Societies: Evolutionary and Comparative Perspectives*. Englewood Cliffs, NJ: Prentice Hall.

Patton, C., and B. Sánchez-Eppler, eds. 2000. *Queer Diasporas*. Durham, NC: Duke University Press.

Peterson, V. S. 1999. "Sexing Political Identities/Nationalism as Heterosexism." *International Feminist Journal of Politics* 1 (1): 34–65. doi:10.1080/146167499360031.

Peterson, V. S. 2010. "Global Householding amid Global Crises." *Politics & Gender* 6: 271–281. doi:10.1017/S1743923X10000073.

Peterson, V. S. 2013. "The Intended and Unintended Queering of States/Nations." *Studies in Ethnicity and Nationalism* 13 (1): 57–68. doi:10.1111/sena.2013.13.issue-1.

Peterson, V. S. 2014a. "Sex Matters: A Queer History of Hierarchies." *International Feminist Journal of Politics* 16 (3): 389–409. doi:10.1080/14616742.2014.913384.

Peterson, V. S. 2014b. "Family Matters: How Queering the Intimate Queers the International." *International Studies Review* 16 (4): 604–608. doi:10.1111/misr.2014.16.issue-4.

Puar, J. K. 2007. *Terrorist Assemblages: Homonationalism in Queer Times*. Durham, NC: Duke University Press.

Puar, J. K., and A. S. Rai. 2002. "Monster, Terrorist, Fag: The War on Terrorism and the Production of Docile Patriots." *Social Text* 20 (3 72): 117–148. doi:10.1215/01642472-20-3_72-117.

Razack, S. H. 2004. "Imperilled Muslim Women, Dangerous Muslim Men and Civilised Europeans: Legal and Social Responses to Forced Marriages." *Feminist Legal Studies* 12: 129–174. doi:10.1023/B:FEST.0000043305.66172.92.

Rutenberg, J. 2001. "Fox Portrays a War of Good and Evil, and Many Applaud." *New York Times*, December 3.

Said, E. 1978. *Orientalism*. London: Penguin.

Sjoberg, L. 2015. "The Terror of Everyday Counterterrorism." *Critical Studies on Terrorism* 8 (3): 383–400. doi:10.1080/17539153.2015.1081756.

Sjoberg, L., and C. Gentry. 2007. *Mothers, Monsters, Whores: Women's Violence in Global Politics*. London: Zed Books.

Weber, C. 2002. "'Flying Planes Can Be Dangerous'." *Millennium* 31 (1): 129–147. doi:10.1177/03058298020310010701.

Weber, C. 2005. "Not without My Sister(S): Imagining a Moral America in Kandahar." *International Feminist Journal of Politics* 7 (3): 358–376. doi:10.1080/14616740500161094.

Weber, C. 2006. *Imagining America at War: Morality, Politics and Film*. London: Routledge.

Weber, C. 2016a. *Queer International Relations*. Oxford: Oxford University Press.

Weber, C. 2016b. "Queer Intellectual Curiosity as International Relations Method: Developing Queer International Relations Theoretical and Methodological Frameworks." *International Studies Quarterly* 60 (1): 11–23.

Weber, C. 2016c. "Queer And/Or International Relations… or Not?" ISQ blog. http://www.isanet.org/Publications/ISQ/Posts/ID/5284/Queer-andor-International-Relationsor-not.

Wiegman, R., and E. A. Wilson. 2015. "Introduction: Antinormativity's Queer Conventions." *Differences* 26 (1): 1–25. doi:10.1215/10407391-2880582.

Beyond binaries: analysing violent state actors in Critical Studies

Shir Daphna-Tekoah and Ayelet Harel-Shalev

ABSTRACT
This article discusses the importance of including the voices of violent state actors in critical research about security and terrorism. Critical Studies tend to avoid narrative research about such actors or to give them "face" and place. However, to understand violence, scholars should listen to, and explore, the narratives of those who are committing violence. The article seeks ways to produce emancipatory knowledge and to be critical without being exclusionary. It discusses the difficulties in deciding who merits the researchers' listening and research focus, and who does not. These issues are explored and contested by presenting an analysis of women combatants' experiences.

Introduction

> War is a time for absolutes: good and evil, right and wrong, "us" and "them". (Yuval-Davis 2001)
> War is the friend of binarisms, leaving little place for complex identities. (Shohat 1992, 8)

Critical Studies on Security in general and Critical Terrorism Studies in particular have engaged with the topics of terrorism and political violence from a number of theoretical and disciplinary perspectives, including Peace Studies, International Relations (IR), Psychology, Social Work, Geopolitics, Feminist Geography, Feminist IR and Area Studies. These various perspectives have allowed scholars to unravel the multitude of ways in which terrorism and political violence impact societies and, at the same time, are deployed as social signifiers to determine identities and boundaries. Such multiple perspectives enable scholars to enter into a deeper debate on these complex political phenomena. Despite the many disciplinary crossovers that define Critical Studies on Security and Critical Terrorism Studies, explicit engagement with violent state actors remains limited. Moreover, critical approaches to security and terrorism often criticise "mainstream" security studies for focusing on elite state actors and ignoring the narratives of social actors. While agreeing with this critique, the current article challenges critical scholars for neglecting research on the narratives of violent state actors.

As scholars who study diverse topics in the field of Feminist IR, Critical Studies on Security and Trauma Studies (Harel-Shalev and Daphna-Tekoah 2016a, 2016b), we found ourselves confronted with a unique personal experience, which later served as the rationale for this article: when we mention to fellow academics that we conduct research about Israeli women activists for peace, the response is one of enthusiasm and great interest. However, when indicating that we also research women combatants in the Israel Defense Forces (IDF), we are aware of discomfort, reluctance to engage in discourse and even anger. This dichotomy led us think about how scholars can be "critical" without being "exclusionary" – about who deserves our attention and empathy and who does not, as we discuss here.

This article is informed by two ideas: first, narratives are profoundly political – they always mark and mask a political moment (Wibben 2011, 64; Elshtain 2000). Choosing to listen to a certain narrative and not listening to another is a political act. Second, some critical scholars consider it their academic mission to produce "emancipatory knowledge", and alongside fulfilling this mission, they also raise questions about so-called "conventional wisdom" and seek to expand knowledge about understudied topics.

Within the research umbrella of Critical Studies, the purpose of this article is therefore to emphasise the importance of including the understudied topic of the voices of violent state actors, such as women soldiers in the IDF, in critical approaches to security and terrorism. The article further discusses the challenges that scholars face during such research. More specifically, we aim to offer and demonstrate alternative ways to produce emancipatory research. Listening to and exploring the narratives of violent actors – such as women in combat – enables emancipatory research to be channelled into three dimensions: (1) problematising the "state" as a unitary actor; (2) challenging the flawed dichotomy between powerful/powerless and offering a necessary problematisation of this rather binary construction that remains inherent in critical approaches; and (3) exposing the trauma of war, even for those fighting for the powerful side, which could possibly undermine the choice of engaging in violence.

The current article is built as follows: the first section addresses the role of critical approaches to security and terrorism in producing emancipatory knowledge, and the second part discusses the benefits of listening to silenced voices with the aim to emphasise the importance of the exploration of violent state actors. The concluding section presents an integrated analysis of research from within a conflict zone and reflects on research on violent state agents. The article emphasises how violent state actors are, in fact, also social actors and how the study of violent state actors can shed new light on studies applying critical approaches to security and terrorism.

Critical approaches to state actors: an exclusionary approach?

As Jean Bethke Elshtain (2000, 31–32) argues, the "[p]ursuit of knowledge will always involve political struggle. The relations between persons of critical mind and society and discipline will always be marked by tension". Similarly, critical studies on security and political violence have raised the issue of "the political responsibility of scholars within security studies" (Eriksson 1999, 311). In fact, studies in the field have observed that Critical Security scholars are themselves political actors (see, for example, Eriksson 1999; Wibben 2011, 2016a). As such, undertaking Critical Studies on Security and exploring specific unexplored topics can mean producing "emancipatory knowledge" (Nunes 2012; Toros 2016; Wibben 2016a; Jackson 2016) and even produce "resistance studies" (Jackson 2016; Toros 2016). Critical theorists attribute to critical reflection the task of unmasking tacit hegemonic assumptions with the aim of interrupting the reproduction of systems of class, race, ethnos and gender oppression (Mortary 2015, 4-5). This "resistance" reorients academic research and practice towards the powerless and the oppressed (Jackson 2016, 125), while raising a challenge to the ways "mainstream" Security Studies often support "intersecting systems of oppression, from racism and sexism to imperialism" (Wibben 2016a, 12).

The ethics and politics of defining security, in both theory and practice, are determined by the choice of the "referent object", namely, "who is being secured?" (McDonald 2016). Critical approaches to security and terrorism may further ask, "whose security is being studied?" (McDonald and Burke 2016, 32). By aiming to study individuals and social actors, rather than elite actors and state actors, critical scholars turn around the focus of IR and expand knowledge about security. Indeed,

> War brings an equality of opportunity for suffering, and there is some debate whether, socially and politically, the account of the direct combatant is or should be privileged in the study of war, or whether the range of experiences of all those caught up in armed conflict should be included. (Woodward and Jenkings 2012, 496)

Critical Studies on Security and terrorism tend to explore and listen to the underdog "side" of the conflict rather than engaging with the powerful and allegedly stronger actors to produce "emancipatory knowledge" (Booth 2005). This line of thought can be seen in various publications in *Critical Studies on Terrorism* (Jackson 2016; Toros 2016, 2017). Jackson (2016), for example, claims that there are numerous potential theoretical benefits that would come from adopting a "resistance studies" framework within Critical Terrorism Studies. In his view, "resistance studies" may reorient academic research and practice towards the powerless and the oppressed. These studies could be used by social movements, human rights groups, protestors, oppressed groups and humanity at large (ibid.). This outlook corresponds well with previous studies that have called for resistance to patriarchy by moving towards more democratic values and deepening our "ethic of care", both in research and in practice (Gilligan 2011).

Yet, while state violence should be resisted (Toros 2016), and critical scholars should indeed resist hegemonic assumptions, one must be aware that such resistance can – and perhaps should – also go through a process of studying and analysing various state actors (Bulmer and Jackson 2016; Chisholm 2016; Harel-Shalev and Daphna-Tekoah 2016a; Daphna-Tekoah and Harel-Shalev 2016) or even of engagement with state actors (Toros 2016). In fact, engagement with violent state actors problematises the assumption that clear boundaries can be drawn between "what is the state" and "who is the citizen", and between "what is the military" and "what is a civilian" (Hedlund 2016; Basham, Belkin, and Gifkins 2015; Bulmer and Jackson 2016). To understand violence, one should speak to those who commit violence (Hedlund 2016). In fact, many of the arguments used in favour of talking with "terrorists" are applicable to why we should be talking to state agents (Toros 2016, 127–8). There is therefore value in studying violent state actors – in exploring their experiences, complexities and silenced voices, as well as in studying the variations among them.

There is a need to generate various kinds of knowledge about violence, state violence and violent state actors. If we agree with the suggestion that drawing attention to some issues and not others makes scholars political actors or even activists (Wibben 2016b; Jackson 2016), we should acknowledge that consciously ignoring a specific kind of knowledge, such as the narratives of violent state actors, might also provide a "certain type of knowledge". In the context of researching violence and state actors, exploring and listening to state actors may produce additional angles of knowledge. We listen to these actors with the aim to critically learn more about political violence.

Disaggregating the state – disaggregating violent state actors

The tendency of critical approaches to security and terrorism to focus on underdog actors and dominated populations can lead, in some instances, to "seeing" the state as a coherent unified actor. When studying political violence and state violence towards social actors and individuals, one should therefore be reminded that states should not be regarded as unified actors. In fact, one should disaggregate state and society before approaching in-depth research on conflicts, security and violence (Migdal 2001; Migdal, Kohli, and Shue 1994)

Struggles for domination in a certain region or state do not always begin with the "in-command" elites of the state, since the state is composed of various actors and various levels. Migdal (2001) indicates that one should not assume that either states or societies act as coherent unified actors. This notion is substantiated by a number of studies that have explored both state violence per se and the various categories of state violence (for example, Ron 1997; 2003; Gordon 2008; Jackson 2008; 2016; Blakeley 2009; Sen 2015; Jarvis and Lister 2014; Varshney and Gubler 2012; Murphy 2013; Hamilton 2011; Sen 2015). States use violence in different forms towards different populations. For instance, even when scholars use the state as the dominant unit of research, they should compare how the implementation of human rights norms, alongside human rights violations, is distributed among diverse groups within the state (Berkovitch and Gordon 2016). Similarly, differences in geographic location, ethnicity, social class, degree of incorporation into the state and religion all have significant implications for the type of treatment populations experience during periods of acute state violence (Ron 1997). For example, even open fire orders can vary in different contexts and regions in the same state in the same period (Ron 2003).

Disaggregation of state actors means looking at the various arms of the state – the judiciary, the government, the forces of law and order, the military, etc. In this context, the military should not necessarily be equated with the government (Migdal 2001). Bulmer and Jackson (2016) warn us to be aware of the dichotomies between the state and society, and between society and the military. In exploring the experiences of veterans, they further advise scholars to avoid the polarity between "militarism" and "anti-militarism". This admonition corresponds well with the aim of Critical Studies on Security to try to avoid binaries (Enloe 2000; Ortbals and Poloni-Staudinger 2014).

Even within the military, one can identify various contradictory forces within its hierarchic patriarchal organisation. Disaggregation of both the state and the military is therefore essential, since within the state and within the military there are likely to be contradicting and competing forces (Levy 2016b; Yefet 2016; Lomsky-Feder and Sasson-

Levy 2015). Moreover, contrary to what one might assume, an increase in civilian control over the military does not necessarily lead to peaceful policies: on the contrary, an increase in civilian control over the military might promote the use of force by legitimising it under specific conditions, such as in a militarised political culture (Levy 2016a). In that sense, there is no dichotomy between the state/military and society. Emancipatory knowledge in this sociopolitical context would not be found in data from society alone but rather from actors from within both society and the military.

In the context of Critical Studies and the transformative agenda of critical approaches to security and terrorism, Bulmer and Jackson (2016, 35) ask "[w]hat if the very resources for the challenging of militarism are to be found in places we least expect?". They recommend that scholars should challenge neat boundaries between militarism and anti-militarism. In addition, they call on researchers to challenge the dichotomised archetypes of veterans "as heroic, stoic, and proud, or conversely, as vulnerable, dysfunctional, and dangerous" (Bulmer and Jackson 2016, 28). Thus, to engage with experiences of war and political violence, one should not hesitate to explore and to listen carefully to veterans' perspectives of war (Bulmer and Jackson 2016; Daphna-Tekoah and Harel-Shalev, 2014, Harel-Shalev and Daphna-Tekoah 2016a, 2016b).

If we take Israel as a case study, we find that a substantial number of studies have explored state violence and Israel's policy in the Occupied Territories (for example, Gordon 2008; Natanel 2016; Ryan 2016; Yiftachel 2013). Residents of the West Bank and the Gaza Strip have all experienced different patterns of Israeli state violence, ranging from warfare, through bombardment, to containment and policing. We hold that state violence should indeed be explored and resisted (Daphna-Tekoah and Harel-Shalev 2017); yet, we suggest that critical scholars should disaggregate the state in the same manner that they disaggregate society or the oppressed. Indeed, some earlier studies have disaggregated the State of Israel in various forms, identifying, for example, various political streams – both right wing and left wing (Mendelsohn 2016). Other studies have drawn distinctions between Israel's policies in various Israeli-controlled geographic spaces (Ron 2003). Ron (1997), and Brym and Maoz-Shai (2009) claim that – in general – state violence should not be regarded as unified, as the violence varies in different areas and different periods. We suggest that any state as a polity should be explored as being composed of various state actors along with various societal actors. An examination of various violent state actors, including war veterans and soldiers – both men and women – may assist us in exploring the important question of how meanings of security shift in different contexts (Stern 2005; 2006; Wibben 2016b).

The gendered cleavages of the state and the military are also important and there has been extensive debate about the participation of women in combat (for example, Kennedy-Pipe 2000; MacKenzie 2013; Elshtain 2000). In parallel, in many countries, there has been an ongoing gradual increase in the numbers of women in combat positions, accompanied by a mixed picture of progress: on the one hand, more roles are opening up to women and, on the other hand, there is a backlash which is manifested in increases in sexual harassment and violence (Duncanson and Woodward 2016, 15). In Israel, women's service in the military became mandatory soon after the creation of the State in 1948. Within this framework, exemptions and unique restrictions have limited *most* women soldiers to non-combat duties (Harel-Shalev and Daphna-Tekoah 2015). This gendered structure of a clear division of labour between men and women that was created by the military and then enforced for many years has had far-reaching consequences for Israeli women, not only in the military but also in all walks of life (Rimlat 2007, 107; Sasson Levy 2003). Within this context, an understudied – and sometimes puzzling – subject is the nature of the experiences of the women who choose to serve in combat or combat-support positions, or, in other words, who choose to become violent state agents (Harel-Shalev and Daphna-Tekoah 2016a, 2016b). What can these women teach us, as scholars, about political violence and the complexities of conflict-ridden areas?

Critical research, silenced voices and women's agency

Critical approaches to security, particularly feminist research, emphasise the necessity to identify silenced voices (Benhabib 1985; Harding 1989; Harel-Shalev and Daphna-Tekoah 2016a; Harel-Shalev 2017; Enloe 2000; 2015; Tickner 2008). Furthermore, feminist and critical scholars stress women's agency in relation to security. As such, women's participation in peace building has been addressed in many scholarly works (such as Helman 1999; Kabasakal-Arat et al. 2004; Farr 2011; Amir 2014; Golan 2015). One should ask, then: why should we not learn and write about women's active participation in war? In practice, women in conflict zones and wars have been analysed mostly through the lens of victimisation and survival, but "their actual participation in redefining the narrative of war" is rarely addressed (Salime 2007, 7; Parashar 2014; Sjoberg 2013; 2016b; Kennedy-Pipe 2000).

Critical scholars and feminist security scholars aim to challenge the construction of women as victims, stressing that they can be agentic, building and redefining security, thereby decentring the state's power over security (Hoogensen and Kirsti 2006; Moser and Clark 2001; Ortbals and Lori 2014). Exploring war and conflict, while focusing on women as war victims and sexual assault victims in the military, is of great importance. Yet, conducting research on violence through the prism of sexual violence towards women, while neglecting other aspects of women's experiences in war, positions women, once again, in the binary category of "powerless" or "victim". To present various narratives of war, Critical Studies on Security and Terrorism must include studies about the experiences of women who commit violence or those who are taking part in a violent environment. Critical Studies on Security must therefore also include women terrorists and women who commit terrorist violence (see Hasso 2005; Yarchi 2014). These terrorists (or freedom fighters) are generally considered to be societal forces rather than state actors in that, by their actions, they resist state power. Recently, yet another dimension has been added to Critical Studies on Security with the appearance of a few studies addressing women as violent state actors, namely, as those who use violence in wars and conflict in various contexts (see Sjoberg 2016b; Harel-Shalev and Daphna-Tekoah 2016a).

In previous research (Daphna-Tekoah and Harel-Shalev 2014, Harel-Shalev and Daphna-Tekoah 2015, 2016a, 2016b; Harel-Shalev et al. 2017), we have given a face to violent state actors by virtue of our involvement in a long-term research effort dealing with women in combat and combat-support positions in the military. Our research – upon which this article is based – uses an in-depth, qualitative, interview-based methodology. Between 2011 and 2017, 85 women participants who had completed their mandatory service in the IDF took part in semi-structured interviews. The veterans who participated in our studies had concluded their service within 10 years of the start of each study. In this series of studies, our approach was guided by scholars (Cohn 1987; Enloe 2010) who have drawn attention to the self-censorship and the shaping of research agendas that can emerge (Gray 2016), in some instances, when scholars engage with state actors. We therefore chose to interview veterans rather than active soldiers, due to our reluctance to enter into direct involvement with (or even dependency on) the military.

As researchers, it is of the utmost importance to us to be bound by the ethical considerations required by our academic institutions but not by any kinds of military or political censorship of the research materials. By interviewing veterans who have recently concluded their service, we can listen to the narratives of state actors, while at the same time acquiring particular knowledge about various forms of state violence and its consequences. By probing the veterans' experiences in the Occupied Territories and on the borders between Israel and Gaza and the West Bank, we were able to reveal more nuanced perspectives of state power, state actors and state violence.

One way to look at women soldiers and women combatants is to see them as state agents; another way is to see them as a part of society, since these viewpoints do not constitute dichotomous divisions. We aimed to listen to the women veterans and to expose their voices – overt and hidden. We learned about their agency and struggles in a patriarchal environment, namely, what it means to be a combatant and what it means to be a woman combatant in a conflict zone in the context of a military occupation during mandatory service.

During our previous and ongoing work on women in the military (Daphna-Tekoah and Harel-Shalev 2014, Harel-Shalev and Daphna-Tekoah 2015, 2016a, 2016b; Harel-Shalev et al. 2017), we have encountered a gap in the theory and methodology of scholars who use Critical approaches to studying security and terrorism. Contrary to the tendency in Critical approaches to security and terrorism, which aims to explore the consequences of violence and conflicts for the oppressed and the weaker parts of society, our focus seeks to expose other marginalised and silenced voices: we explore the understudied experiences and positionalities of women combatants who participate in violent armed conflicts. These women combatants – by their very service in military roles in a hierarchic patriarchal organisation – become party to state violence. However, one should note that although women combatants take part in state violence, they are also subordinated to a societal order built on masculine hegemonic assumptions. In a way, they are thus both oppressed and oppressors.

As mentioned earlier, Critical Studies on Security aim to produce "emancipatory knowledge" (Nunes 2012; Toros 2016; Wibben 2016a; Jackson 2016) and even to generate "resistance studies" (Jackson 2016; Toros 2016). Yet, to be critical about state power and military power does not necessarily mean avoiding the narratives of violent state actors. As Basham, Belkin, and Gifkins (2015) suggest, to be critical about power is to be "sceptically curious" about its character, representation, application and effects. In line with Enloe's (2000; 2015) writings, in approaching military power as a question, rather than taking it for granted, Critical Studies on Security have the mission to explore beyond the role of the military as the protector of the nation from foreign threats (Basham, Belkin, and Gifkins 2015; Gray 2016).

By exploring women combatants who serve in conflict zones, in a masculine militarised environment, we can analyse and challenge various binaries, such as protected versus protecting, agent versus subject, and strength versus vulnerability. These particular binaries represent patriarchal settings and conceptions (Gilligan 2011; Enloe 2000). Our research approach to intentionally engage with violent state actors continues to speak to the critical security literature. We aim to uncover multiple positions of women in the sociopolitical context of women combatants and, like Sjoberg (2013) and Ortbals and Poloni-Staudinger (2014), we think it is worthwhile to explore the relations between state, violence and gender structures.[1]

Exploring the "bad guys": narratives of state actors

The research was conducted against the dichotomy between the state/government version of reality and a critical perspective of the armed conflict between Israel and the Palestinians (and the occupation of the West Bank and Gaza). Our research goals were partly aimed at unmasking war's "true face" (Harari 2005), and partly at exposing various narratives. Women combatants can provide an alternative story about war and conflict that is beyond the "heroic mask for war, which hid some of its ugliest features" (Harari 2005, 44–48). According to Harari, the secrets of war are consistently "made known only to those select men who passed its bloody initiation rites and became warriors, and who were consequently given a privileged place in society" (Harari 2005, 48). Although some civilians throughout history have tried to expose and unmask stories of wars and conflict, the power of the male military cult is still immense (Harari 2005).

Given this perspective, we believe that it is of outmost importance to study and reveal women combatants' narratives of war and political violence, which are outside of the manly "cult": such a perspective could lead to a different understanding of security, armed conflicts and terrorism. Moreover, with regard to trauma, scholars and experts addressing post-traumatic stress disorder following exposure to traumatic events in the battlefield tend to focus on explaining the development of the post-traumatic stress disorder, rather than looking at how and why the state had sent the combatants into the battlefield. We choose to present critical perspective on different aspects of war and violence and to ask the question: what do war and armed conflict do to the allegedly stronger side? (Daphna-Tekoah and Harel-Shalev 2017; Harel-Shalev et al. 2017; Bulmer and Jackson 2016).

By analysing the experiences of women combatants who have recently been released from mandatory service, we seek to learn about and shed light on various aspects of violence, political violence and conflict. To begin with, these narratives help us see that soldiers do not automatically accept state policy, and some of them criticise military options. The veteran combat women tended to criticise state policy while describing their experiences. This led us to the understanding that state actors should not be regarded as a unified collective, identified with the state. For instance, Suzanna shared with us her frustrations and insecurities, and described for us the type of incident that caused her to break during her combat service:

> the kind of incidents that you don't have any control over. These kinds of incidents in which we sit in the war room and we are informed about our first casualties, and you can do

nothing. These are the things that bring me down - to watch the news, and to understand the no-one [the government] is actually doing something right … Other things that bring me down are visits of … politicians who come here [to the war room on the border] and take pictures, to ask their [senseless] … questions, and at one point, it really interfered with our work … in order to gain political profit.

Some of our interviewees shared a quite similar perspective to Jackson's view (Bulmer and Jackson 2016), mentioned earlier, regarding the flawed dichotomy between society and the veteran, on the one hand, and the flawed identification of veterans with the "state", on the other. Suzanna's perspective teaches us about her doubts and criticisms and the frustration she experienced from her military service. In the context of complying with conscription at the age of 18 (or facing a jail sentence), she continued to share her thoughts with us:

You ask yourself - wait, do we have to go in [to Gaza]? …. Who benefits from this move? …. you understand that the prime minister will not go into Gaza himself … but those who will go in and get killed are kids [young soldiers]. They [politicians] run their business up there and we are the ones getting hit by the missiles. They sit in Jerusalem in the parliament, and YOU are here, you don't have a choice. You look at the soldiers and they are actually kids, you don't see them as men. I will never forget the guy I saw on Friday, and he was just a kid, he looked like a 12-year-old kid in a soldier's costume. And you know that he will go into Gaza in two hours from now, you want to hold him, and tell him: wait here, I will call your mom to take you home … When you hear on the radio that there are casualties, it is devastating, it breaks you … You feel like a pawn in a board game, that people are moving you around …. Everyone suffers …. Let us resolve this conflict already.

The above narratives further *problematize the "state" as a unitary actor* and corresponds with the recent query of Toros (2016): "[i]s the whole state venture as such [violent]?". We thus ask: should all parts of the state be considered in the same way? Is the entire state not worthy of critical scholars' research focus? The narratives of the women veterans indicate that "states" should not be seen as unitary actors, but as composed of various individuals, communities, institutions and much more (Migdal 2001; Toros 2016).

Our research has indeed disaggregated violent state actors and exposed their various positionalities, thus challenging the assumption that the state is a coherent unit. It further challenges the flawed *powerful/powerless* dichotomy. We find that at the same time that woman soldiers are taking part in violent conflict and occupation, they are also struggling with many challenges outside the battlefront. In terms of positionalities, they are struggling to function in a masculine hierarchic organisation, they reveal maternal attitudes, they often have to cope with male chauvinism, and they express various voices and narratives regarding their experiences. In addition, some women soldiers are required to cope with additional challenges, one of which is sexist remarks, as Hila, a lieutenant colonel, emphasised,

I participated in a classified discussion with high-ranking generals, and as I began to present my data, someone interrupted with a comment related to his wife and myself. I answered sharply: "Is there anyone else here in the room who wants to comment on women, so let us finish with that and then I will be able to continue." From that time onwards, I didn't hear anymore comments like that.

The narratives of the women veterans enable us to illustrate the problematisation of the binary construction that still often dwells in Critical approaches. On the conflict in Gaza, Suzanna said,

> It is complicated, very complicated, there is no black and white. You are so sorry for them [the Palestinians] during the war. … And on the other hand, you are also angry, since you [want to] say to them "get up! Do something! [against Hamas]", and then you realize that they cannot get up and do something. It is complicated. And what do I think? I think it is bad from both sides, our side and their side.

Suzanna, who is a combat veteran and a member of the reserve forces, is also – in her civilian life – a graduate student in political science. She shared with us her thoughts about the harsh period during her service near Gaza: "[i]s there anyone in the country who cares about the fact that my M.A. thesis has not been written?". She criticised both her professors for a lack of empathy and political leaders for sending her and her comrades to serve inside or near the Gaza Strip. Suzanna's narrative emphasises the women's perspectives in terms of being a state agent, while at the same time being a part of society – a person, a woman. This outlook further emphasises the flawed binary of powerful and powerless, while at the same time resisting the equation and identification of the veterans with the state. Listening to women combatants and analysing their narratives exposes and reveals various power relations in the military environment. While being indispensable part of the military and the state, the women were not blind to the other side of the conflict (Harel-Shalev and Daphna-Tekoah 2016a, 182).[2] Adina, a combat medic, who served in Gaza, stated,

> You see a house demolished, 99% of the people who live there are not the ones to blame; still, people were shooting from that location, you can see that their lives [the Palestinians] are being ruined.

Similarly, Jana shared with us her narrative:

> I had a lot of empathy toward the Palestinian side. In terms of security, I saw several unjustified shootings from our side, in which hurting other people was too easily accepted. I had reservations regarding the military actions, but I have much more criticism regarding the politicians who sent the military to be there in the first place.

In their war narratives, most women veterans tend to share in detail the dilemmas that they faced during their service (Harel-Shalev and Daphna-Tekoah, forthcoming). Roni shared her ethical dilemmas in a war room (in this case, an operations war room between Israel and the Gaza Strip):

> There were so many dilemmas there [in the war room] … There was a situation in which we had concrete information about the location of a "wanted terrorist" and they wanted to take him down, but on the roof, there were three kids; they put them there to play soccer, and we saw them standing there, and we knew who was inside the building. I remember the brigade commander and the other officers holding their heads, and we all had to cope with a serious dilemma … they didn't know what to do. It was the lives of three kids versus "something" that could save many lives, but in the end, they didn't do it, they didn't shoot …. I saw with it my own eyes …

Feminist scholars suggest that violence is poorly understood through the lens of state-centred security thinking; it could perhaps be better understood if we were to begin asking questions around the damage that can occur at the convergence of competing identity claims (Stern 2005; Wibben 2016a). Evaluation of these processes among societal forces is indeed important and crucial, but it could also be applied to state actors. Such identity struggles may exist within state actors, regarding their various positionalities in conflict zones. An example of such an identity struggle may be found in Talia's narrative (also quoted in Harel-Shalev and Daphna-Tekoah 2016a, 181):

> I was in charge at a check-point in the West Bank, near a settlement, and we received concrete information that a terrorist from Nablus was planning a terror attack. We got his picture and all the information we needed. There was a lot of pressure, and many Palestinians wanted to cross. We did not send soldiers home for the weekend; there was a lot of stress. And then we saw a Palestinian walking toward the check-point, and one settler jumped at him and started beating him. You immediately think – what if this Palestinian is the terrorist? Yet, I grabbed one of my [male] soldiers and we separated the two. I pushed the settler away, and he shouted at me that I was a "whore" and complained that I had touched him. I had exactly one second to decide what to do ... I knew that I am supposed to protect human life. By the way, later on that day, my soldiers caught the terrorist with the explosives.

The narratives of the women veterans revealed a far more nuanced view than could be obtained simply by identifying the veterans with "the state". In fact, many of the narratives reflected the veterans' struggles to deal with competing identity claims during their mandatory military service – identities as an Israeli, a soldier, an occupier, a woman and a human being.

Beyond the description of the conflict, the dilemmas and the violence involved, gendered elements were interwoven into the veterans' narratives, which could hint at their insecurities: the women expressed gratitude for the roles that had been given to them by the hegemonic hierarchic military system, but it was apparent that they were trapped in patriarchic conceptions and notions. Mali, who served in war rooms and was in charge of intelligence visual systems, stated,

> I think this is the most operational role that a young woman could be positioned in; the closest to hostile activities, closest to operational incidents, closest to confidential information. A role that has influence. If you say something to the battalion commander, he will take your advice seriously. It is really remarkable. An 18-year-old girl, advising the battalion commander ... you learn how to stand up for yourself, you learn to insist that if you think that some info is important ... you will not allow some other soldier to disregard your opinion. If something bad happens, it is your responsibility, so you really learn how to insist and stand up for yourself.

While some of the veterans were proud of their pioneering roles in an array of combat positions, others had internalised patriarchal norms and were grateful for – and even surprised at – the authority given to them. These findings may be related to the fact that "violent state actors" are also social actors. They serve to underline the notion that – along with the important task of studying oppressed and dominated communities – researchers should not neglect individuals who are representatives, to some degree, of state power, but who are also an integral part of the social forces in that state. These veterans often feel "insecure" in this context, rather than "powerful". In fact, the contribution of such individuals was often disregarded by the military and their fellows. The gendered elements of their status in the military are prevalent in their experiences. For example, Karine, an intelligence officer in a war room, who served both near the border with Gaza and in the West Bank, described her role and responsibilities while managing intelligence in a war room:

> When I arrived, it was after the "Arab Spring" had erupted, and all the mess [in the Middle East] ... Intelligence was affected by it ... the military was aiming at understanding how it would affect us ... If one talks about counter terrorism, I didn't need to go far to Iran to think about what is happening, I had it here. I "lived the conflict" on a daily basis. Allegedly, I was a non-combat soldier, but I stood there armed, in a ceramic vest, at the entrance to the army base inside a conflict zone. They might say I was a non-combat soldier, but I served inside a conflict zone and I WAS a combatant.

Basham (quoted in Baker et al. 2016, 2) critically explains how the majority of studies in IR seem somehow to be devoid of people. She further states that mainstream IR is "populated by insights from and into the actions of elite actors, and more critical work, particularly feminist scholarship, sheds light on the diverse lived conditions ... of different social actors". Encounters with people whose lives have been shaped in diverse ways by militaries and by militarism complicate the understanding of violence. Our interviews indicate that women soldiers could be, and should be, analysed as both violent state actors and as social actors. To study political violence merely from the perspective of the oppressed does not provide a full accounting of the phenomenon and will not enable a full unmasking of war and armed conflicts. Both types of research – of social actors and of state agents – are necessary if we are to gain knowledge on armed conflicts – their presence and their consequences.

Finally, our interviews uncover the *trauma* of war for those fighting for the so-called "powerful side", as is typified in the description of a traumatic event experienced by Jana, an officer who served in the Gaza Strip before Israel's disengagement from Gaza:

> I think that they drove on top of explosives. The explosives on the road triggered the explosives that were in the military vehicle, and the [men] combatants exploded into tiny pieces. A day later, another heavy vehicle with explosives was shot at, and five soldiers evaporated. I remember that I felt that blast. It was so strong. The visual memories that are stuck in my head are the other soldiers crawling on the road, looking for body parts of dead soldiers ... I remember that [when it happened] ... I entered the war room and one of the women soldiers shouted out that the vehicle had evaporated. I remember saying to her: "what do you mean?" She said – evaporated. One minute it was there, and the next minute it was gone. A shock ... the brain cannot comprehend this event. ... An entire military vehicle, with five soldiers in it, gone ... evaporated ... inconceivable.

Jana later described how she often wakes up, years after her release from the military, with memories of Israeli soldiers crawling on the road, looking for body parts of their comrades – the dead soldiers – and with many other traumatic memories (also quoted in Harel-Shalev and Daphna-Tekoah, forthcoming). The trauma of war for those fighting for the so-called powerful side was prevalent in the veterans' narratives. These narratives presented us with a question: are Jana's experiences less worthy of investigation because she is a one of the "occupiers"? The "stronger" side? A violent state actor? We think not.

The consequences of war are often silenced. Perhaps, if the traumatic narratives of combatants and of violent state actors were "out there", being heard, being louder, then perhaps these voices could have a stronger political impact on both state and society, including decision-makers. It is thus apparent that a deeper and more critical analysis of war trauma among veterans is needed (Daphna-Tekoah and Harel-Shalev 2017). Particularly in intractable conflicts (Kriesberg 1993), each side of the conflict tends to concentrate its own narrative, pain and struggles while neglecting the other side's narrative, pain and struggles. Studying the pain, traumas and difficulties of the soldiers and exposing the price of war, occupation and armed conflict may shake the narrative of the state, decision-makers, and political actors and may therefore contribute to the scope of resistance studies by undermining the option of engaging in violence.

Thus, our findings can be considered as emancipatory knowledge for societies involved in conflict, occupation and war, and for societies in which women serve in the military. In addition, we reveal the narratives of state actors whose views are not necessarily identical with the official state narrative. The narratives both problematise the "state" as a unitary actor and, at the same time, challenge the flawed dichotomy between the so-called powerful and the powerless. Finally, the narratives expose the traumatic experiences of the so-called powerful side – by addressing the consequences of occupation, violence and war – and may assist society to reflect about its actions and perhaps undermine the choice of engaging in violence.

Research from within the conflict – reflexivity and critical thinking

In Eurocentric thought and inquiry, "war" and "peace" tend to be sharply distinguished (Barkawi 2016, 201), whereas in non-Western societies, war and peace are often interwoven together into social, economic, political and cultural life. As Barkawi observed, in non-Western areas, "[w]hether there is war or peace may not be a question susceptible to a yes or a no; 'peacetime' may be shot through with relations of force and war" (Barkawi 2016, 202). In conflict-ridden areas, when one discusses political violence, one should grasp that violence does not merely occur during extraordinary periods; it is part of ordinary everyday life. The Israeli–Palestinian conflict is an ongoing conflict, and – unlike the research trips that many scholars undertake for ethnographic research – our research trip is here and now within this conflict zone.

As MacKenzie (2011) observed, "locating yourself in your work is not about narcissism or personal biography … reflexivity should place emphasis on the ways in which the consumption, exchange, and witnessing of emotions through research alters and affects the researcher and the research process …" (692). During the research process, we – as scholars – constantly reflect and ask ourselves: are we being militarised? (Enloe, quoted in Schouten & Dunham 2012). Are we capturing the combatants' narratives with curiosity (Enloe 2004)? How do we react to narratives that are not exactly what we wish to hear? Are we empowering our research participants? Are we promoting violence by studying violent state actors? We are indeed aware that while engaging with violent state actors, we could be exposing ourselves to a risk of scholarly militarisation (Enloe 2010). In the following section, we grapple with these questions.

Reflection is not merely an intellectual exercise (Mortari 2015, 4–5). Reflexivity offers the context within which information has been produced; it is a strategy that exposes power in research (Chisholm 2016; Nencel 2014; MacKenzie 2011), as it requires one to pay attention to "how the researcher is socially situated, and how the research agenda/ process has been constituted" (Ramazanoglu and Holland 2002, 118). We agree with

Bulmer, who states that feminist researchers believe in an "engaged scholarship which aims to transform the world through a critical praxis which is collaborative and democratic and takes seriously the emotional and personal" (Bulmer, in Bulmer and Jackson 2016, 36). During the exploration of the veteran combatants' experiences, we used narrative analysis to produce a nuanced representation of the situation. In parallel, we constantly reflected on the narratives and on our questions and responses to the data and interviews.

Let us now return to our particular and perhaps unique insider/outsider status as women, as researchers in the field of Critical Studies on Security, and as researchers of women violent state actors. Insight that impinges on our specific situation has been offered by a number of scholars. Fieldwork (Toros 2008) and ethnography (Chisholm 2016) situate researchers amongst the community they are researching, as either active participants or observers, or a combination of the two. Traveling to conflict zones offers researchers an important opportunity to produce empirically rich research on militarised communities and on ongoing conflicts (Parashar 2014; MacKenzie 2011; Gray 2016). Chisholm (2016) mentions that her representations as an outsider impacted on how she could access a security community and the knowledge produced. Gray (2016) further complicates this stand, while exploring domestic abuse in the British Armed Forces and engaging with military personnel.

In contrast to scholars whose study of conflict zones involves traveling from their home countries to an area of conflict and then returning home, we grew up and live in a conflict zone. Our representation is both one of insiders from within Israeli society and, at the same time, one as civilians from "the outside" conducting critical feminist academic research on the military.

Beyond listening to our research subjects, we are aware that we should also to listen to ourselves. Living in a militarised environment for an extended period impacts upon the research questions one asks and the research one can conduct; similarly, the context in which the research is situated impacts upon the whole research process (Cohn 1987; Chisholm 2016; Enloe 2015; Golan 2015). Chisholm (2016), who conducted a long field study, warns scholars of being emotionally and intellectually invested in the understandings of the security that they are supposed to examine critically. This task was similarly challenging and difficult for us.[3]

While reflecting on the question of whether we are militarising knowledge through our work, we reviewed several aspects of our research process. First, we looked at other studies that worked closely with veterans, since the above issues are not exclusive to our own research: other recent studies have raised these same complexities. For example, David Jackson, a British war veteran, indicated in an article co-authored with Sarah Bulmer, that he was proud of his service in the military, but still felt angry at the lack of political responsibility taken by the government for the aftermath of war. He further emphasises, "I would agree that as soon as you place these complicated concepts within neat boundaries, you silence many of those who stand in no man's land. It is this troubling space that I like to inhabit" (Bulmer and Jackson 2016, 36). Just as Bulmer and Jackson call for the need to explore and reveal complex and silenced voices about war and conflict, so, too, are our research and methodology aimed to identify and analyse voices of Israeli veterans. This perspective demonstrates that veterans themselves are not as militarised as one may assume. We believe that such studies may assist scholars to produce a nuanced prism of the state violence phenomenon and the consequences of war. Yet, at the same time, we are aware that we should still constantly ask ourselves: are we empowering violence and militarism? Are we able to free our research from patriarchal norms? Are we justifying or glorifying violent state actors?

To answer these complex questions, some thoughts come to mind. Critical approaches to security and terrorism make a crucial contribution to challenging conventional wisdoms in various disciplines and academic research. They demand of scholars to be curious, to doubt and to interrogate so-called "obvious" assumptions (Enloe 2014). Second, feminist scholars and activists have often been associated, and sometimes also self-identified, with peace-oriented approaches, anti-war sentiments and pacifism (Åhäll 2016, 4; Enloe 2015). As feminist peace-oriented critical scholars, we offer here an alternative perspective of women who serve in the army, as their national duty – by compulsory service – and who experience on a daily basis a variety of practices that are both complicated and diverse. Third, at the same time, we are aware that we could be militarising knowledge by focusing on soldiers of an occupying regime. By exposing and revealing their silenced voices and by presenting a framework of narratives that focus on women as competent actors and not as fragile or necessarily as victims of sexual abuse and harassment in a patriarchal militarist environment, we are aware that we might be empowering them and their stories. We thus struggle with the idea that by being attentive to their stories, we might be promoting a "heroic mask for war, which hid some of its ugliest features" (Harari 2005, 44–48) in the context of a military occupation. This is precisely the narrative that we wished to resist. How, then, can our research be considered as resistance research?

Revealing the traumas and the scars of the soldiers and exposing the price of war, occupation and armed conflict, by exposing the narratives of veterans relating to their mandatory military service, may undermine the option of engaging in violence by shaking the narrative of the state and of political actors. By so doing, we could contribute to the scope of emancipatory knowledge and resistance studies. Particularly in the context of a military occupation and violent conflict, the question of "who deserves our attention and empathy in critical studies" is further sharpened by the acknowledgement of the complex position of women combatants as both *state agents* and *social actors*.

There is a tendency, even in critical research, to interpret veterans' experiences as one-dimensional, being generally related to "violent state actors", without disaggregation, and listening to the narratives of violent state agents is considered as almost taboo territory for critical scholars of Security and terrorism. Feminist contributions to Security studies have a different "entry-point" to the study of militarisation (Åhäll 2016, 2). These studies tend to ask how militarisation as a security practice forms part of sense making in the everyday. Critical and feminist studies on security and conflicts examine the normalisation process of militarisation in society (Enloe 2000). As such, the soldiers in the current research "naturally" joined the army and served in various roles, but still they had reservations and criticism about state policy.

In our research, we constantly ask ourselves: are we being held captive to the notion of gender equality and inequality in the military, rather than critically appraising the whole system? This questioning is well illustrated in the oft-cited article of Catharine MacKinnon. She portrays the dilemma in an imaginary after-life encounter between a woman combat soldier and a feminist woman activist: "[t]he feminist says to the [woman] soldier, 'we fought for your equality.' The soldier says to the feminist, 'oh, no, we fought for your equality'". In their dialogue, both fight for acknowledgement of their relative contributions to promoting women in society (MacKinnon 1987, 35; quoted in Harel-Shalev and Daphna-Tekoah 2015, 69).

This dilemma is also linked to the question of women's agency. Feminist theorising about agency in the context of political violence is a crucial element in feminist and critical studies on security (Sjoberg 2016a). According to Enloe (2015), particularly in a militarised society, one can trace a tendency of unquestioning admiration of a masculinised military institution. The side effect of such a process is the minimising of analytical curiosity, especially a feminist-informed sceptical curiosity. Critical feminist analysis of state actors (within the military) – particularly in a militarised society such as Israel – can expose silenced narratives beyond "conventional wisdom". "To be skeptical, is to be energetically wary of simplistic descriptions and superficial explanations - both from within the state and from the outside… Things are always more complicated than they are being portrayed" (Enloe 2015, 7). Moreover, by documenting knowledge about women soldiers as violent state actors, we can contribute to scholarly assessment and understanding of various elements of conflict, violence and terrorism. Seeking a dialogue with various state actors and, particularly, engaging with the "military community in a genuine dialogue that deepens our understandings of militarization and war, and actively intervening in those processes and subjecting them to critique" lies at the heart of critical studies and feminist praxis (Bulmer in Baker et al. 2016, 5).

The narratives of the interviewees force us to question our pre-conceptions regarding many aspects of war, violence and occupation. Clearly, fieldwork and ethnography are conditioned through the ways in which the researchers themselves relate to the security communities and how they carefully work to maintain such access in dynamic and shifting political and social environments (Toros 2008; MacKenzie 2011; Chisholm 2016). The notion that the role of the critical scholar in security studies is to be "consciously critical – questioning underlying assumptions, investigating things that conventional commentators typically leave unexplored" (Enloe 2015, 3) is the overriding consideration that guides us on our research journey.

According to Wibben (2016a, 1), "[a]cknowledging that framing issues in particular ways and drawing attention to some issues and not others, makes us in part political actors". As Israeli feminist and critical scholars, we feel obligated to study these topics. We thus engage critically with violent state agents in various ways with the aim to produce emancipatory knowledge. As scholars from within the conflict who have access to combat veterans, we feel obligated to access this data and to interrogate this topic from a critical perspective. Moreover, we have the responsibility to do so, since revealing these narratives can further the understanding of violent state actors and can call into question existing assumptions. This stance, we believe, leads us to a better understanding of Israeli society, in which spillovers of state violence change societal norms and characters (Golan 2015).

This article should therefore also be read as a scholarly call to pay more attention to the need to avoid binary assumptions in the study of political violence and terrorism. Exploring the narratives of state actors who participate in armed conflict and war from different perspectives – whether the ethics of care among soldiers, attitudes towards state policy, cracks, rifts and contradictions within state institutions, or challenges inherent in the roles of women combatants – can shed new light on violence and armed conflict in various areas of study. This exploration can contribute not merely to critical approaches to the study of terrorism, but also to the critical study of trauma, gender, politics and security.

Notes

1. We felt the need to engage with different narratives of violence and state violence, particularly those of women in the military. We are aware that within the spectrum of women's experiences as state actors, there are numerous differences between the experiences of non-combat and combat soldiers (Kennedy Pipe 2000; Harel-Shalev et al. 2017; Lomsky-Feder and Sasson-Levy 2015; Rimlat 2007) and equally numerous differences between mandatory military service and the service of military professionals (Lomsky-Feder and Sasson-Levy 2017).
2. At the same time, most of the expressions of empathy and care were expressed towards the veterans' comrades. As in other narratives of soldiers in wars and military occupations, the veterans that we interviewed usually did not refer to the other side of the conflict (Woodward and Jenkings 2012).
3. An important additional consideration that impacted our work was the obligation we felt to omit several testimonies from within the conflict that could have hurt both sides and could have incited violence. Narratives that could harm the already fragile relations between Israelis and Palestinians were thus omitted from our analysis. In addition, so as to respect the families of the casualties on both sides and to protect the anonymity of our interviewees (who could have been identified easily by anyone who is familiar with the conflict and its most controversial incidents), some facts were intentionally omitted from our published work.

Funding

This work was supported by the Israel Science Foundation [160/15];

References

Åhäll, L. 2016. "The Dance of Militarisation: A Feminist Security Studies Take on 'The Political'." *Critical Studies on Security* 4 (2): 134–168. doi:10.1080/21624887.2016.1153933.

Amir, M. 2014. "Women Speaking of National Security: The Case of Checkpoint Watch." *International Political Sociology* 8 (4): 363–378. doi:10.1111/ips.2014.8.issue-4.

Ann, T. J. 2008. "Gender in World Politics." In *The Globalization of World Politics: An Introduction to International Relations*, edited by J. Baylis, S. Smith, and P. Owens, 262–277. Oxford: Oxford University Press.

Arat, Z. K., N. Chazan, M. A.-D. Shamas, and R. N. Tarazi. 2004. "Women for Ending Israeli Occupation in Palestine and for Building Peace." *International Feminist Journal of Politics* 6 (3): 515–523. doi:10.1080/1461674042000235645.

Baker, C., V. Basham, S. Bulmer, H. Gray, and A. Hyde. 2016. "Encounters with the Military." *International Feminist Journal of Politics* 18 (1): 140–154. doi:10.1080/14616742.2015.1106102.

Barkawi, T. 2016. "Decolonising War." *European Journal of International Security* 1 (2): 199–214. doi:10.1017/eis.2016.7.

Basham, V. M., A. Belkin, and J. Gifkins. 2015. "What is Critical Military Studies?." *Critical Military Studies* 1 (1): 1–2. doi:10.1080/23337486.2015.1006879.

Benhabib, S. 1985. "The Generalized and the Concrete Other: The Kohlberg-Gilligan Controversy and Feminist Theory." *Praxis International* 4: 402–424.

Berkovitch, N., and N. Gordon. 2016. "Differentiated Decoupling and Human Rights." *Social Problems* 63: 499–512. doi:10.1093/socpro/spw020.

Blakeley, R. 2009. *State Terrorism and Neoliberalism: The North in the South*. London: Routledge.

Booth, K., ed. 2005. *Critical Security Studies and World Politics*. London: Lynne Rienner.

Brym, R. J., and M.-S. Yael. 2009. "Israeli State Violence during the Second Intifada: Combining New Institutionalist and Rational Choice Approaches." *Studies in Conflict & Terrorism* 32 (7): 611–626. doi:10.1080/10576100902961797.

Bulmer, S., and D. Jackson. 2016. "'You do not live in my skin': embodiment, voice, and the veteran." *Critical Military Studies* 2 (1–2): 25–40. doi:10.1080/23337486.2015.1118799.

Chisholm, A. 2016. "Ethnography in Conflict Zones: The Perils of Researching Private Security Contractors." In *The Routledge Companion to Military Research Methods*, edited by A. J. Williams, N. Jenkings, R. Woodward, and M. F. Rech, 138–152. London: Routledge.

Cohn, C. 1987. "Sex and Death in the Rational World of Defense Intellectuals.„ *Signs: Journal of Women in Culture and Society*, 12(4): 687–718.

Daphna-Tekoah, S., and A. Harel-Shalev. 2014. "Living in a Movie – Israeli Women Combatants in Conflict Zones –A Multilayered Analysis." *Women's Studies International Forum* 44 9 (2): 26–34. doi:10.1016/j.wsif.2014.03.002.

Daphna-Tekoah, S., and A. Harel-Shalev. 2016. "The Politics of Trauma Studies: What Can We Learn From Women Combatants' Experiences of Traumatic Events in Conflict Zones." *Political Psychology*. doi:10.1111/pops.12373.

Duncanson, C., and R. Woodward. 2016. "Regendering the Military: Theorizing Women's Military Participation." *Security dialogue* 47 (1): 3–21. doi:10.1177/0967010615614137.

Elshtain, J. B. 2000. *Real Politics: At the Center of Everyday Life*. Baltimore: John Hopkins University Press.

Enloe, C. 2000. *Manoeuvres: The International Politics of Militarizing Women's Lives*. Berkeley: University of California Press.

Enloe, C. 2004. *The Curious Feminist: Searching for Women in a New Age of Empire*. Berkeley, CA: University of California Press.

Enloe, C. 2010. "The Risks of Scholarly Militarization: A Feminist Analysis." *Perspectives on Politics* 8 (4): 1107–1111. doi:10.1017/S1537592710003233.

Enloe, C. 2014. *Bananas, Beaches and Bases: Making Feminist Sense of International Politics*. Berkeley, CA: University of California Press.

Enloe, C. 2015. "The Recruiter and the Sceptic: A Critical Feminist Approach to Military Studies." *Critical Military Studies* 1 (1): 3–10. doi:10.1080/23337486.2014.961746.

Enloe, C. 2012. "Theory Talk #48: Cynthia Enloe on Militarization, Feminism, and the International Politics of Banana Boats." In *Theory Talks*, edited by P. Schouten and H. Dunham, May 22. 2012. http://www.theorytalks.org/2012/05/theory-talk-48.html

Eriksson, J. 1999. "Observers or Advocates?: On the Political Role of Security Analysts." *Cooperation and Conflict* 34 (3): 311–330. doi:10.1177/00108369921961889.

Farr, V. 2011. "UNSCR 1325 and Women's Peace Activism in the Occupied Palestinian Territory." *International Feminist Journal of Politics* 13 (4): 539–556. doi:10.1080/14616742.2011.611661.

Gilligan, C. 2011. *Joining the Resistance*. Cambridge: Polity Press.

Golan, G. 2015. "Militarization and Gender in Israel." In *Gender and Peacebuilding: All Hands Required*, edited by M. P. Flaherty, T. G. Matyók, S. Byrne, and H. Tuso, 212–228. Lanham: Lexington Books.

Gordon, N. 2008. *Israel's Occupation*. Berkeley: University of California Press.

Gray, H. 2016. "Researching From the Spaces in Between? The Politics of Accountability in Studying the British Military." *Critical Military Studies* 2 (1–2): 70–83. doi:10.1080/23337486.2016.1127554.

Hamilton, K. 2011. "The Moral Economy of Violence: Israel's First Lebanon War, 1982." *Critical Studies on Terrorism* 4 (2): 127–143. doi:10.1080/17539153.2011.586199.

Harari, Y. N. 2005. "Martial Illusions: War and Disillusionment in Twentieth-Century and Renaissance Military Memoirs." *The Journal of Military History* 69 (1): 43–72. doi:10.1353/jmh.2005.0023.

Harding, S. 1989. "Is There a Feminist Method?." In *Feminism and Science*, edited by N. Tuana, 17–32. Bloomington: Indiana University Press.

Harel-Shalev, A. 2017. "Gendering Conflict analysis - The case of Minority Women and Muslim Women's Status in India." *Ethnic and Racial Studies* 40. doi:10.1080/01419870.2017.1277028.

Harel-Shalev, A., and S. Daphna-Tekoah. Forthcoming. "A Room of One's Own (?) in Battlespace - Women Soldiers in War Rooms."

Harel-Shalev, A., and S. Daphna-Tekoah. 2015. "Gendering Conflict Analysis: Analyzing Israeli Female Combatants' Experiences." In Chap. 4 in *Female Combatants in Conflict and Peace*, edited by S. Shekhawat, 69–83. London: Palgrave Macmillan.

Harel-Shalev, A., E. Huss, S. Daphna-Tekoah, and J. Cwikel. 2017. "Drawing on Women's Military Experiences and Narratives – Women Soldiers' Challenges in the Military Environment." *Gender, Place and Culture* 1–16. doi:10.1080/0966369X.2016.1277189.

Harel-Shalev, A., and S. Daphna-Tekoah. 2016a. "Bringing Women's Voices Back In: Conducting Narrative Analysis in IR." *International Studies Review* 18 (2): 171–194. doi:10.1093/isr/viv004.

Harel-Shalev, A., and S. Daphna-Tekoah. 2016b. "The 'Double-Battle': Women Combatants and Their Embodied Experiences in War Zones." *Critical Studies on Terrorism* 9 (2): 312–333. doi:10.1080/17539153.2016.1178484.

Hasso, F. S. 2005. "Discursive and Political Deployments by/of the 2002 Palestinian Women Suicide Bombers/Martyrs." *Feminist Review* 81: 23–51. doi:10.1057/palgrave.fr.9400257.

Hedlund, A. 2016. "Why study the 'bad guys'?" *Open Democracy*. Accessed 9 May 2016. https://www.opendemocracy.net/beyondslavery/anna-hedlund/why-study-bad-guys.

Helman, S. 1999. "From Soldiering and Motherhood to Citizenship: A Study of Four Israeli Peace Protest Movements." *Social Politics* 6 (3): 292–313. doi:10.1093/sp/6.3.292.

Hoogensen, G., and S. Kirsti. 2006. "Gender, Resistance and Human Security." *Security Dialogue* 37 (2): 207–228. doi:10.1177/0967010606066436.

Jackson, R. 2008. ""The Ghosts of State Terror: Knowledge, Politics and Terrorism Studies." *Critical Studies on Terrorism* 1 (3): 377–392. doi:10.1080/17539150802515046.

Jackson, R. 2016. "To Be or Not To Be Policy Relevant? Power, Emancipation and Resistance in CTS Research." *Critical Studies on Terrorism* 9 (1): 120–125. doi:10.1080/17539153.2016.1147771.

Jarvis, L., and M. Lister. 2014. "State Terrorism Research and Critical Terrorism Studies: An Assessment." *Critical Studies on Terrorism* 7 (1): 43–61. doi:10.1080/17539153.2013.877669.

Kennedy-Pipe, C. 2000. "Women and the military." *Journal of Strategic Studies* 23 (4): 32–50. doi:10.1080/01402390008437811.

Kriesberg, L. 1993. "Intractable conflicts." *Peace Review* 5 (4): 417–421. doi:10.1080/10402659308425753.

Levy, Y. 2016a. "How Civilian Control May Breed the Use of Force." *International Studies Perspectives* 0: 1–18. doi:10.1093/isp/ekv020.

Levy, Y. 2016b. "Religious Authorities in the Military and Civilian Control: The Case of the Israeli Defense Forces." *Politics & Society* 44 (2): 305–332. doi:10.1177/0032329216638063.

Lomsky-Feder, E., and O. Sasson-Levy. 2017. *Israeli Women Soldiers and Citizenship: Gendered Encounters with the State*. New York: Routledge.

Lomsky-Feder, E., and O. Sasson-Levy. 2015. "Serving the Army as Secretaries: Multi-level Contract and Subjective Experience of Citizenship." *British Journal of Sociology* 66 (1): 173–192. doi:10.1111/1468-4446.12102.

MacKenzie, M. H. 2011. "Their Personal is Political, Not Mine: Feminism and Emotion." *International Studies Review* 13 (4): 691–694.

MacKenzie, M. H. 2013. "Women in Combat: Beyond 'Can They?' or 'Should They?': Introduction." Critical Studies on Security 1 (2): 239–242. doi:10.1080/21624887.2013.814838.

MacKinnon, C. A. 1987. "Difference and Dominance: On Sex Discrimination." In Feminism Unmodified: Discourses on Life and Law, edited by C. A. MacKinnon, 32–45. Cambridge, MA: Harvard University Press.

McDonald, M. 2016. "Whose Security?: Ethics and the Referent." In *Ethical Security Studies*, edited by Jonna Nyman and Anthony Burke 32–45. London: Routledge.

Mendelsohn, B. 2016. "Israel and Its Messianic Right: Path-Dependency and State Authority in International Conflict." *International Studies Quarterly* 1–12. doi:10.1093/isq/sqv015.

Migdal, J. S. 2001. *State in Society: Studying How States and Societies Transform and Constitute One Another*. Cambridge: Cambridge University Press.

Migdal, J. S., A. Kohli, and V. Shue. 1994. *State Power and Social Forces: Domination and Transformation in the Third World*. Cambridge: Cambridge University Press.

Mortari, L. 2015. "Reflectivity in Research Practice: An Overview of Different Perspectives." *International Journal of Qualitative Methods* 14 (5): 1–9. doi:10.1177/1609406915618045.

Moser, C. N. O., and F. Clark. 2001. *Victims, Perpetrators or Actors?: Gender, Armed Conflict and Political Violence*. London: Zed Books.

Murphy, E. 2013. "Class Conflict, State Terrorism and the Pakistani Military: The Okara Military Farms Dispute." *Critical Studies on Terrorism* 6 (2): 299–311. doi:10.1080/17539153.2012.748481.

Natanel, K. 2016. "Border Collapse and Boundary Maintenance: Militarisation and the Micro-Geographies of Violence in Israel–Palestine." *Gender, Place & Culture* 23 (6): 897–911. doi:10.1080/0966369X.2015.1136807.

Nencel, L. 2014. "Situating Reflexivity: Voices, Positionalities and Representations in Feminist Ethnographic Texts." *Women's Studies International Forum* 43: 75–83. doi:10.1016/j.wsif.2013.07.018.

Nunes, J. 2012. "Reclaiming the Political: Emancipation and Critique in Security Studies." *Security Dialogue* 43 (4): 345–361. doi:10.1177/0967010612450747.

Ortbals, C. D., and P.-S. Lori. 2014. "Women Defining Terrorism: Ethnonationalist, State, and Machista Terrorism." *Critical Studies on Terrorism* 7 (3): 336–356. doi:10.1080/17539153.2014.956014.

Parashar, S. 2014. *Women and Militant Wars: The Politics of Injury*. London: Routledge.

Ramazanoglu, C., and J. Holland. 2002. *Feminist Methodology: Challenges and Choices*. London: Sage Publications.

Rimlat, N. 2007. "Women in the Sphere of Masculinity: The Double-Edged Sword of Women's Integration in the Military." *Duke Journal of Gender, Law & Policy* 14: 1097–1119.

Ron, J. 1997. "Varying Methods of State Violence." *International Organization* 51 (2): 275–300. doi:10.1162/002081897550366.

Ron, J. 2003. *Frontiers & Ghettos: State Violence in Serbia and Israel*. Berkeley: University of California Press.

Ryan, C. 2016. "Gendering Palestinian Dispossession: Evaluating Land Loss in the West Bank." *Antipode*. doi:10.1111/anti.12280.

Salime, Z. 2007. "The War on Terrorism: Appropriation and Subversion by Moroccan Women." *Signs* 33 (1): 1–24. doi:10.1086/518370.

Sasson-Levy, O. 2003. "Feminism and Military Gender Practices: Israeli Women Soldiers in 'Masculine' Roles." *Sociological Inquiry* 73 (3): 440–465. doi:10.1111/soin.2003.73.issue-3.

Sen, S. 2015. "Bringing Back the Palestinian State: Hamas Between Government and Resistance." *Middle East Critique* 24 (2): 211–225. doi:10.1080/19436149.2015.1017969.

Shohat, E. H. 1992. "Dislocated Identities of an Arab-Jew." *Movement Research: Performance Journal* 5. (Fall-Winter). 8.

Sjoberg, L. 2013. *Gendering Global Conflict: Toward a Feminist Theory of War*. New York: Columbia University Press.

Sjoberg, L. 2016b. *Women as Wartime Rapists: Beyond Sensation and Stereotyping*. New York: New York University Press.

Sjoberg, L. 2016a. "Gender-based Violence in War." In *Handbook on Gender and War*, edited by S. Sharoni, J. Welland, L. Steiner, and J. Pedersen, 175–193. Cheltenham: Edward Elagar Publishing.

Stern, M. 2005. *Naming Security – Constructing Identity: "Mayan Women" in Guatemala on the Eve of "Peace."*. Manchester: Manchester University Press.

Stern, M. 2006. "'We' the Subject: The Power and Failure of (In)Security." *Security Dialogue* 37 (2): 187–205. doi:10.1177/0967010606066171.

Toros, H. 2008. "Terrorists, Scholars and Ordinary People: Confronting Terrorism Studies with Field Experiences." *Critical Studies on Terrorism* 1 (2): 279–292. doi:10.1080/17539150802184652.

Toros, H. 2016. "Dialogue, Praxis and the State: A Response to Richard Jackson." *Critical Studies on Terrorism* 9 (1): 126–130. doi:10.1080/17539153.2016.1147775.

Toros, H. 2017. " "9/11 is alive and well": How Critical Terrorism Studies has Sustained the 9/11 Narrative." *Critical Studies on Terrorism* 10 (2): 203–219. doi:10.1080/17539153.2017.1337326.

Varshney, A., and J. R. Gubler. 2012. "Does the State Promote Communal Violence for Electoral Reasons?." *India Review* 11 (3): 191–199. doi:10.1080/14736489.2012.705634.

Wibben, A. T. R. 2016a. "Opening Security: Recovering Critical Scholarship as Political." *Critical Studies on Security* 4 (2): 137–153. doi:10.1080/21624887.2016.1146528.

Wibben, A. T. R., ed. 2016b. *Researching War: Feminist Methods, Ethics and Politics*. London: Routledge.

Wibben, A.T.R. 2011. *Feminist Security Studies: A Narrative Approach*. New-York: Routledge.

Woodward, R., and K. Neil Jenkings. 2012. "This place isn't worth the left boot of one of our boys': Geopolitics, Militarism and Memoirs of the Afghanistan War." *Political Geography* 31 (8): 495–508. doi:10.1016/j.polgeo.2012.10.006.

Yarchi, M. 2014. "The Effect of Female Suicide Attacks on Foreign Media Framing of Conflicts: The Case of the Palestinian–Israeli Conflict." *Studies in Conflict & Terrorism* 37 (8): 674–688. doi:10.1080/1057610X.2014.921768.

Yefet, K. C. 2016. "Synagogue and State in the Israeli Military: A Story of 'Inappropriate Integration." *The Law & Ethics of Human Rights* 10 (1): 223–294.

Yiftachel, O. 2013. "Colonial Deadlock or Confederation for Israel/Palestine?." *Middle East Insights No. 87, National University of Singapore*. January 4, 2013. https://mei.nus.edu.sg/index.php/web/publications/mei-insights/43/2013/P15.

Yuval-Davis, N. 2001. "The Binary-War." *OpenDemocracy.net*. Accessed October 25 2016. https://www.opendemocracy.net/conflict-war_on_terror/article_89.jsp.

"Academics for Peace" in Turkey: a case of criminalising dissent and critical thought via counterterrorism policy

Bahar Baser, Samim Akgönül and Ahmet Erdi Öztürk

ABSTRACT

On 11 January 2016, 1128 academics in Turkey and abroad signed a petition calling on Turkish authorities to cease state violence in mainly Kurdish populated areas of the country, which had been under curfew and an extended state of emergency. The petition received an immediate reaction from President Recep Tayyip Erdoğan, who accused the signatories of treason and terrorist propaganda. He subsequently demanded that public prosecuters launch an investigation. Criminalisation of the petition has been exacerbated by disciplinary action by universities against many of the signatories. Many have suffered insults, arrest, detention or suspension as a result of the ensuing smear campaign. This massive crackdown on academic freedom has been masked by discourses of counterterrorism, which have also been deployed to criminalise dissent more generally in Turkey as a part of a process of rapid "democratic retrenchment" since 2013. This article is an attempt to put the criminalisation of academics within the larger framework of human rights violations, increasing curtailments of academic freedom and rising authoritarianism in Turkey. It argues that the prosecution of the signatories of the petition is an extension of an established tradition of targeting academic freedom in times of political crisis in Turkey but is also a product of growing authoritarianism under the ruling party and President Erdoğan. It shows that counterterrorism laws can be extended far beyond eliminating security threats by instrumentalising them to suppress dissent in a declining democracy.

Introduction

It is the responsibility of intellectuals to speak the truth and to expose lies. This, at least, may seem enough of a truism to pass over without comment.

Noam Chomsky (1967)

On 11 January 2016, 1128 academics from 89 universities in Turkey and all around the world signed a petition[1] calling on the Turkish authorities to cease state violence in the mainly Kurdish populated areas of the country which were under curfew and an extended state of emergency. The text criticised the Turkish state's use of violence in the region and asked the government to prepare conditions for peace negotiations. Those negotiations broke down in June 2015 when both sides returned to violence after an almost six years on and off ceasefire. The petition also criticised the Turkish state for contravening its own laws and violating international treaties. The conflict reached boiling point in the second half of 2015, when the Turkish military clashed with the Kurdistan Workers' Party (*Partiya Karkerên Kurdistan* – PKK) and its urban youth wing, *Tevgera Ciwanen Welatparêz Yên Şoreşger* (The Patriotic Revolutionary Youth Movement – YDG-H). The petition was opened for signatures around this time, while non-mainstream news agencies were reporting civilian casualties on a daily basis. Moreover, as documented by a recent United Nations Report prepared by the Office of the United Nations High Commissioner for Human Rights (OHCHR), serious human rights violations occurred during the curfews, and entire residential areas were cut off from public reach and the movement of lay people was restricted (OHCHR Report 2017, 2). The report estimates that the number of displaced people as a result of clashes and curfews was between 355,000 and half a million (ibid., 4).

As Sozeri (2016) points out, neither the claims about the Turkish state's conduct nor the demands for restitution laid out in the petition were particularly novel. It nevertheless caused uproar in Turkey, so much so that it marked something of a turning point, presaging the official crackdown that would soon follow. Right after the petition was released, Turkish President Recep Tayyip Erdoğan accused the academics of treason in one of his public addresses and invited the judiciary to respond: "I call upon all our institutions: everyone who benefits from this state but is now an enemy of the state must be punished without further delay" (Schiermeier 2016). The judiciary, under the influence of the president, wasted no time in launching public prosecutions against many of the academics who had signed the peition. The signatories were accused under Turkish counterterrorism laws of "terrorist organisation propaganda". Furthermore, the Council of Higher Education (*Yüksek Öğrenim Kurumu* – YÖK) directed the universities to conduct disciplinary investigations which were followed in short order by police raids at academics' homes and university offices, resulting in dismissals, arrests and detentions (Uğur 2016). The accusations did not let up, however, with signatories of the petition further condemned for insulting the Turkish state and engaging in terrorist acts (Altıparmak and Akdeniz 2017, 13). As a reaction to this stigmatisation and witch-hunt, around 1000 academics added their names to the petition in solidarity with the first group, increasing the total number of signatories to more than 2000.

This was surely not the first attack on freedom of speech, nor was it the first crackdown on academic independence in Turkey. In the past, limitations on the right to publish or teach on "sensitive" political issues have been widely reported and prison time has often served as punishment for academics challenging the state's narrative on the Kurdish Question[2] or the Armenian Genocide, which together constitute the "third rail" in Turkish politics.[3] However, the "Academics for Peace" petition marked a new era. Whereas violations of academic freedom in the past had typically been sporadic and unsystematic, the government's approach to using counterterrorism discourse as a weapon against dissent promised suppression of academic freedom on an unprecedented scale.

As Flader (2016) points out, the shocking wave of anticipatory obedience by the judiciary, higher education institutions and university rectors highlights how far authoritarianism in Turkey has reached over the last years. The failure of the peace process also paved the way towards less reconciliatory attitutes by the government against the opposition. Indeed, as DeVotta (2015, 211) argues, civil wars and counter-terror practices might create an authoritarian shift if the conflict endures. Although terrorism and counterterrorism has been a fundamental part of Turkey's vocabulary since the 1980s (Barrinha 2011), it has been taking new shapes and forms under the ruling Justice and Development Party (*Adalet ve Kalkınma Partisi* – AKP), and this incident coincided with a new era in Turkey where the definition of the concept of "terrorism" has been stretched so far that it can be employed against anyone who fails to toe the party line.

This article contributes to discussions of how counterterrorism laws can be utilised by states to suppress ideas and groups that contest official narratives. It shows that those in power not only utilise laws but also engender a discourse around counterterrorism that blurs the boundaries between actual terrorism and civil disobedience, and by doing that, they arbitrarily limit freedom of speech. The narrative created around these laws can be instrumentalised to criminalise certain group and individuals. This article focuses on this very point and asks how so-called counterterrorism laws and the discourse born out of them have enabled state authorities, the judiciary and the police to suppress dissent and freedom of speech in Turkey. It argues that the prosecution of the signatories of the petition is a continuation of long-term violations of academic freedom in Turkey as well as a consequence of the growing authoritarianism under the ruling party and President Erdoğan.

The article will first detail the key background events that paved the way for the petition, with a specific focus on growing authoritarianism and the return to heightened securitisation prompted by the failure of the peace process. The following section will then focus on the situation of academic freedom in Turkey in general in order to demonstrate that the violation of academic freedoms is not a recent phenomenon and then analyse the "Academics for Peace" group, the petition and the developments in the aftermath of its press release. The article's main focus is this specific petition, its background and its consequences. A final section is also dedicated to the developments aftermath of the failed coup attempt in Turkey in July 2016, which engendered a massive purge in Turkish academia which surely affected the signatories of the petition.

Turkey's authoritarian shift and the end of the peace process

Hegemonic authoritarianism in Turkey

Turkey's authoritarian shift forms part of a broader wave of "democratic retrenchment" across the global since the 2000s. Weak democratic systems in the Balkans, Russia, Latin America and rising right-wing movements in most Western countries are visible general trends across the world (Levitsky and Way 2002). In this regard, since the end of the Cold War, scholars have tried to define these regimes by employing different concepts such as semi-democracy (Case 1993), virtual democracy (Norris and Jones 1998), illiberal democracy (Zakaria 1997) and soft authoritarianism (Means 1996; Winckler 1984). Each of these concepts point to the decay of democracy in one way or another. Despite holding elections regularly, such regimes neglect the basic tenants that we have come to associate with contemporary liberal democracies. Instead, elections become instruments to legitimise increasing authoritarianism (Schedler 2006, 6–19). In Turkey, the concentration of power in the hands of President Erdoğan as a "dominant leader" through the instrumentalisation of state apparatuses and the ruling AKP's hegemony over civil society and the media are the important pillars of Turkey's new authoritarianism. The AKP's hegemonic political project is increasingly being referred to as "New Turkey".

The AKP, founded in 2001, came to power in 2002 and rose on the back of a highly promising reform agenda. It increased its popularity not just in Turkey but also abroad by framing its demands and goals in line with those the European Union made of Turkey in its membership bid. Their actions were praised and they were depicted as the fresh political elite who could put Turkey on the path to rapid democratisation. The AKP then quickly emerged as Turkey's dominant political party, winning landslide victories until the elections of June 2015. Despite a noticeable loss of support at the June 2015 poll, the party was able to reconsolidate its power following a snap election in November 2015. This election received much criticism from international and domestic observers who pointed to "irregularities in the campaign, including media bias and self-censorship, misuse of state resources to support Erdoğan's election bid, lack of transparency in campaign finances, and voter fraud" (see Freedom House Turkey Country Report, 2016).

Lately, the AKP's rule has received much criticism from the opposition, civil society organisations and non-mainstream media in Turkey, as well as the international community. The AKP and its influential former leader (and current Turkish president) Erdoğan have transformed Turkey into a de facto presidential system in which the president assumes more and more control over the executive, legislative and judicial branches, a move that is both perturbing and polarising (Öztürk 2014). As Yesilada (2016, 19) very well summarises, the positive environment of the early 2000s when the AKP came to power and promised certain reforms has been replaced by "a grim picture of illiberal political developments that are characterized by President Erdoğan's power grabs, loss of judicial independence, and electoral manipulations to achieve the desired election outcome that favoured Erdoğan and the Justice and Development Party". The final objective appears to be a full "executive presidency" in which all power is concentrated in the hands of the president. Authors such as Esen and Gümüşcü (2016) define the current situation as *competitive authoritarianism* by arguing that Turkey no longer satisfies even the minimal requirements of democracy. Akkoyunlu and Öktem (2016) also define Turkey as a country where there is personalisation of executive power, weakening of democratic checks and balances, less free and fair electoral competition, and the imposition of stricter constraints on freedom of expression and civil liberties. They also underline that there is a growing use of the state's coercive capacity to suppress various forms of violent and non-violent dissent.

The AKP's leaders manipulated Turkey's weak post-2008 democratic system to advance an agenda that was in fact anti-democratic and authoritarian. During the last decade, dozens of activists, academics, politicians, journalists and others have been detained simply for disagreeing with government policies, or for opposing Erdoğan's discourses on political, economic and social matters. In this regard, the (Economist Intelligence Unit's 2015) Democracy Index defined Turkey as a hybrid regime that combines democratic procedures and autocratic practices. In a similar fashion, the 2015 report of Freedom House ascertained that media freedom in Turkey deteriorated at an alarming rate in this year. The World Justice Project's 2016 Rule of Law Index ranks Turkey 99th out of 113 countries, which implies the absence of a significant judicial check on government and the presence of governmental interference in judicial processes (Rule of Law Index, 2016). The AKP government utilised its control of the judiciary to punish critical reporting and political opposition via the country's famous anti-terror law (Patton 2007, 339–34), which has been both disproportionate and ill-tailored (Dearden 2016). The term is stretched such that its reference point is no longer the law, the Turkish constitution, or international norms and regulations. More than 2000 legal cases were opened with the allegations of "insulting the President" against people who criticised Erdoğan on social media and elsewhere. Turkey has become an example of how democratically elected governments can take undemocratic paths to cling to power and how counterterrorism policies can go hand in hand with authoritarianism on the path to one-person rule. The AKP and its leader Erdoğan emerged as the two key elements in this context (Keyman and Gümüşcü 2014).

It is true that the AKP retains an autonomous party structure on paper. At the same time, it would be fair to say that Erdoğan and the party have become almost synonymous (Özbudun 2014, 157). As mentioned, during Erdoğan's term as president, he has openly declared his ambition to switch the political system from a parliamentary democracy to a presidential one. In Giorgio Agamben's terminology, Erdoğan could be thought of as having instrumentalised "exceptional circumstances" to present himself in the public domain as an "exceptional leader" – the only one who can steer Turkey past the rocky shoals on its present course (Agamben 2005, 40). Of course, many dimensions of the economic and foreign policy crises that Turkey faces at present are in fact, at least in part, of Erdoğan's own making, which makes his claims to "exceptional" leadership that much more ironic. After almost 15 years in power, Erdoğan has established a network of control across the entire Turkish state of which he is the "central node". Moreover, the continuation of the civil war in the southeast of the country combined with the nationalistic sentiments of the majority of the Turkish population and the lack of resistance from either the parliament or the judiciary have produced a toxic political environment in which extreme sentiments find fertile soil. In this regard, counterterrorism discourse also emerges as a useful tool to suppress dissent.

Turkey under the Erdoğan presidency is by no means the only example of political instrumentalisation of crisis in the pursuit of power. DeVotta (2015, 210–11) notes, for example, how Sri Lanka's illiberal democratic regime transitioned to a soft-authoritarian one during the Sri Lankan civil war and the way in which counterterrorism discourse against the Tamil Tigers was formative in that process. By suggesting that exceptionalism fosters democratic retrenchment, he also claims that "civil wars justify counter-terror practices, and the longer the conflict the more draconian these practices can become" (DeVotta 2015, 210–11). The decades-long war between the PKK and the Turkish state has created an atmosphere of insecurity, polarisation and mistrust in Turkey. Erdoğan's and the ruling party's politics works by activating the fears of the population and thus relies heavily on societal consensus regarding the "threat" emerging from violent Kurdish separatism. As Altıparmak and Akdeniz (2017, 104) note, since the collapse of the peace process, counterterrorism has become the token excuse to limit freedom of speech and assembly. The concept of "terror" is so vague that academics, members of parliament, actors, artists, journalists and others can easily be targeted with accusations of making "terrorist propaganda". The authors claim that Turkey, still, does not have the legal infrastructure that could be used to accommodate these definitions used by the state authorities that strongly violate human rights. Due to the many cases that have been sent to the European Court of Human Rights, Turkey had to make a lot of modifications in its laws which basically limited the ground to arbitrarily use these laws. However, in the time of crises, the state does not shy away from bending the law accordingly.[4]

In this regard, the case of "Academics for Peace" may have disturbed the governing party's agenda by openly criticising its actions in national and international platforms. The punishment for this "impudence", then, was justified within the framework of counterterrorism and Turkish nationalism.

The end of the peace process

The roots of the Turkish–Kurdish conflict can be traced back before the fall of the Ottoman Empire and the foundation of the Turkish Republic in 1923. As a result of nation-building efforts in the early republican era, a number of harsh measures were implemented to suppress any kind of dissent against the newly emerging and fragile authority of the state, with the aim of creating a unified nation under one flag from an ethnically, religiously and linguistically divided country. Therefore, the Turkish–Kurdish conflict can be understood as part of continuous resistance against the Turkish state's assimilation policies. These policies have resulted in the systematic suppression of Kurdish identity, and subsequently, a demand for the recognition and restitution of this group's basic political, cultural and linguistic rights.

Over the last few decades, the conflict turned violent, making it the country's primary political challenge, not to mention a high priority security problem that threatens the country's territorial integrity. There has been an armed conflict between the Turkish state and the Kurdish armed group, the PKK, since the early 1980s. For a long time, the Turkish state had a "no negotiation with terrorists" approach and opted for a military solution. Particularly in the 1990s, South-East Turkey was ruled under constant state of emergencies where extra-judicial killings, disappearances and deportations became the norm. Kurdish politicians, journalists, activists and other human rights activists were criminalised throughout this whole period and were frequently tried for "supporting terrorist propaganda". Overall, nearly 50,000 people were killed in this armed conflict and it is estimated that up to 2 million Kurds were displaced, lost their properties and suffered from the consequences of this low-intensity civil war (see Uluğ and Cohrs 2017, 4).

The AKP came to power in 2002 and its rise to power was a turning point in Turkey for many reasons. It started implementing a conservative agenda, and at the same time, "taboo" topics such as Kurdish identity and peace negotiations were opened to discussion. The AKP gradually began implementing reforms to accommodate Kurdish identity in order to align itself with the membership ideals of the European Union. After 2009, the AKP first started with a reform process which was called the "Kurdish Initiative". A state TV channel broadcasting in Kurdish was opened and several departments at universities started offering curriculum in Kurdish. The AKP also ended the state of emergency as a gesture of goodwill to show that they were determined to find a peaceful solution to this problem. In the meantime, the AKP decided to implement a policy of negotiation with the PKK. Between September 2008 and 2011, there had been several meetings in Oslo between high-level representatives from the National Intelligence Agency (MIT) and top PKK leaders in the company of international mediators. These talks collapsed in 2011; however, talks about talks continued until June 2015, with several ceasefires, visits to the imprisoned leader of the PKK by HDP (People's Democratic Party) representatives and various parliamentary commissions which prepared reports for potential roadmaps.

The peace process officially ended due to the lack of commitment from both sides on certain issues. For instance, the PKK has never completely withdrawn from Turkey as any lasting peace will require it to do, while the government has failed to implement the reforms that were demanded by the Kurdish side and which were promised by the government. However, the impact of the June 2015 elections was the last nail in the coffin of the peace process. The AKP, in losing the absolute majority of votes in that poll, sought to burnish its nationalist credentials to appeal to that segment of Turkey's electorate that is most susceptible to nationalistic appeals in advance of rescheduled elections in November 2015. As the violence resumed, attacks on both sides were reported and several high-profile bombings in Ankara and Istanbul took place. A state of emergency was declared in certain parts of Turkey and this led to gross human rights violations as there had been extensive civilian casualties.

Turkish security forces used heavy artillery, tanks and other armed vehicles, while the PKK's youth wing, YDG-H, dug trenches (sometimes filled with explosives) and planted barricades in order to limit access by the Turkish security forces to their neighbourhoods (Human Rights Watch 2015). During what the state authorities called "security operations", many Kurdish civilians – including women, children and elderly – were killed. Human Rights Watch reports that more than 100 civilian deaths were recorded while many people suffered multiple injuries. In December, they also reported that these numbers were likely to increase due to the heavy clashes (Human Rights Watch 2015). The Human Rights Foundation of Turkey published a press release on 9 January 2016 that reported that 58 round-the-clock, open-ended curfews in around 20 districts and 7 cities (covering more than 1 million residents) in southeastern Turkey had been officially confirmed. The Foundation's statement indicates that during these curfews, basic human rights have been violated and around 150 civilians including women, children and elderly were killed.

An OHCHR report revealed that 2000 people were killed in the context of security operations between July 2015 and December 2016. As the report suggests, this number would include "close to 800 members of the security forces, approximately 1200 local residents, of which an unspecified number may have been involved in violent or non-violent actions against the state" (OHCHR Report 2017, 2). The report also stated that they managed to document "numerous cases of excessive use of force, killings, enforced disappearances, torture, destruction of housing and cultural heritage, incitement to hatred, prevention of access to emergency medical care, food, water and livelihoods, violence against women, and severe curtailment of the right to freedom of opinion and expression as well as political participation" (ibid.). The report suggests that "it appears that the domestic protection of human rights in South-East Turkey has effectively been non-functioning since at least July 2015, as demonstrated by the reported lack of a single investigation into the alleged unlawful killings of hundreds of people over a period of 13 months between the late July 2015 and the end of August of 2016" (OHCHR Report 2017, 3).

"We won't be a party to this crime!"

The role of public intellectuals in tumultuous times

What happened to the signatories of the "Academics for Peace" petition makes us question the role of public intellectuals in dark times. The petition was criticised by fellow academics for many reasons, including for its tone, its content, its wording and its supposed bias. Some academics also claimed that scholars should stay neutral in these cases. The question of "neutrality" in times of conflict raises serious questions, however. Is a deliberate nonchalance in the face of massive human rights violations the same thing as staying "neutral"? Or, as Chomsky (1967) pointed out, is it the public intellectual's duty to expose deceit and falsehood? Is it the duty of academics to speak truth to power?

Petitions, anti-war campaigns, open letters, protests and boycotts are among many other strategies that have been used by academics to criticise certain governments or states throughout history. For example, the *Manifesto of the 121* – an open letter penned by 121 intellectuals, academics, reporters and journalists (including Jean-Paul Sartre) in France, and published by the magazine *Vérité-Liberté* in 1960 – stands out for its historical importance. Sartre did not organise the petition, but his participation was crucial (Leak 2006). The *Manifesto* called on the French state and the French people to acknowledge that conflict was a legitimate struggle for independence by the Algerian people, and denounced the use of torture by the French military. It also called on the authorities to respect French conscientious objectors to the conflict. After the petition, no retribution was brought on Sartre; however, other signatories of the *Manifesto* were dismissed from their posts (Leak 2006; Schalk 1991). Moreover, as Schalk (1991, 106) points out,

> *Le Monde* printed in its entirety a countermanifesto of October 1960 that condemned the work of 'the professors of treason,' accused of being a 'fifth column' that draws its inspiration from 'foreign propaganda.' This manifesto was signed by nearly three hundred intellectual supporters of Algerie francaise, including seven members of the French Academy. But at that time readers could only speculate as to the exact nature of 'treason' supposedly perpetrated by these 'professors.'

Surely it is possible to find other examples of these sorts of open letter/manifestos/petitions. Chomsky's "political interventions" have become the stuff of legend (Giroux 2016, 179). He was at the forefront of opposition against the Vietnam War, writing numerous articles on the issue. The 1965 "teach-in" on the Vietnam War at the University of Michigan was also a remarkable step towards showing dissent against war mongering at higher education institutions.[5] Also, in early 1967, more than 5000 US scientists signed a petition asking the President to stop using certain types of weapons which were said to be inhumane (Krane 2011, 4).

Academics have long intervened in peace processes as well. For example, during the apartheid period in South Africa, a group of Stellenbosch University academics formed a group called the "Stellenbosch '85 Discussion Group", chaired by Professor Sampie Terreblanche. This was a group apart from the more classic leftist "anti-status quo" group of academics, who often found themselves threatened and excluded from university campuses if they were against the apartheid regime and who often risked being sacked by the university administration or being detained by the police. The academics within the Stellenbosch group, in contrast, held "priviledged" positions in South African society. Yet, they decided to criticise the apartheid regime in spite of the risks to their personal reputation and position. Some members of this group, such as Prof. Willie Breytanbach and Prof. Willie Esterhuyse, also participated in clandestine meetings with ANC representatives in the United Kingdom, which gradually paved the way for a peaceful reconciliation period in South Africa.[6] Around two dozen intellectuals who were mostly based at Stellenbosch University even had a meeting with then President P.W. Botha. The discussion group showed that the perceptions of the Afrikaner elite were changing and was also a clear signal to the political elite that they were losing the support of the intellectuals (see Horowitz 1991, 79).

More recently, a group of Israeli academics published a petition in 2014 criticising Israeli state policies in Gaza. The signatories declared their desire that it "be known that they utterly deplore the aggressive military strategy being deployed by the Israeli government". They argued that state violence is creating more divisions between the two communities and the bloodshed is preventing a peaceful solution which is the only alternative to end the conflict. Similar to the "Academics for Peace" petition in Turkey, they stated that "Israel must agree to an immediate cease-fire, and start negotiating in good faith for the end of the occupation and settlements, through a just peace agreement" (Statement by Israeli Academics July 2014).

Turkish and Kurdish intellectuals have written similar petitions, manifestos and open letters. The *Aydinlar Dilekcesi* manifesto stands out in this regard. After the 12 September 1980 coup, Turkey established a comprehensive martial law regime under the management of the country's military-dominated National Security Council (*Milli Güvenlik Konseyi* – MGK) and high numbers of detentions, political restrictions and torture were reported across the country. Furthermore, media and intellectual freedoms were radically restricted during the period of military rule. In response, in May 1984, a group of intellectuals presented a petition criticising this state of affairs to both the presidency and the Grand National Assembly of Turkey (*Türkiye Büyük Millet Meclisi*– TBMM). Popularly known throughout the country as the "Intellectuals" Petition', it was in fact originally titled "Observations and Requests about the State of Democracy in Turkey" (*Türkiye'de Demokratik Düzene İlişkin Gözlem ve İstemler*). It was signed by 1383 scholars, authors, actors, poets and artists. The petition stated the importance of freedom of thought and speech for Turkey's democratic future. It highlighted the issue of torture in prison – describing this as a crime against humanity – and demanded a general amnesty to those convicted of "thought crimes". The reaction of the Turkish state bears repeating and has echoes of today's situation. The Martial Law Command immediately prohibited further publication of the petition and opened a case against 56 of the most prominent of the signatories, including the author Aziz Nesin, the journalist Uğur Mumcu, the scholar Yalçın Küçük and Hikmet Çetin, a former politician. The first trial was held in August 1984 and all the suspects were acquitted in February 1987 (see Index on Censorship, 1984).

Another controversial political campaign has been the "Özür Diliyorum" (I Apologize) campaign, launched as an online petition in 2008. The campaign's principal objective is to prompt a public discussion about the 1915 Armenian Genocide – as mentioned, a highly politically sensitive issue in Turkey – by calling for a collective national apology for the events and expressing regret and sorrow for the loss felt by the victims and the injustice caused. Four prominent public intellectuals – Ahmet İnsel, Baskın Oran, Cengiz Aktar and Ali Bayramoğlu – authored the campaign declaration, which read, "[m]y conscience does not accept the insensitivity showed to and the denial of the Great Catastrophe that the Ottoman Armenians were subjected to in 1915. I reject this injustice and for my share, I empathize with the feelings and pain of my Armenian brothers. I apologize to them". After a short period, the petition garnered more than 30,000 signatories online, prompting reactions from the key political players – including then Prime Minister Erdoğan, who was critical – and widespread public discussion and debate. Most of the signatories received death threats. Furthermore, the Office of the Public Prosecutor launched an investigation into the crime of "public humiliation of the Turkish nation" regarding the campaign, but it did not turn it into an official case.

The "Academics for Peace" petition is no different to the examples provided above in terms of scope and intentions. However, it has arguably been the most impactful of all, although not as intended. Rather than drawing attention to the plight of civilian Kurds in southeastern Turkey, it has provoked a vicious reaction from the state and some segments of civil society. Moreover, the authorities' crackdown has been facilitated by the petition itself, which provides a wholesale list of academics in numerous institutions in Turkey who disapprove of the government's approach to the Kurdish Question after the failure of the peace process. The tremendous courage of these scholars has been met, therefore, with retribution and malicious intent.

Academic freedom in Turkey

Academic freedom is under threat all around the world, something scholars have been bringing to the attention of the academe and the wider public for more than a decade. Nehring and Kerrigan (2016) observe that this phenomenon is not limited to authoritarian countries; even liberal democracies are becoming less and less secure for academic freedom and freedom of speech. Henry A. Giroux's (2016) criticism towards neoliberalism and its impact on higher education institutions is remarkable. His examination of current academic practices indicates, in his view, the emergence of a new age of authoritarianism. Even in so-called liberal societies, critical thinking is not welcome at institutions of higher education where academic indifference towards injustice and violence is becoming the norm. Critical thinking, he contends, is increasingly "criminalised" across the globe: "[a]cademics who function as critical public intellectuals have always posed a threat to authoritarian states and corporate entitites, just as the institutions in which they worked were viewed as a threat to authoritarian powers" (Giroux 2016, 118). Turkey is no exception here, and even when the trends of democratisation were moving in a positive direction, academics faced intense pressure to eschew the public dissemination of "dangerous thinking" (Giroux 2016). It is worth, therefore, detailing in brief the story of academic freedom in Turkey in order to contextualise recent events surrounding the "Academics for Peace" petition.

As mentioned, heavy limits on academic independence have been a feature of the Turkish political scene long before the rise of the AKP. University campuses were the site of the most contentious and often violent ideological confrontations between leftists and rightists during the period of "radicalisation" of Turkish politics in the late 1960s and 1970s. In response, the military regime established after the 12 September 1980 coup established a state authority – *YÖK* to "monitor" universities and ensure institutionalised state control over the higher education institutions (Gocek 2016). While YÖK did not function as an apparatus of direct "thought control", it nevertheless had something of a "chilling effect" on academic conduct and publication. Moreover, in the wake of Turkey's authoritarian turn, the existence of YÖK has provided the AKP with a ready-made state apparatus capable of clamping down hard on academic freedom. As Gocek (2016) states, "[s]ince educational institutions are among the most significant places for research, their control becomes crucial in autocratic states. Rulers want to closely monitor access to knowledge and therefore to power". Indeed, the space in which academics can conduct research and contribute to political discussions in Turkey has been radically constricted. The "Academics for Peace" petition was simply the proverbial straw that broke the camel's back in relation to academic freedom and the Kurdish Question.

The deteriorating situation of Turkish academic freedom after 2010 has not gone unheeded. The International Working Group on Academic Liberty and Freedom of Research in Turkey (Groupe international de travail – GIT: "*Liberté de recherche et d'enseignement en Turquie*") was founded in 2011 in the wake of the arrest of Prof. Busra Ersanli on charges of "terrorist propaganda". This initiative of Turkish-born scholars (often working abroad) and international partners was established to monitor and expose further attacks on academics in Turkey. By early 2012, the initiative had established chapters in Germany, Switzerland, France and North America. The group called for solidarity with Turkish academic colleagues, a petition signed by hundreds of academics (*GIT Turkiye, Akademik Ozgurlukler Icin Birlesme Cagrisi*). GIT also launched a series of reports on violations of academic freedom in Turkey, the first of which was published in 2012b (*GIT, Akademide Hak Ihlalleri*).

The work of GIT indicates that the solidarity shown towards the "Academics for Peace" drew on a base already established with networks such as the Academics Solidarity Platform and the Foundation University Workers' Solidarity Network (GIT Report 2016, 2). The report states that

> In the absence of academic freedom, one cannot speak of the autonomy of universities as institutions of higher education. Institutional autonomy alone is not sufficient to safeguard free thought and free research. A university may thrive, in a universal sense, only in the presence of both scientific and institutional autonomy. (GIT Report 2016, 7)

The report places contemporary events in historical context by detailing the general degradation of academic freedom in Turkey, especially in moments of historical political crisis (GIT Report 2016, 9). It further notes that

> After the year 2000, the ruling political powers established their own administrations at universities, step by step, and at every level. They never refrained from exerting pressure and applying censorship with regard to 'sensitive topics' which have existed since the

founding of the republic. Moreover, they widened the scope of repression at universities by means of introducing 'brand new sensitive issues'. (GIT Report 2016. 9)

Already in 2012, the GIT's 2012a "Call to Unite for Academic Freedoms" stated that academic research was being hindered by direct and indirect obstacles and that those academics lecturing on subjects that are considered taboo in Turkey faced particular difficulties. Underlining the urgent need for safeguarding freedom of expression and research, the call announced that the GIT Turkey will fight against oppression on academia. The GIT Report (2016) reveals that the sensitive topics which the academics are not allowed to touch upon in their academic work changes from one period to another, not only depending on who the ruling party is but also on the changing dynamics of politics in Turkey. Many violation cases from all over Turkey are mentioned in GIT Reports which demonstrate that counterterrorism narratives have been used to criminalise academics and delegitimise their academic work way before the petition was publicly announced in January 2016.

For instance, a PhD thesis on the Kurdish issue and the Kurdish language was derecognised by Marmara University in Istanbul with the university stating that the PhD thesis has been contradicting with the Turkish Constitution's articles that cannot be amended (Abbott 2012). The PhD candidate then defended her thesis in Lund University in Sweden. Another academic has won a large research grant to work on the Kurdish Question and civil society but his university did not let him pass the ethics committee because they found his topic controversial. Another academic asked an exam question to his students about the PKK leader Öcalan and his views and this was considered to be "terrorist propaganda". An investigation has been launched against him (GIT 2012b). These types of violations of academic freedoms also continued after the petition. One professor at Akdeniz University resigned in April 2016 because her student's thesis subject on the role of women in peacebuilding was deemed "dangerous" by the university (*Diken* 29 April, 2016). These incidents show that the failure of the peace process has also paved the way for the criminalisation of concepts such as peace, peacebuilding or negotiations.

The "Academics for Peace" petition uproar: criminalisation, targeting and investigations into "terrorist propaganda"

The "Academics for Peace" group differed somewhat from previous civil society initiatives such as the GIT. Although there is an overlap among the members of these initiatives, the "Academics for Peace" group's principal concern was not academic freedom per se, but rather the question of justice for the Kurds. The group came together in 2012 just before the so-called peace process had started between the PKK and the Turkish state. They were a loose network rather than a registered non-governmental organisation and lacked any distinct hierarchy or organisation. The members of this initiative wanted to emphasise that there is very little known about the dynamics of the Turkish–Kurdish conflict in Turkey and they wanted to prepare a road map for enhancing peace and reconciliation at the societal level. During the peace process, they also voluntarily contributed to the production of knowledge on these issues.[7]

Erdoğan's strong reaction to the petition alarmed YÖK and prosecutors immediately. In his talk, he stated that "[d]espite all of these facts, this crowd, who calls themselves academics, accuses the state through a statement. Not only this, they also invite foreigners to monitor developments. This is the mentality of colonialism" (*Hurriyet Daily News*, 12 January 2016). In an echo of reactions to the 1960 *Manifesto of the 121* in France, the president labelled the signatories "ignorant" and "so-called intellectuals" and accused them of being a "fifth column", and of disseminating a "colonisers' mentality". "Hey, you so-called intellectuals! You are not enlightened persons, you are dark. You are nothing like intellectuals. You are ignorant and dark, not even knowing about the east or the southeast. We know these places just like we know our home addresses", he said, reiterating his position that Turkey's problem is "not a Kurdish one, but one of terror". YÖK's official response to the petition announced that "[t]he declaration issued by a group of academics that describes our state's ongoing struggle against terror in the southeast as 'massacre and slaughter' has put our entire academic world under suspicion". It followed this by stating that "[t]his declaration cannot be associated with academic freedom. Providing the security of citizens is the primary responsibility of the state" (*Hurriyet Daily News*, 12 January 2016).

Immediately following the YÖK statement, 30 academics were detained. Their houses were raided by anti-terror squads within the police department. Their belongings, including books, computers, mobile phones and other research materials, were confiscated. Apart from the criminal investigations, universities were also forced to open disciplinary inquiries into the signatories. In January and February, around 100 academics learned that they were being investigated by their institutions. During the investigations, many academics were questioned for their political views and a majority of the universities who opened probes did not treat this as a matter of freedom of speech or academic freedom (Human Rights Watch, 16 March 2016).

What was crucial about this ordeal was also the targeting and stigmatising of academics as a collective. Erdogan's reaction echoed in the mainstream media who duly published reports and op-eds criminalising the academics and what they stand for. News channels kept talking about the petition for a long time, and broadcasts showed names, affiliations and photos of the signatories; some news programmes even reviewed academics' social media on live TV highlighting, for example, tweets that might be deemed anti-government or critical of President Erdoğan. A newspaper gave a full page with these academics' names and affiliations. They had full disclosure, making them vulnerable. The propaganda surely had an impact on the public and how they perceived this petition. Some academics reported that they received threats from students, neighbours and even random strangers. Their office doors at universities were marked with red signs which stated "terrorist academics" were not welcome at the universities. Many received emails or social media mentions and messages full of death threats and swear words. Some had to empty their offices at the university, leave their homes or even cities in order to protect themselves (Sozeri 2016). For instance, in Eskişehir, a mannequin was hanged over a highway with a banner stating "[d]eath penalty to the PKK Academics" (*Haberler*, 24 April 2016). A cyber lynching was also put into force against the academics in social media outlets. While these were happening, the prosecutors were demanding information from signatories about the identity of the "mastermind" of the petition (Flader 2016). The signatories were told during the interrogations that they are accused of taking orders from Bese Hozat, a PKK commander. Their argument was that the terminology used in the petition mirrored the "terrorist organisation's vocabulary".

Moreover, a mafia leader who is known as a full-throated supporter of the AKP regime made a declaration on his blog page titled "The So-Called Intellectuals, The Bell Will Toll for You First". In this post, he issued a horrific threat: "[w]e will spill your blood in streams and we will shower in your blood" (*Hurriyet Daily News*, 14 January 2016). Various politicians from the AKP also stated that the declaration itself has been drafted by the PKK and the academics have been taking orders from the PKK leadership. Their main criticism was that the petition has not criticised the PKK but solely directed its demands to the Turkish government. Indeed, many columnists picked up on this issue and claimed that the petition lacked academic rigour because it was "biased" and it was only directed to the Turkish government without any criticism towards the PKK. The president and his supporters also claimed that the academics used "terrorist jargon" similar to the discourses of the PKK.

In an attempt to delegitimise the petition even further, a counter-petition was prepared by pro-government academics calling themselves "Academics for Turkey". Their petition refused to criticise military action in southeast Turkey and instead declared full support for state policy against the PKK (see Sozeri 2016). Various universities put both direct and indirect pressure on their staff to sign the petition, and many did so simply in order not to be stigmatised in their respective institutions.

Moreover, during the investigations, many academics were subjected to bullying and mobbing. Some were forced to withdraw their signatures in order to prevent further criminalisaiton and investigations. In other cases, signatory academics withdrew their signatures voluntarily in order to detach themselves from these discussions. Some have done so legally with a press release while others preferred to stay anonymous. Human Rights Watch interviewed signatory academics during investigations and revealed the injustices they were facing. For instance, an assistant professor of sociology was suspended from Düzce University a day after Erdoğan's first speech. She learnt about her suspension from the university website without an official notice. Moreover, police raided her home and office and took her computer and other belongings. She testified before the Düzce public prosecutor and a court imposed a travel ban, preventing her from going abroad and to continue her academic work. Another academic from Van Yüzüncü Yıl University was taken into custody and spent a night in jail. Although he has German citizenship, he was also subject to a court-ordered travel ban. The university also informed him that his contract would not be renewed. Other academics from the same institution were also given court-ordered travel bans while criminal investigations were ongoing (Human Rights Watch Report, 2016). Fifteen scholars from Kocaeli University and three from Uludağ University have been detained and their houses raided by the police. These examples were multiplied as the investigations continued.

Critics of the "Academics for Peace" petition made two points. The first set of criticisms argued that the tone was unprofessional and harsh and that the petition only addressed criticisms towards the Turkish state while pointedly avoiding discussion of PKK activity and violations of rights. The second set emphasised the choice of wording. Use of the word "massacre" – in the context of the apparent "deliberate and planned massacre" by the Turkish state – was argued to be disproportionate. Many columnists and journalists joined the "Academics for Peace" in making these criticisms.

However, the petition still received tremendous support locally and internationally.[8] For instance, the "Academics for Peace" initiative also received several prizes, including the Palm Prize for free speech, the Aachen Prize, The Middle East Association's Academic Freedom Award.

The pending trial and precariousness: resisting arrests, deportation and defamation

Counterterrorism emergency measures have already become a part of the daily routine in Turkey (Barrinha 2011). Flader (2016) takes the Turkish state's reactions to the petition one step further, however, describing them as an example of *Gleichschaltung*, the process – originally developed by the Nazis – of eliminating all opposition within the political, economic and cultural institutions of the state and establishing control over all aspects of society. In an interview, signatory academic Dr Murat Ozbank also underlined the similarities between the current purge in Turkey and the *Gleichschaltung* in Nazi Germany by focusing on the totalitarian direction that Turkey is taking by suppressing the opposition both in political circles and civil society (Evrensel, 7 February 2016).

Among the signatories, Esra Mungan, Muzaffer Kaya, Kıvanç Ersoy and Meral Camcı were called in for questioning and were arrested on 14 March 2016, two months after the petition press release. They were accused of "making terrorist propaganda" under the Counter-Terrorism Law (Article 7/2) (Altıparmak and Akdeniz 2017, 15). The obvious reason behind their detention and arrest was that they publicly read the petition one more time even though it had been criminalised. At the time of the arrests, Camcı was abroad but she returned and joined her colleagues in jail in order to show solidarity. After these academics were arrested, President Erdoğan publicly endorsed an extension of the legal definition of a terrorist:

> It might be the terrorist who pulls the trigger and detonates the bomb, but it is these supporters and accomplices who allow that attack to achieve its goal. The fact their title is politician, academic, writer, journalist or head of a civil society group doesn't change the fact that individual is a terrorist. (Abbott, Nature, 16 March 2016).

After five weeks of imprisonment and solitary confinement, the three scholars were brought before the court. The accusations included taking orders from the PKK leaders, legitimising the PKK, accusing the Turkish state for committing massacres, and preparing ground for inviting United Nations observers to the Turkish territory among others. Initially charged under counterterrorism laws, the prosecutor inexplicably changed tack and sought to frame the prosecution under the infamous Article 301 of Turkey's legal code that prohibits "insulting Turkey and Turkishness". The judge adjourned the case to 27 September and the trial was then delayed through to the end of December 2016 and then to March 2017, and then again to 18 July 2017 in order for the prosecutors to obtain the necessary permission from the Ministry of Justice to proceed with a prosecution under Article 301.

Events have also shown that foreigners are as vulnerable as local Turks to prosecution. Chris Stephenson, a British computer scientist at Bilgi University who protested against the arrests of the four academics mentioned earlier, was himself detained in March 2016. He elected to leave Turkey while awaiting a deportation order. He was escorted to his plane in the presence of a police officer. He had been detained after police found leaflets publicising Kurdish New Year celebrations on 21 March (*Newroz*) in his possession. This publicity material was also considered "terrorist propaganda". He was then told he would be able to return to Turkey but would have in that case to face trial.[9] The well-planned strategy behind the arrest signalled to the foreign and domestic audience alike that (1) foreign nationals would not be exempted from prosecution simply on account of their citizenship status; (2) anyone who publicly supports the Kurds or voices criticism of the Turkish state's or government's actions towards them is vulnerable to arrest and prosecution; and (3) diplomatic tensions can be avoided when foreigners are implicated because Turkey is able to fall back on the "counterterrorism" justification. Therefore, showing dissent as a foreign national risks deportation, detention, harrassment or loss of employment, on top of the stigmatisation dished out by the mainstream media. The signal to all Westerners living in Turkey was clear.

The criminalisation of academics through counterterrorism discourse is the handiwork of five principal state institutions and actors: the president, the AKP government, mainstream media outlets (newspapers, TV channels), the judiciary and the police, and YÖK and the universities. Social media has also been deployed widely by pro-AKP trolls. The aim of this defamation campaign against academics is collective character assassination. By insulting an entire profession as "dissidents", delegitimising their demands, criminalising intellectual dissent by cultivating a hostile anti-intellectual environment and stigmatising anyone who would oppose government policies on the Kurdish issue, the state seeks to bring academics to heel.[10]

The whole debate on the petition also drew attention away from the plight of Kurdish civilians in the region, making the academics and *their* freedoms the issue. At times, therefore, the discussion about freedom of speech and academic autonomy overshadowed the original purpose of the petition, which was to stop state violence in the region. Similarly, the international solidarity campaigns cast light on the fundamental rights of academics leaving the Kurdish issue largely tangential to the main discussion. Many solidarity declarations asked the Turkish government to immediately stop persecuting academics, yet failed to mention the human rights abuses going on against the Kurdish population in Turkey.

The outcome of the debate showed the long-standing vulnerability and precarious existence of academics in Turkey. The absence of job security and the ease with which they can be dismissed from universities because of their political views has always been at issue. Moreover, the debate exposed in no uncertain terms the lack of capacity universities have to defend academic freedom generally and their staff's freedom of speech in particular. Oppression of academics became more visible than ever before. Moreover, the "subcontracting" of monitoring and surveillance of academic conduct to the public – including, tragically, students themselves – takes matters to a new level. Before the petition, there had been isolated cases of students reporting lecturers who criticised the government or taught on controversial issues. However, under the new dispensation, students who come forward are amply rewarded for demonstrating their allegiance to the AKP and President Erdogan. Sadly, student snitches and informants now join university rectors, heads of departments and other bureaucrats as enforcers of state policy against academic freedom. A June 2016 incident at Bilgi University in which a student recorded his professor criticising President Erdogan and passed the recordings to the mainstream media stands as a case in point. Because of this duplicity, the professor was dismissed from the university (*Diken*, 18 June 2016).

The course of events once more proves the hegemonic influence of President Erdogan in almost every field – the judiciary, security services, universities, media and parliament. It is also clear that orthodox understandings of terrorism are still very strong in Turkey and that the peace process never really succeeded in breaking the Turkish reflex of seeing the Kurds as the "enemy within". While the ease with which it is possible to gin up nationalist fervour through media maniupulation makes this an obvious strategy for the government, the entire process overlooks just how counterproductive these hyper-nationalist strategies have proven in the past, only serving to make the conflict more toxic and likely more protracted (Barrinha 2011, 164). Indeed, given that the AKP launched the peace process precisely because it realised that the policies of the past would no longer work, the return to type speaks volumes about the government's political desperation.

The failed coup attempt and the academic purge that followed

The 15 July 2016 coup attempt in Turkey was undoubtedly one of the most significant events in the country's recent history. According to testimonies and popular news, a group of flag officers of Turkey's army attempted an overthrow of Erdoğan and the AKP government (Adams 2016). AKP politicians and the mainstream media blame the Gülen Movement (GM)[11] for plotting this coup attempt. However, the jury is still out on whether the putschists were drawn only from Gülenist cliques in the military or whether the revolt in the ranks was more widespread.

Turkey, of course, has suffered long periods of military tutelage and a variety of different types of military intervention in politics. This particular coup attempt, however, was distinctive. Five days after the coup attempt, the AKP government declared a state of emergency for three months and President Erdoğan announced it to the public as a positive step and as an opportunity to clean up pro-Gülenist people from the public sector (Jones and Kandemir 2016). The state of emergency was later prolonged for another six months. Although on paper the state of emergency seems to be related to the putsch, it is fair to argue that President Erdoğan has been using his emergency powers to overhaul most of the opposition groups and potential social and political targets. The need to protect the Turkish nation and state in these exceptional circumstances gives a patina of legitimation to these moves.

On the one hand, according to figures released by the Turkish media, the putsch involved 8651 officers or 1.5 per cent of armed forces' personnel (Pitel 2016). On the other hand, in the first two weeks of the state of emergency, multiple universities and hundreds of civil society associations, media centres and companies were shut down. Additionally, thousands of teachers in their probation period were let go, thousands of passports were annulled and hundreds of people – including journalists, scholars, judges, bureaucrats and state officials – were suspended under investigation and/or arrested, including many Alevis, leftists and Kemalists who did not have any relations with the Gülen movement. The government made these moves on the grounds that the accused had aided and abetted the coup attempt. Moreover, members of the HDP, including the party's co-leaders and elected mayors, which is considered to be a pro-minority left-wing party in Turkey, have been arrested and put in jail, dashing hopes for a renewal of the peace process. These arrests showed very clearly that the purge was intended to go much beyond the Gülenist circles.

Following the failed coup, more than a hundred thousand civil servants were expelled from public service, thousands detained, and arrested. More than a dozen universities were closed down and academics have been dismissed. Expulsion from public service results in being banned from taking up office in public institutions or corporations, the confiscation of passports and, if deemed necessary, the confiscation of property. Expulsion from a university deprives the academic of the right to submit an associate professorship application, which in Turkey can be obtained without institutional affiliation. In addition to those dismissed before the coup, more than 300 signatories of the "Academics for Peace" petition were expelled from public service through state of emergency decrees between September 2016 and February 2017.[12] Others who are not suspended have to live under heavy pressures and mobbing at many universities all around Turkey. Some are constantly pressured to withdraw their signatures. As Altıparmak and Akdeniz (2017, 71) accounts, there is no available information on what kind of methods were used to prepare the emergency decrees to suspend these academics. Nobody has access to the information on proofs which criminalised these academics and others in order to be mentioned in these decrees. As the authors argue, the only reason why these academics have been dismissed was because they signed the petition. This situation is surely against the European Court of Human Rights' Article 10 on the freedom of speech. The emergency decrees violate not only freedom of speech, but also the right to fair trial and protection of privacy (Altıparmak and Akdeniz 2017, 73).

As elected opposition politicians are arrested, and academics are suspended and banned from public service, there is massive surveillence of social media accounts and the political climate in Turkey becomes all the more totalitarian. In the post-putsch period, the "undesirables" of the newly emerging regime are being silenced in order for a "New Turkey" – in which there is no room for concepts such as democracy, peace or freedom of speech – to be born.

Concluding remarks: contesting oppression and creating venues of resistance as academics

The "Academics for Peace" petition was published in an open letter format in January 2016, with the aim of making a call for peace and asking the Turkish state to return to the negotiating table with the Kurdish armed movement, the PKK. The initiative was a loose one with no hierarchical structure. The petition was distributed through social media and signed by academics who thought they could make a change, despite the fact that it is very unlikely with a petition. The reaction from the president, state institutions, YÖK and the university rectors and heads of departments was not proportionate and it aimed at criminalising the signatory academics for being critical of the state's official policies. Counterterrorism law has been used in conjunction with the politics of fear, in order to stigmatise this whole group as "terrorist sympathisers", discourage others to show dissent and to instruct authorities to take measures against those who dare to speak out. The reactions to the petition also managed to scare away the "people in the middle" who were neither in line with state's actions in the southeast region of Turkey but who dared not sign a document saying as much. They are buried in silence.

As mentioned earlier, after almost a year, the prosecution of these signatory academics continues and there are still pending charges against them for "terrorist propaganda" and "insulting Turkey". Most of the signatories have not given up on their demands and have created various avenues of resistance in order to demonstrate that their cause was a just one. While the court cases are pending, universities also try to make their job harder by not allowing them to attend international conferences, sabbaticals or other visits. Some have lost their passports during the recent purge and are subject to travel bans. Some academics are also taken out of conference programmes because they are signatories (Kural, Bianet, 7 April 2016). In the meantime, individual applications to institutions such as Scholars at Risk or the Scholar Rescue Fund skyrocketed.

Those who have been dismissed from their universities find it hard to find another job as other institutions hesitate to employ signatory academics. Their criminalisation continues by the mainstream media and other state institutions. They are forced to live a "civil death" in Turkey by being deprived of their basic rights. The unfair treatment and mobbing also caused one academic[13] to commit suicide which was exemplary in terms of showing the psychological damage that this process is having on the signatories. Some academics also started a hunger strike demanding the lifting of the state of emergency and returning to their academic posts, among others.

They are finding "solidarity academies" where they teach for free or they find "people without campus" initiatives in order to pursue their academic ideals by underlining that they do not need an institution for intellectual activities. Some academics in Eskişehir even founded a musical band and sing-songs for peace. Some prominent academics such as Baskın Oran have opened court cases against President Erdoğan for slander (*Qantara*, 29 June 2016). It can be said that the "Academics for Peace" initiative is a social movement in the making in Turkey.

Surely, the oppression, lack of employment and sense of insecurity drive many academics to look for alternatives abroad. Especially after the putsch, there has been a brain drain of academics from Turkey. Countries such as France, Germany and Czechia have declared their support for the academics who are oppressed by the ruling regime. Not only persecuted academics but also some who have never been openly critical are leaving. Time will show whether this is temporary or permanent. To our dismay, many intellectuals are also surrendering their civic courage and intellectual capacities to the dictates of the regime which is becoming authoritarian. This is precisely the outcome Giroux (2016, 156) predicted for US academia under the impact of neoliberalism. As long as the culture of fear flourishes in Turkey, it seems as if the hope for improvements in academic freedom, freedom of speech and room for critique fades day by day.

Notes

1. The text was initially written in an open letter format rather than a petition. The signatories included prominent non-Turkish scholars such as Noam Chomsky, Judith Butler, Slavoj Žižek, Immanuel Wallerstein, Etienne Balibar and David Harvey. The full text is available at http://bianet.org/english/human-rights/170978-academics-we-will-not-be-a-party-to-this -crime.

2. Prof. Ismail Besicki is one of the remarkable examples. He served 17 years in prison for his writings on the Kurds. The imprisonment of Prof. Busra Ersanli in 2011 is also a case in point.
3. "For example, when the the German Parliament passed the Armenian Genocide resolution anonymously on June 2, 2016, university presidents came under pressure to issue public statements supporting Turkish foreign policy" (Gocek 2016).
4. For a detailed account of analysis on the petition from a human rights perspective, see Altıparmak and Akdeniz (2017, 101–139).
5. For more info, see http://michiganintheworld.history.lsa.umich.edu/antivietnamwar/.
6. First author's personal contact with Prof. Willie Esterhuyse and Prof. Willie Breytenbach, October 2016, Stellenbosch, South Africa.
7. See their website: https://barisicinakademisyenler.net/node/1.
8. A complete list of solidarity messages can be found here: http://internationalsolidarity4academic.tumblr.com/page/2.
9. YÖK has cancelled Dr Stephenson's work permit in March 2017. He worked in Turkey for 18 years. In the time of writing this article, he is preparing for appeal. Other foreign academics who were working in Turkey and who were signatories to the petition have also lost their work permits.
10. It also bears noting that these types of smear campaign in Turkey frequently happen and in rare cases result in political murders. The cases of Hrant Dink, an Armenian journalist in Turkey, and Tahir Elci, a Kurdish lawyer and human rights activist, are examples of how far stigmatisation can go. For more information on the case of Hrant Dink, see Freely (2007), and for the case of Tahir Elci, see Darici (2016).
11. The Gülen Movement is a political-religious network organised under the ideas of Fethullah Gülen. Even though the Movement has been trying to show itself is an inter-religious and dialogue-based civil society, it has two different faces that are indirectly connected each other. While the civil face is mostly based on philanthropy and cultural dialogue activates, the political face is aiming to reach power via controlling the bureaucratic mechanisms in Turkey that has reach the pick point during the AKP period.
12. One should make a distinction between the academics who were suspended by the emergency decrees because of their alleged connections to the GM and the others who were the signatories of the decision. Also, some of the suspended academics had no connections to the movement but they were employees of higher education institutions which were allegedly linked to the GM. Although all groups are affected by the authoritarian tendencies in Turkey and they had to endure unfair detentions and suspensions, the main reason behind their dismissals is different. The signatories are targeted by the government and the president, and consequently by other state apparatuses due to their stance on human rights issues in Turkey. Their political stance on the Kurdish Question and how to tackle with the creeping authoritarianism in Turkey also is clearly distinct from the GM and its supporters. The GM and its media apparatuses have also instrumentalised the counterterrorism rhetoric until they broke up their alliance with the AKP government and their attitude has been systematically criticised by most of the signatories of the petition.
13. Mehmet Fatih Traş was a research assistant at Cukurova University. He committed suicide in February 2017 as a result of psychological trauma after being dismissed from his job.

Disclaimer

Two authors of this paper are signatories of the petition. However, in no way do the authors represent "Academics for Peace" as a group and the authors wish to underline that this article solely reflects their personal assessments and viewpoints. None of the statements made or opinions expressed in the article can be attributed to the signatories, collectively or individually, of the "Academics for Peace" petition.

Acknowledgements

The authors would also like to thank the anonymous reviewers Dr Burcu Togral and Didem Oral for their valuable comments on the earlier versions of this article.

Disclosure statement

No potential conflict of interest was reported by the authors.

Funding

Bahar Baser wishes to thank the South African National Research Foundation for funding her research. This article was written while she was a visiting postdoctoral fellow at the Faculty of Military Science, Stellenbosch University. Ahmet Erdi Öztürk and Samim Akgönül wish to thank the research centre DRES of the University of Strasbourg for excellent work conditions provided during the writing process of this article.

References

"Academics Comment on President's Wording". 2016. *Bianet*, January 14.
"Al sana akademik özgürlük: 'Barış' tezi geri çevrildi, danişman istifasini verdi". 2016. *Diken*, April 29.
Abbott, A. 2012. "Turkey Cracks down on Academic Freedom", *Nature*, July 3.
Abbott, A. 2016. "Turkish Academics Were Jailed for 'Making Terrorist Propaganda'", *Nature*, March 16.
Adams, S. 2016. "Turkey Coup 2016 Explained: What Happened and What Is a Military Coup?", *Mirror*, July 18.
Agamben, G. 2005. *State of Exception*. Chicago, CA: University of Chicago Press.
Akkoyunlu, K., and K. Öktem. 2016. "Existential Insecurity and the Making of a Weak Authoritarian Regime in Turkey." *Southeast European and Black Sea Studies* 16 (4): 505–527. doi:10.1080/14683857.2016.1253225.
Altıparmak, K., and Y. Akdeniz. 2017. *Barış İçin Akademisyenler: Olağanüstüzamanlarda Akademiyi Savunmak*. Istanbul: Iletisim Yayinlari.
"Barış için imza atan Murat Özbank: Korkup sustukça, korktuğumuz başimiza gelir". 2016. *Evrensel*, February 7.
Barrinha, A. 2011. "The Political Importance of Labelling: Terrorism and Turkey's Discourse on the PKK." *Critical Studies on Terrorism* 4 (2): 163–180. doi:10.1080/17539153.2011.586203.
"Bilgi'den kovulan akademisyen: Mahremiyetime saldırılmış hissediyorum", 2016. *Diken*, June 18.

Case, W. 1993. "Semi-Democracy in Malaysia: Withstanding the Pressures for Regime Change." *Pacific Affairs* 66 (2): 183–205. doi:10.2307/2759366.

Chomsky, N. 1967. "The Responsibility of the Intellectuals", *The New York Review of Books*, February 23.

Darici, H. 2016. "Of Kurdish Youth and Ditches." *Theory & Event* 19: 1.

Dearden, L. 2016. "President Erdogan Says Freedom and Democracy Have 'No Value' in Turkey amid Arrests and Military Crackdown," *Independent*, Mar 18.

DeVotta, N. 2015. "From Counterterrorism to Soft-Authoritarianism: The Case of Sri Lanka." In *Critical Perspectives on Counter-terrorism*, edited by, M. Lister and L. Jarvis, 210–230. London: Routledge.

Economist Intelligence Unit's 2015 "Democracy Index, Turkey," http://country.eiu.com/turkey.

"Erdogan slams academics over petition, calls Chomsky to Turkey". 2016. *Hurriyet Daily News*, January 12.

"Erdogan's Freedom of Speech." 2016. *Qantara*, June 29.

Esen, B., and S. Gümüşcü. 2016. "Rising Competitive Authoritarianism in Turkey." *Third World Quarterly* 37 (9): 1581–1606. doi:10.1080/01436597.2015.1135732.

Flader, U. 2016 "Voices from the Dark: The Academics' 'Peace Petition' and the Remnants of Opposition in Turkey", *Movements@Manchester*, February 24.

Freedom House, Freedom in the World. 2016. *Turkey Country Report*. https://freedomhouse.org/sites/default/files/FH_FITW_Report_2016.pdf

Freely, M. 2007. "Why They Killed Hrant Dink." *Index on Censorship* 2: 15–29. doi:10.1080/03064220701334477.

Giroux, H. A. 2016. *Dangerous Thinking: In the Age of New Authoritarianism*. New York: Routledge.

GIT Turkey. 2012a. *Call to Unite for Academic Freedoms*.

GIT Turkey. 2016. *"Academic Rights Violation Report III: May 2013-May 2015*.

GIT Turkiye. 2012b. *Akademide Hak Ihlalleri Dosyasi: Turkiye'de Arastirma Ve Egitim Ozgurlugu Uluslararasi Calisma Grubu*.

Gocek, F. M. 2016. "Why Turkey Wants to Silence Its Academics?" *The Conversation*, July 27.

Horowitz, D. L. 1991. *A Democratic South Africa? Constitutional Engineering in A Divided Society*. Berkeley: University of California Press.

The Human Rights Foundation of Turkey, Factsheet on Declared Curfews in Turkey between 11 December 2015 and 8 January 2016, http://en.tihv.org.tr/fact-sheet-on-declared-curfews-in-turkey-between-11-december-2015-8-january-2016/.

Human Rights Watch Report. 2015. *Turkey: Mounting Security Operation Deaths*. https://www.hrw.org/news/2015/12/22/turkey-mounting-security-operation-deaths

Jones, G., and A. Kandemir 2016 "Turkey's Erdogan Announces Three-Month State of Emergency," *Reuters*, July 20.

Keyman, E. F., and S. Gümüşcü. 2014. *Democracy, Identity, and Foreign Policy in Turkey*. Basingstoke: Palgrave Macmillan.

Krane, M. S. 2011. "The Responsibility of Intellectuals: Chomsky and Student Opposition to the Vietnam War." *Young Historians Conference*. https://www.pdx.edu/challenge-program/sites/www.pdx.edu.challenge-program/files/KRANE-TheResponsibilityofIntellectuals.pdf

Kural, B. 2016. "İmzacı Üç Akademisyene Konferans Engeli", *Bianet*, April 7.

Leak, A. 2006. *Jean-Paul Sartre*. London: Reaktion Books.

Levitsky, S., and L. Way. 2002. "The Rise of Competitive Authoritarianism." *Journal of Democracy* 13 (2): 51–65. doi:10.1353/jod.2002.0026.

Means, G. P. 1996. "Soft Authoritarianism in Malaysia and Singapore." *Journal of Democracy* 7 (4): 103–117. doi:10.1353/jod.1996.0065.

Nehring, D., and D. Kerrigan 2016. Introduction: Academic Freedom in Crisis, *Social Science Space*, September 2.

Norris, P., and D. Jones. 1998. "Virtual Democracy." *Harvard International Journal of Press Politics* 3: 1–4. doi:10.1177/1081180X98003002001.

Office of the United Nations High Commissioner for Human Rights, Report on the Human Rights Situation in South-East Turkey: July 2015 to December 2016. Published in February 2017.

Özbudun, E. 2014. "AKP at the crossroads: Erdoğan's majoritarian drift." *South European Society and Politics* 19 (2): 155–167. doi:10.1080/13608746.2014.920571.

Öztürk, A. E. 2014. "The Presidential Election in Turkey: History and Future Expectations." *Contemporary Southeastern Europe* 1 (2): 110–118.

Patton, M. J. 2007. "AKP Reform Fatigue in Turkey: What Has Happened to the EU Process?" *Mediterranean Politics* 12 (3): 339–358. doi:10.1080/13629390701622382.

"Petition by 1,383 intellectuals to the President of Turkey". 1984. *Index on Censorship*, 13:5, 5–10.

Pitel, L. 2016. "Erdogan Uses State of Emergency to Overhaul Turkey's Military", *Financial Times*, August 2.

"Probe launced into mafia leader's 'bloodbath' threats against academics".2016. *Hurriyet Daily News*, January 14.

Rule of Law Index. 2016. *World Justice Project*. Turkey. https://worldjusticeproject.org/sites/default/files/documents/RoLI_Final-Digital_0.pdf

Schalk, D. L. 1991. *War and the Ivory Tower: Algeria and Vietnam*. Lincoln: University of Nebraska Press.

Schedler, A. 2006. *Electoral Authoritarianism: The Dynamics of Unfree Competition*. Boulder, CO: Lynne Rienner Publishers.

Schiermeier, Q. 2016. "Turkish Scientists Rocked by Accusations of Supporting Terrorism", *Nature*, January 18.

Statement by Israeli Academics. 2014. *Shift in Opinion Over Boycott of Israel*. July 24, 2014. https://www.timeshighereducation.com/comment/letters/shift-in-opinion-over-boycott-of-israel/2014726.article

Sozeri, E. K. 2016. "Two Petitions Two Academia: Turkish Loneliness and the Universal Values." *Translate for Justice*.https://translateforjustice.com/2016/02/01/two-petitions-two-academia-turkish-loneliness-and-the-universal-values/

"Trafik Levhasina Cansiz Manken Astilar, Uzerine "Idam" Yazdilar". 2016. *Haberler*, April 24.

"Turkey: Academics Jailed For Signing Petition". 2016. *Human Rights Watch*, March 16.

Uğur, M. 2016. "Academic Freedom under Threat in Turkey", *Times Higher Education*, April 14.

Uluğ, O. M., and J. C. Cohrs. 2017. "Examining the Ethos of Conflict by Exploring the Lay People's Representations of the Kurdish Conflict in Turkey." *Conflict Management and Peace Science* 1–22. doi:10.1177/0738894216674969

Winckler, E. A. 1984. "Institutionalization and Participation on Taiwan: From Hard to Soft Authoritarianism?" *The China Quarterly* 99: 481–499. doi:10.1017/S0305741000017148.

Yesilada, B. 2016. "The Future of Erdoğan and the AKP." *Turkish Studies* 17 (1): 19–30. doi:10.1080/14683849.2015.1136089.

Zakaria, F. 1997. "The Rise of Illiberal Democracy." *Foreign Affairs* 76 (6): 22–43. doi:10.2307/20048274.

ⓐ OPEN ACCESS

The geography of pre-criminal space: epidemiological imaginations of radicalisation risk in the UK Prevent Strategy, 2007–2017

Charlotte Heath-Kelly ⓘ

ABSTRACT
This article explores geographical and epistemological shifts in the deployment of the UK Prevent strategy, 2007–2017. Counter-radicalisation policies of the Labour governments (2006–2010) focused heavily upon resilience-building activities in residential communities. They borrowed from historical models of crime prevention and public health to imagine radicalisation risk as an epidemiological concern in areas showing a 2% or higher demography of Muslims. However, this racialised and localised imagination of pre-criminal space was replaced after the election of the Conservative-Liberal Democrat coalition in 2010. Residential communities were then de-emphasised as sites of risk, transmission and pre-criminal intervention. The Prevent Duty now deploys counter-radicalisation through national networks of education and health-care provision. Localised models of crime prevention (and their statistical, crime prevention epistemologies) have been de-emphasised in favour of big data inflected epistemologies of inductive, population-wide "safeguarding". Through the biopolitical discourse of "safeguarding vulnerable adults", the Prevent Duty has radically reconstituted the epidemiological imagination of pre-criminal space, imagining that all bodies are potentially vulnerable to infection by radicalisers and thus warrant surveillance.

Introduction

In studying the counter-radicalisation practices which constitute the UK's Prevent strategy, academics have explored the deployment of pre-crime interventions, targeted disruption, rehabilitation, and risk assessment upon individuals and groups (Elshimi 2015; De Goede and Simon 2012; Gutowski 2011; Heath-Kelly 2013; Kundnani 2009; Lindekilde 2012). The Prevent strategy is, as the name suggests, a series of preventative measures used against persons thought to be at higher risk of becoming terrorists, or showing signs of "extremism" (understood by the Home Office as the ideological and behavioural precursor to political violence). This article traces the imagination of radicalisation risk in UK government policy since the rushed emergence of Prevent after the

---

This is an Open Access article distributed under the terms of the Creative Commons Attribution License (http://creativecommons. org/licenses/by/4.0/), which permits unrestricted use, distribution, and reproduction in any medium, provided the original work is properly cited.

2005 London bombings. It argues that shifts in the Prevent strategy reveal the reconceptualisation of pre-crime in British counterterrorism.

Initially, the Prevent pathfinder programme of 2007–2008 performed pre-criminal intervention in the form of community engagement activities and community policing, undertaken by local authorities in seventy areas considered high-risk by the Office for Security and Counterterrorism (OSCT) (Local Government Association 2008, 2; Thomas 2012). But this localised geography of pre-criminal intervention was de-emphasised (not abolished) in 2010, once the Conservative and Liberal Democrat coalition government took power and commissioned the Prevent Review. In the context of their economic austerity agenda, the implementation of Prevent through the Department for Communities and Local Government ended. Prevent delivery was centralised in the OSCT, ostensibly to simplify its delivery and reduce the allocation of funding for community engagement activities. Labour's localised imaginations of extremism risk in residential communities were then side-lined by the government's new "Prevent duty". This new policy imagines extremism risk *nationally*, inserting "radicalisation awareness" into already existing national structures for safeguarding vulnerable adults[1] in health care and schools.

In both eras of counter-radicalisation, the prevention of terrorism was understood to operate in an explicitly "pre-criminal space" – a phrase that occurs four times in NHS England's *Prevent Training and Competencies Framework* (Goldberg, Jadhav, and Younis 2016; NHS England 2015). This term is left largely undefined, standing as an empty, but central, signifier in the governmental discourse of preventative (yet banal) intervention upon lives rendered simultaneously risky and vulnerable-to-becoming-terrorist (Heath-Kelly 2013a). But how is pre-criminal space constituted in the imagination of policy-makers, and how have crime prevention programmes been adapted to deliver this form of counterterrorism?

Pre-criminal measures trace their ancestry to crime prevention measures of the mid-twentieth century which used data on prior criminal conduct, school drop-outs and economic deprivation to model the probability of future offending (McCulloch and Wilson 2016, 9). An area's potential to experience crime became predictable and calculable through statistical analysis. As I will show in the next section, crime prevention was imagined through local geographies, statistical data and the calculative rationality of risk. In the 1990s, criminal justice embraced the predictive turn, shifting further away from traditional models of retrospective intervention by bringing forward the threshold of criminal responsibility. Acts undertaken *in preparation for* criminal offending, or anti-social conduct imagined as prelude to future offending, became punishable in-and-of-themselves (ibid., 9–25).

The practice of pre-criminal justice as pre-emption develops from these earlier statistically oriented models. In the context of the securitisation of crime, and the War on Terror, pre-crime has since introduced a specifically anticipatory form of policing. In the early 2000s, US and UK police were awarded new powers to pre-emptively detain suspects in counterterrorism investigations for significant periods of time. As McCulloch and Wilson point out, pre-crimes are crimes which have not happened and are not imminent (ibid., 25). With no crime scene evidence or materials demonstrating preparation for a criminal act, the evidence underwriting arrest is replaced by the role of suspicion. If police intelligence places a suspect on a nascent trajectory towards terrorist offending, or if one's travel data or financial transactions trigger the digital systems which monitor for flagged behaviours or deviations from standard patterns (Amoore and Marieke 2005; De Goede, Marieke 2012), then pre-emptive intervention can occur.

The politics of knowledge which construct trajectories of extremism and radicalisation are vastly important to the performance of pre-criminal intervention under the Prevent Strategy. This article explores how imaginative geographies of extremism risk have changed throughout 10 years of the Prevent Strategy, outlining the shift from Prevent's localised pre-criminal intervention in residential neighbourhoods to the national roll-out of the Prevent Duty. The 2015 Prevent Duty invoked a nationalised imagination of pre-criminal space. It appropriates national structures of education and healthcare to apply preventative surveillance to all citizens, for their own protection (Home Office 2015b). It calls this "safeguarding vulnerable adults" against terrorism. The Prevent Duty thus securitises *all* bodies as potentially vulnerable to contamination by extremism (even if Muslim and brown bodies still make up the majority of referrals made to the police).

The nationalised imaginary of extremism risk in the Prevent Duty deviates from traditional surveillance and profiling – which begins its work by imagining a defined suspect group. Even if the Prevent Duty ends up targeting brown bodies, its calculative rationality does not begin by imagining them as the location of radicalisation risk. Instead, the nationalised Prevent Duty replicates a big data logic found in the digital arena – it prioritises the scale of a vast sample size, rather than beginning from the suspect community imaginary we have come to expect from counterterrorism pro-grammes (Hillyard 1993; Pantazis and Pemberton 2009; Ragazzi 2016). But, because schoolteachers and health-care professionals are not immune to Islamaphobic media discourses, they apply their duties of suspicion unequally and replicate the stigmatisa-tion of brown bodies found in Labour's Prevent Strategy.

In this way, the performance of pre-crime in Prevent has moved towards algorithmic logics of detection and inductive profiling (Heath-Kelly 2016). A calculative shift has occurred which imagines pre-criminal space nationally, and Prevent's deployment has been reorganised and extended to fit this landscape.

British governments and their approaches to counter-radicalisation

The Prevent agenda was first invented by Tony Blair's government in 2006. It was the first example of a counter-radicalisation strategy in Europe or America. It was pre-existed by the de-radicalisation interventions of the Saudi Arabian regime which has, since 2004, attempted to un-teach "deviant" interpretations of Islam through religious re-education in prisons (Boucek 2008). Yet, Saudi Arabia's rehabilitation of prison populations is an example of criminal prevention rather than pre-crime intervention; it relies on statistical data about offending rates to predict future crime risk (McCulloch and Wilson 2016). It utilises the *statistical calculative rationality* of crime prevention. This makes the UK's counter-radicalisation strategy the first to take on an explicitly *pre-crime* formulation of prevention (as opposed to statistically targeted rehabilitation measures). Without the use of statistical data on offending rates, Blair's Prevent strategy imagined a pre-criminal space within British Asian residential areas where extremism risk necessitated intervention.

The originality of the Prevent Strategy must be understood within the context of the London bombings of 2005 and the failed tube bombing which immediately followed. The government was thrown into a panicked search for methods to prevent suicide bombers who, unlike previous generations of militants, possessed few links to established organisations. Traditional surveillance, suppression and infiltration techniques from the campaign against the Provisional Irish Republican Army (IRA) could not be replicated. In this knowledge and policy vacuum, the discourse of radicalisation emerged to explain the seemingly individualised and disconnected pathways of citizens into armed militancy (Heath-Kelly 2013a; Kirby 2007; Sageman 2004; Sedgwick 2010). In response to this new discourse of decentralised threat, Blair's government introduced the Prevent strategy as an anticipatory programme of counter-radicalisation, deployed by local authorities to identify and counter extremist influences.

Early Prevent documentation explicitly framed counter-radicalisation as deploying community cohesion and moderate Islam against extremist influences, to bring about preventative effects through community resilience:

> It is not for government to intervene in theological debates, but there is a role for government in [...] providing effective campaigns to confront extremist ideologies; promoting local role models able to counter negative imagery and comment; promoting understanding of the benefits that Muslims have brought to local areas; promoting understanding and acceptance of key shared values, and promoting dialogue and engagement between communities in support of those values. (Department of Communities and Local Government 2007, 5)

The Department for Communities and Local Government oversaw the initial Prevent "pathfinder" pilot of 2007/8 which targeted intelligence gathering and community engagement activities at 70 local communities mapped as high-risk for producing extremists (Department of Communities and Local Government 2007; see the Appendix for the 70 priority areas defined by central government as high risk in 2007). The demographic make-up of areas funded by the Prevent Pathfinder programme in 2008–2009 suggests that their "extremism risk" and level of funding was directly constituted in relation to their numbers of Muslim residents (Kundnani 2009, 13–4).

As I will show in following sections, early Prevent operations under Labour governments redeployed the rationales of public health and criminal prevention models from the nineteenth and twentieth centuries. Here, communities were profiled as sites for health and policing interventions according to their statistically generated risk score for vulnerability to diseases or crime. The public health and pre-crime typologies of primary, secondary and tertiary preventative interventions were directly carried over into Labour's Prevent strategy, constituting a heat-map of vulnerability to extremism based upon community demographics.

However, this did not last. Under the Coalition and subsequent Conservative governments, the apparatus and operations of counter-radicalisation have shifted. While capacity building within communities and community policing still occurs, Prevent planning and implementation has been considerably centralised in the Home Office since 2010. Local authorities have been cut out, now existing only as bidders for Home Office created Prevent activities and funds for their implementation. Furthermore, the new Prevent safeguarding duty[2] is not applied exclusively to/through British Asian residential communities, but through the national systems of education and health care.

Of particular interest here is the 2011 Prevent Review undertaken by the Coalition government. The Coalition took office in 2010, after 13 years of Labour Party governments. Labour had previously implemented the Prevent Strategy through the Department for Communities and Local Government (DCLG), relying upon methods and assemblages previously used to deploy "community cohesion" (interventions designed to effect cross-community reduction of tensions) (Thomas 2012; Thomas 2014). The administrative geography of Prevent under Labour was heavily associated with local authority delivery of workshops and events that promoted "moderate Islam" in residential communities; Prevent governed through community, if you will.

The Coalition introduced a raft of austerity measures to reduce public spending, including the severing of Prevent's delivery through the DCLG – removing the link to integration work and ownership of Prevent work by local authorities. The Prevent review centralised control of Prevent delivery within the Office of Security and Counter-Terrorism (OSCT) (Thomas 2014). Indeed, it de-emphasised "community" as the landscape for counterterrorism and moved Prevent towards administration through *whole-of-population* institutions (schools, universities and health-care premises). While "community" has not totally disappeared as the mechanism through which Prevent is delivered and articulated, and local variations exist in Prevent-funded community development (Therese et al. 2016), residential community has been deemphasised in favour of nationalised imaginations of terrorism risk and pre-criminal intervention.

As I will show, this is unusual. Prevent now embeds the reporting of deviance in national organisations because they have a high level of public contact. It defends this massively increased surveillance of the population by arguing that larger sample size is beneficial to counterterrorism. This logic is alien to crime prevention models which used statistical data to allocate risk scores to discrete areas. As such, post-2011 Prevent reflects an epistemology more common to big data and algorithmic tools.

Digital methods and epistemologies prioritise the collection of huge datasets and utilise computerised techniques to partition and reassemble the data scraps. Rather than reducing sample size and narrowing down onto suspect groups, the epistemology behind complexity science invokes the potential *within* huge data sets. The human eye cannot detect patterns at this scale, but complexity epistemology advocates that machines can identify correlations which have previously remained hidden (Amoore and Piotukh 2016). While the Prevent strategy does not utilise algorithms as such, the reworking of its administration and deployment suggests an influence of big data epistemological discourse on planners and policymakers (Heath-Kelly 2016) – one which has played a role in Prevent's shifting geography of pre-crime.

While the epistemological and geographical imagination of extremism risk within Prevent is shifting towards nationalisation, I do not want to suggest that all ethnicities are equally made suspect by Prevent as a result. This article does not claim that white British and British Asians find themselves equally exposed to suspicion or intervention. Rather, it models the shift towards whole-of-population subjection to, and mass responsibilisation for, the Prevent Strategy. Prevent no longer begins from the assumption that pre-criminal interventions should target particular residential areas, even if its nationalisation still disproportionately stigmatises and affects British Muslims. An epistemological and geographical shift has occurred in the imagination and pre-emptive mapping of extremism risk.

An epidemiology of radicalisation under labour

Pre-crime interventions have a long history. They did not begin as counterterrorism tactics, but have historically taken the form of crime reduction initiatives deployed upon "high-risk" areas and cases. And these crime reduction initiatives themselves rely upon prior discourses and methods of public health and preventative medicine. Antecedent public health strategies of the nineteenth and twentieth centuries produced geographical epidemiologies of threats to population health such as cholera. Importantly, these public health geographies utilised a tripartite frame to categorise the population, one which was directly carried over into pre-crime interventions and counter-radicalisation (of the New Labour era, 1997–2010).

At the "primary" level, preventative public health measures target the health of the *general population* vis-à-vis a threat or contaminant (rather than the sick, or a group thought highly likely to become sick). The general conditions which enable disease are the object of intervention. For example, a "primary" measure includes the introduction of a sewer system to manage human waste, thereby acting at the level of the entire population to prevent illness. "Secondary" preventative measures are localised interventions performed upon individuals and groups *showing early symptoms of disease*, or *at high likelihood* of contracting illness. This is a more focused intervention aimed at prevention contagion within particular communities. Finally, "tertiary" prevention is directed towards those *already suffering from a disease* – to cure them, rehabilitate them and prevent reoccurrence (Brantingham and Faust 1976; Van Dijk and Jaap 1991).

This public health geography of prevention is thus constituted around notions of proximity and contagion. Those already sick are found at the centre, whereas secondary health interventions pre-emptively target those deemed to be in proximity to contagions, and primary interventions intervene upon general enabling conditions at the level of the population.

These public heath typologies were directly transplanted from epidemiology to crime prevention efforts of the mid-twentieth century. Crime became something statistically predictable, inherently geographic and preventable in policy terms. As in public health, the primary level of crime prevention identified the general conditions that enable crime to occur. Primary crime prevention measures were then applied to the general population – whether or not they were deemed likely to become criminals or victims of crime – introducing neighbourhood watch policies and televised crime awareness campaigns (Van Dijk and Jaap 1991). The lacking awareness of crime in the broader population was here constituted as an enabling condition of crime.

The secondary level of crime prevention engaged in the early identification of potential criminals. It generated pre-crime demographics from statistical modelling of population data. Geographies of future offenders were produced from school drop-out figures, the locations of pockets of economically disadvantaged and untrained youths, and sometimes even the presence of citizens with physical and mental disabilities (Brantingham and Faust 1976). This particularly offensive symptomology is drawn from 1960s' crime prevention initiatives in the United States, but all secondary crime prevention produces knowledge by analysing the statistical correlates of crime (school exclusion, economic disadvantage) and then reversing the analytic temporality – to assume that the correlative symptom *increases the probability of* crime. This generates a risk score.

In such correlative analysis, an epidemiological geography of crime was created – a map of supposed pre-crime areas and demographics. These spaces were then targeted with job training, education interventions and social activities which supposedly promoted resilience and civic responsibility.

Finally, tertiary prevention was transplanted from the already-diseased of public health to the convicted offenders of criminal justice. Even this tertiary level was considered preventative (rather than simply punitive), because the judicial response to crime aimed at the reduction of recidivism through the separation of offenders from the population (imprisonment), rehabilitation programmes and treatment programmes for addiction (Van Dijk and Jaap 1991).

The three levels constitute a geographical model of offending risk and criminal prevention through statistics. The calculative rationality underpinning public health interventions and "criminal prevention" is the statistical paradigm which emerged in the nineteenth century. This model replaced Enlightenment faith in human nature, natural law and determinative causality (Hacking, Ian 1990). In the statistical paradigm, *probabilities* are used to calculate the chance of future disorder or illness and then to direct appropriate political interventions. Probability science involves abstracting from the individual case to the level of all cases. Through the collection of crime figures, poverty statistics and school-leaving data, base rates of statistical probability ("regularities" within a large population) can be produced. This produces knowledge about likely futures. This knowledge production is simultaneously a mapping exercise – creating a geographical model of risk and pre-criminal intervention.

The same epidemiological typology of prevention can be directly mapped onto the early years (2007–2011) of the UK Prevent Strategy. Under the Labour governments of the early twenty-first century, counterterrorism prevention was (hurriedly) deployed through the geography of primary, secondary and tertiary interventions, constituting an imagined, epidemiological geography of extremism risk.

One of the first official steps in terrorism prevention involved the increased responsibilisation of the general public for preventing terrorism. In the style of *primary* pre-crime interventions upon the general "enabling conditions" of crime, the public were tasked with reporting suspect packages and behaviour to the police through public awareness campaigns. Posters and tannoy announcements adorned the walls and filled the concourses of public transport networks, instructing citizens to report any suspicious activity or packages to the British Transport Police. Coaffee and Rogers (2007) have described this as the post-September 11 intensification of previous emergency planning doctrines, where individual citizens are now called upon to play a role in urban risk management. Coaffee's work also points to governmental perception that openness, as a condition of unfettered movement within cities, enables terrorism to occur. In this geographical reading of threat mobility, governments turn to material objects like "rings of steel", bollards and cordons to protect financial districts and parliaments (Coaffee 2004).

In this conceptualisation of primary-level terrorism prevention, the general conditions which enable crime to occur are the non-suspicious attitude of the population and the relative openness of the urban environment. To combat the threat of terrorism, both population and urban infrastructure are adapted to disrupt the malicious intents of deviants. These primary-level preventative measures were also used by the British Government with regard to the IRA campaign.

After these primary-level interventions in the domestic arena failed to prevent the London bombings of 2005, the British government adopted the secondary and tertiary levels of pre-crime intervention – making their innovative leap into pre-crime. Policymakers and media constituted the "radicalisation" discourse to explain how, and why, British nationals would bomb London. The discourse relies upon the imagination of a (disruptable) socialisation process of peer-pressure and ideological change which leads to terrorism – a model very different to previous research in Terrorism Studies on protest movements and root causes.[3] The individualised discourse of radicalisation emerged immediately after the London bombings (Kundnani 2015; Sedgwick 2010), and imagined the process by which British citizens could turn against their own government, under the influence of "extremist ideology" and disenfranchisement.

Counter-radicalisation interventions were aligned with the secondary level of prevention under the Labour governments: they mapped those considered *likely to develop* symptoms of terrorism. But what statistical data could be used to model the chance of terrorists emerging in a given area? Unlike public health interventions, imaginative geographies of radicalisation risk struggle to generate predictive statistical models. As Mark Sageman (2016) has convincingly argued, cases of terrorism are too few and far between to construct the base rate upon which a statistical model relies. Unlike the predictive modelling of burglary and street crime, there are not enough terrorists to produce statistical models of terrorism and allocate risk scores to areas. In this vacuum, residential demographics substituted for the statistical base rate of previous crime prevention models.

In 2007, Prevent funding was provided to seventy local authorities in relation to the numbers of Muslims in their area. If an area had been 5% comprised of Muslims in the 2001 census data, or more, then it qualified for the new Prevent funds (Thomas 2014). This threshold was later reduced to 2%, according to Paul Thomas (ibid.). This funding-according-to-demographic clearly demonstrates the reductive and offensive association of Muslims and British Asian communities with extremism potential by central government. The number of Muslims was understood as a precursor to terrorism by the government, given the stated faith of the 9/11 hijackers and the 7/7 London bombers. The demographic of residential communities became constituted as the secondary level of intervention – the "at-risk" population requiring preventative intervention.

Prevent funding from central government was used to fund a wide variety of social and training activities for British Asian residential communities, including language courses, training in accessing local services, sports, and cross-community work – operating in parallel with assemblages of "community cohesion" (Kundnani 2009; Thomas 2010). Policies of "community cohesion" had been introduced after riots in British Asian areas of Northern cities in the summer of 2001. Despite these riots being provoked by white nationalist agitators, the Cantle report on the disturbances advocated preventative measures which would (among other things) reduce community self-segregation. To build cross-community engagement, community cohesion policies funded local "shared events", as well as "arrival packs" for new residents (Kundnani 2009; Worley 2005). The distribution of Prevent funding to local authorities according to population demographics, to projects mirroring community cohesion assemblages, saw the creation of a Prevent geography where race (even if not mentioned by name) constituted the key condition for potential contagion. Prevent mapped British Asian communities as being "at risk of becoming risky" (Heath-Kelly 2013) in the style of public health interventions on communities thought likely to become sick. Prevent then deployed local organisations to build resilience to extremism in these areas and trained favoured "moderate" figures to this end.

The original "Preventing Violent Extremism" documentation was reasonably open about the government's perception of British Asian communities as spaces of ideological conflict and vulnerability, advocating the promotion of moderate voices against extremist narratives (Department of Communities and Local Government 2007). The funding of educational and social activities through a counterterrorism remit was intended to build the "resilience" of these communities to violent extremism – increasing their resistance to problematic ideologies and enabling them to challenge extremist viewpoints (Home Office 2009).

The language of resilience as resistance to extremist ideologies directly parallels the language of contagions and the fostering of immunity. Unlike community cohesion work, however, voluntary organisations and local authority staff working with Prevent money soon became uncomfortable with the expectation to pass information about communities and individuals to the police (as well as the embedding of counterterrorism officers in service delivery). The national government's initial attempt to fund community cohesion work and Prevent work in equal measure steadily gave way to the dominance of securitising actors and perspectives at both local and national levels (Thomas 2014). In Birmingham, for example, the introduction of Prevent saw a leading Counterterrorism Unit officer transplanted into the Council Equalities Division to manage the project funding – causing great alarm about the implicit surveillance of communities being undertaken (Therese et al. 2016). In the interaction between national and local governments, the Home Office applied pressure upon local authorities to adopt Prevent reporting measures (national indicator 35) and tip their practice towards monitoring British Asian communities rather than community cohesion activities (Thomas 2010).

The congruence of surveillance with the funding of community events should not surprise us, once we note the translation of the tripartite model of criminal and epidemiological prevention. Once communities are mapped as locations of secondary contagion likely to develop symptoms, even well-intentioned activities dedicated to capacity building and resilience are situated within the securitised prevention of deviance. Underneath the ambiguous language of "community" and the fluffy funding of sports lurked a very real governance agenda of secondary crime prevention designed to intervene upon those considered likely to develop symptoms of radicalisation. Surveillance is the obvious counterpart to community integration in this model.

In the Labour era, one might describe Prevent's "secondary-level interventions" as the meeting point between "community cohesion" (which promoted integration and cross-community relations through voluntary organisations) and "community policing". Both operate at the secondary level of crime prevention, targeting those groups who have been designated as vulnerable to future disorder through statistical modelling exercises. Community policing is an approach to law enforcement which maximises collaboration with local residents, responding to neighbourhood grievances in exchange for the facilitation of flows of information about crime. It constitutes areas of pre-crime through statistical modelling and then embeds officers in the community to reduce the threat of potential deviance. This type of policing originally had roots in the prosecution of neighbourhood crimes but was adapted to counterterrorism in post-7/7 Britain (Klausen 2009). As Klausen argues, policy-makers favoured bolstering the relationship between British-Asian communities and police to both improve the potential flow of counterterrorist intelligence and also mitigate any damage resulting from operations and arrests.

Such national policy on counterterrorism had the effect of constituting Muslim neighbourhoods as both "stakeholders" in and suspects of the Prevent agenda. They were implicitly portrayed as both at-risk (and deserving of additional resourcing and support) and risky (to be surveilled as potential threats) (Heath-Kelly 2013). Furthermore, this command that communities engage with the state, via their local police, produced binary identities *within* communities on the basis of co-operation. As Basia Spalek and Alia Imtoual argue, community engagement practices produced binaries of legitimate/illegitimate, moderate/radical Muslims (Spalek and Imtoual 2007). The early geography of Prevent thus constituted British Asian residential neighbourhoods as locations of secondary intervention on its heat map of pre-crime (see Kundnani 2009 and the Appendix), before allocating privileged status to certain members of those neighbourhoods though their collaboration with prevention endeavours.

These dynamics speak to the second meaning of "community policing", alluded to in recent work by Francesco Ragazzi as "policed multiculturalism", whereby the policy performatively enacts and constitutes the "community" it names (Ragazzi 2015). Here, counterterrorism officers police the boundaries of the community through designations of who, and who does not, count as a relevant stakeholder. Simultaneously, however, community engagement is also a productive deployment of power; members of "engaged" communities self-nominate to take on roles in the adjudication and monitoring of conduct, as well as the promotion of a self-defined "moderate" Islam (Ragazzi 2016).

This perspective is an important corrective to the "suspect community" thesis which highlights the legal and cultural assemblages which constitute ethnic groups as potentially dangerous and subject to exceptional treatment (Breen-Smyth 2014; Hickman et al. 2011; Hillyard 1993). As Ragazzi, Spalek and Imtoual and other scholars show, the constitution of a community as suspicious is not simply a disciplinary action performed from outside; rather, collusory conduct is also induced from community members who are awarded privileged status in exchange for cooperation. But whatever the specificities of counterterrorism dynamics in communities rendered suspect, there can be little doubt that Prevent's early geography conforms to a secondary-level pre-crime model. Communities identified as more vulnerable to becoming deviant were made subject to pre-crime interventions of capacity building, integration workshops and surveillance (Kundnani 2009). The epidemiological model fits.

Finally, the tertiary level of British counterterrorism under Labour acted upon those *already* made "radical". To refer back to the original conceptualisation of tertiary crime prevention, it intervenes upon convicted offenders to reduce their reoffending risk through long-term incarceration and/or rehabilitation (Brantingham and Faust 1976). In a further study of the translation of public health models to crime prevention, van Dijk and Jaap confirmed that tertiary crime prevention acts upon offenders and ex-offenders through rehabilitation and treatment programmes (1991). This tertiary level of crime prevention also maps onto the Saudi deployment of theological corrections upon prisoners, to prevent future offending.

In Brantingham and Faust's (1976) terms, the tertiary dimensions of British counter-terrorism under the Labour governments were demonstrated in the open-ended detention of terrorism suspects under control orders and TPIMs.[4] These house-arrest programmes were efforts to prevent potential deviance through immobility. Their geography is largely a secret one. The artist Edmund Clark recently exhibited his work "Control Order House" at London's Imperial War Museum, speaking directly to the proliferation of secretive residential detention (2013). Clark's photographic exhibition explores the mundane, stripped bare existence of the residence under indefinite legal curfew. It conveys the silent worlds of such detention which exist secretly alongside us, in every town and city, mapped by the Home Office and Police but unknown to the population.

Other tertiary measures also existed and continue to exist. The Channel programme of multi-agency rehabilitation interventions for those showing signs of extremism has a similar tertiary geography of secrecy; like control order houses, its presence is ever-present yet unseen by the public. The Association of Chief Police Officers maintains organisational control over Channel – which is described as a multiagency collaboration between local authorities, educational partners, health services partners, social services, children's services, police and offender management partners to "divert people away from the risk they face before illegality occurs" (Home Office 2012, 4). It is a de-radicalisation programme present in every local authority, focusing on the rehabilitation of those thought to be on the path towards terrorism through mentoring and counselling by an approved community peer.

But, unlike normal criminal rehabilitation of offenders, counterterrorism has *brought tertiary prevention forward in time*: into the pre-terrorist stage. Convicted terrorists are not made subject to Channel (they are imprisoned); rather, it is those categorised *as moving towards violent extremism* who are subjected to Channel interventions. This premature deployment of rehabilitation upon the potential offender speaks to the underlying temporal confusion of the radicalisation discourse: knowledge cannot identify the tipping point when illiberal thought and behaviour produces terrorism. In this grey-zone, Prevent performatively constitutes a new category of offender (Heath-Kelly 2013; Sageman 2016) – the pre-criminal "terrorist" requiring rehabilitation before they commit a crime. The epidemiology of radicalisation risk introduces the treatment stage before crime, or even criminal preparation, has occurred. The imagination of pre-criminal states brings forward the threshold of deviancy and intervention, enabling the "rehabilitation" of persons reported to police by community leaders for holding political or religious views deemed suspicious.

To conclude, under post-9/11 Labour governments, the deployment of pre-criminal interventions largely followed the tripartite structure of previous criminal and public health models of prevention – albeit, with racialisation replacing the statistical knowledge which underwrote previous eras of criminal prevention. Separate measures were deployed at each "level" of intervention: public information campaigns at the primary level of the general populous; community workshops and community policing at the secondary level of residential communities deemed vulnerable; and preventative-rehabilitation deployed upon those considered already affected by radical contagion at the tertiary level. The Labour governments translated criminal prevention and community cohesion models into counterterrorism, but reworked them around a different calculative rationality: statistical prediction was replaced by the imagination of pre-criminal space and epidemiological vulnerability attached to race. This endorsement of pre-emption and pre-crime was to become even more pronounced in the subsequent Coalition and Conservative eras.

Nationalising pre-criminal space: prevent under the conservatives

Since the election of the Coalition government in 2010, the geographical application and the epistemology of the Prevent strategy has changed. Upon election in May 2010, all secondary-level Prevent work was immediately suspended pending the Prevent Review of 2011.[5] This official review explored Labour's counter-radicalisation structures, then permanently removed responsibilities for the Prevent Strategy from the Department of Communities and Local Government (DCLG) and instead passed them to the Home Office under the OSCT. The Coalition Government decided that previous Labour administrations had muddled the delivery of two separate areas of policy: community integration and counterterrorism (Home Office 2011, 1). This can be interpreted as a direct criticism of Prevent's secondary level of crime prevention. The Coalition and Conservative governments' geography of counterterrorism has largely de-operationalised residential communities in the delivery of Prevent, removing the DCLG from operations and reducing the number of local authorities funded to deliver Prevent activities from 70 to 28.

Alongside the continuation of limited community engagement activities, Prevent is now deployed through Research Information and Communications Unit (RICU) messaging from the OSCT and through whole-of-population institutions of health care and education. The Prevent Duty (the legal duty to report suspicions of radicalisation) has operated in all schools, health-care premises and universities since at least 2015, but in priority areas since 2011.

This has split the administration of the Prevent Strategy between localised community focused engagement (which works from an assumption about suspicious locales and identities) and the national level (which acts upon the whole of population). To some degree, particularly ethnicities are still imagined as pre-criminal and epidemiologically vulnerable, despite the wider roll-out of Prevent surveillance to all citizens. For example, RICU messaging has been deliberately targeted at particular ethnicities and age ranges thought to be higher risk for extremism. The RICU of the Home Office, founded in 2007 and led by Commander Steve Tatham, was previously responsible for psychological operations at the Ministry of Defence (Sabir 2017). After undertaking research projects on British Muslim communities and online habits, Sabir describes how the unit began deploying covert anti-radicalisation messaging towards young males of Pakistani, Bengali and Somali ethnicity. This messaging was delivered covertly by employing several PR firms (Breakthrough Media Network; Bell Pottinger) to disseminate the unit's propaganda – obscuring the source.

Given the ethnic profiling undertaken by RICU, we can clearly see that the secondary level of pre-crime intervention has not been discarded altogether. Racial profiling still informs the delivery of preventative interventions and the supposed building of "resilience" to extremism. Furthermore, a reduced number of local authorities (70 reduced to 28) still receive some central government funding to deliver Prevent interventions and capacity building upon their populations (Thomas 2014). The government advises that intelligence agencies and police have identified these 28 areas as "hot spots" of the greatest vulnerability, but publicly available maps of their location are unavailable. We can, however, assume that the 28 hot spots are drawn from the 70 areas listed as high risk for extremism in 2007 though (Appendix).

Both the materials and funding for Prevent work are now drawn from central government sources, with local authorities effectively being paid to deliver Home Office content with little agency. A recent leak of Home Office documents regarding Prevent activities conducted in 2015 confirms this reading (Home Office 2015a). It shows that the central-government-funded local authorities and outreach organisations to deliver centrally produced content, including school plays about a Muslim Imam deployed with the British Army, the training of Muslim women in countering extremist rhetoric, and videos shown in schools and youth centres about boys who make bad choices and join jihadist or far right organisations. The 28 local authorities were used like local franchises for the delivery of the Home Office's message.

The delivery of government workshops by youth workers and civil servants, within areas designated high-risk areas requiring secondary-level intervention, speaks to Francesco Ragazzi's research on the securitisation of social policy in Western Europe during the War on Terror (Ragazzi 2017). In the delivery of these secondary interventions, and the tertiary performance of "rehabilitation" upon the radicalised by multi-agency panels (the Channel programme), we can recognise Ragazzi's argument that social policy has been securitised. The securitising move relies upon the historical trust placed in social care professionals by populations, which is then used to introduce counterterrorism policing and surveillance-masked-as-social-care into suspect residential communities.

However, the model of securitised social work captures the Labour government's Prevent Strategy better than it does the Conservative. While the post-2011 Prevent arena still deploys some elements of secondary-level intervention (identifying 28 high priority local areas for Home Office produced content, targeting particular ethnicities with RICU messaging), the remainder of the policy operates according to a different epistemological logic. Through the Prevent Duty, the secondary level of epidemiology (vulnerability to infection) has become blurred with the primary (the generalised conditions which enable the spread of disease within human populations).

The major development in the Conservative government's Prevent Strategy has been the 2015 Prevent Duty (Home Office 2015b). This Duty has legally enforced a requirement on all schools, nurseries, health-care premises and universities to have "due regard" for preventing terrorism. All schools must be aware of radicalisation risks, report signs of radicalisation to their police contact and teach "British values" to the children. Health-care premises are also required to roll out Prevent training to all staff with safeguarding duties and to report signs of radicalisation to their police contact. The Prevent Duty Guidance specifies that

'Safeguarding' is the process of protecting vulnerable people, whether from crime, other forms of abuse or (in the context of this document) from being drawn into terrorist related activity. (Home Office 2015b, 21)

In one discursive move, protecting vulnerable adults from abuse has been merged with nationwide counterterrorism monitoring. This biopolitical imagination of pre-criminal space constitutes vulnerable bodies as potential terrorists. We are all now "vulnerable bodies" though, because one's status as vulnerable is defined circularly by one's adoption of extreme views. One must *already have been vulnerable*, prior to being flagged as a potential radical, otherwise such pathological views could not have developed. As such, the deployment of counter-radicalisation through the Prevent Duty blurs the primary and secondary levels of criminal prevention/public health intervention. *Every community is vulnerable to extremist infection and criminal proclivity; the general epidemiological enabling condition is reworked as human existence itself.*

At the moment, universities have lighter responsibilities under the 2015 Prevent Duty (Home Office 2015b) and are not required to train academic staff in the detection and reporting of radicalisation (although some choose to roll out the Government's WRAP training). In the view of my own institution, each university is required to perform a radicalisation risk assessment, put structures in place to deal with any reports of radicalisation, have an external speaker vetting process and to give government Prevent training only to "key" members of staff (usually interpreted as the student residences, counselling and security teams). The Prevent Duty thus lurks in the background of student–institutional interaction, unlike its overt deployment within schools and health-care premises.

By July 2016, the Home Office confirmed that 550,000 doctors, nurses and teachers had received Prevent Workshop to Raise Awareness of Prevent training (Jeory and Cockburn 2016). The number of social sector professionals given responsibility for counterterrorism continues to rise with the prolonged roll-out of Prevent training – and one could make the argument that social policy has indeed been further securitised. However, in making that argument, one also needs to account for the geographical shift in the implementation of the Prevent strategy. The vast network of doctors, nurses, lecturers and teachers now incorporated into counterterrorism reporting are not service providers only to the ethnicities and residential communities made suspect in Labour's era. They aren't only implementing their training upon designated high-risk groups; rather, the mechanics of the Prevent Duty are present in the social services provided to the whole-of-population.

Of course, Muslims are still constructed as a suspect community by Islamaphobic media reporting and government statements (such as David Cameron's "muscular liberalism" address of 2011). However, the developments of Conservative Prevent policy appear to be de-emphasising residential communities as a starting point for pre-criminal intervention, in favour of national Prevent delivery through social service providers. Prevent's geographical application has changed, merging the previously distinct categories of primary and secondary implementation.

The Prevent Duty also represents a dramatic epistemological shift away from statistical calculative methods. Statistical models of crime prevention could never support such a whole-of-population roll-out, because actuarial rationalities subtract from general population data to identify specific locations of probable threat. Instead of isolating particular areas of contagion and intervention, the Prevent duty now prioritises the responsibilities of national social care facilities for counterterrorism surveillance. This has had the effect of massively increasing the number of referrals made to Channel. Police and local authorities encounter a far larger amount of data about extremism as a result of this geographical expansion. For example, the number of referrals made to the Channel de-radicalisation programme has skyrocketed since the introduction of the Prevent Duty. For example, between 1 January and 31 December 2015, 3955 people were reported to Channel – a massive increase on previous years, up 209% from the referral of 1281 people in 2014. The 3955 referrals in 2015 is more even than the sum of 3943 referrals made *in the preceding eight years* (NPCC n.d.)!

These dramatic increases were the result, and apparently the intention, of the new Prevent geography. Indeed, the revised Prevent strategy describes schools and clinics as potential assets for counterterrorism because of their huge numbers of contacts with the population:

> 1.3 million NHS workers have contact with over 315,000 patients daily and some 700,000 workers in private and voluntary healthcare organisations see many thousands more [...] *Given the very high numbers of people who come into contact with health professionals in this country, the sector is a critical partner in Prevent.* There are clearly many opportunities for doctors, nurses and other staff to help protect people from radicalisation. The key challenge is to ensure that healthcare workers can identify the signs that someone is vulnerable to radicalisation, interpret those signs correctly and access the relevant support. (Home Office 2011, 83–5; emphasis added)

This prioritisation of scale is indicative of a move from actuarial (statistical) modelling towards an algorithmic or big data rationality. As such, the geographical shift in Prevent is also an epistemological one. In the digital realm of inductive calculation, data is *not* used to calculate probability. Induction works according to different logics to produce imaginations of risk. Louise Amoore's work on the UK e-borders programme has been pivotal in exploring algorithmic security calculation, showing how digital analytics combine discrete and unrelated pieces of data (like travel histories and methods of payment) to constitute possible futures of risk or normality (Amoore 2011). These data "scraps" generate patterns and correlations. The mode of inductive calculation associated with algorithmic prediction involves the ingestion, partitioning and machinic reassembly of vast amounts of data – transforming them into knowledge "spoken" into being by the algorithmic process (Louise and Piotukh 2015). Complexity becomes the modality of calculation, because it is presumed that such heterogeneity (on such a vast scale) has the potential to reveal new patterns and connections between previously disparate factors (Comfort et al. 2010; Heath-Kelly 2016).

Despite the usual restriction of algorithmic rationalities to the digital realm, there are reasons to believe that big data discourse has informed the geographical shift in Prevent strategy interventions, within the context of the Conservative austerity drive. First, the deployment of Prevent through the entire social services network renders the whole-of-population as an object of surveillance, despite no fears that the entire British population is about to rebel. Scale has been prioritised, and referral numbers have rocketed. Scale has become a modality of pre-crime intervention.

Second, the training given to social professionals does not train them to recognise a static risk profile of radicalisation symptoms. As I have shown elsewhere, the training is confused, vague and does not provide a profile of the radicalised subject (Heath-Kelly 2016). Indeed, NHS policy on Prevent emphasises that a static risk profile would not capture the nebulous and shifting character of radicalisation and thus staff must instead use their "professional judgement" to detect terrorists (NHS England 2015). This is interesting because it suggests the adoption of an inductive modality common to big data epistemologies. Here, prevent surveillance is understood to *generate* the terrorist profile rather than responding to it. Through prolific contacts with the public, social professionals are thought able to distinguish the radical from the normal. In this paradigm, their embeddedness in vast flows of contact (data) renders them as potential counterterrorism assets, capable of organically noticing the future radical (despite a constantly shifting profile) and alerting the police.

The geographical shift in Prevent is thus accompanied by altered epistemological commitments. The prioritisation of scale, and the refusal to limit the remit of Prevent to the reporting of defined symptoms, indicates a non-actuarial calculative rationality. Vast swathes of social workers are expected to intuit the presence of radical tendencies, rather than to report profiled behaviours.

Indeed, if Prevent were still embedded in a statistical calculative rationality, it would have been discarded as a failure. In 2016, 90% of NHS referrals to Channel were assessed by the Police as not related to terrorism or extremism. The referrals were instead reclassified as requiring other types of safeguarding intervention (housing, drug and alcohol rehabilitation). As such, the training given to teachers, doctors and nurses is not producing referrals that are taken seriously by police, and yet the roll-out of Prevent to all social workers continues unabated. It is not considered politically or statistically problematic that the misfire rate of Prevent surveillance in the NHS is 90%.

How can such high numbers of inappropriate referrals be tolerated without necessitating a change in the Prevent Duty? These features can only be treated as unimportant if statistical modelling no longer informs Prevent's epistemology. The national roll-out of Prevent and the ambivalence towards the 90% misfire rate betrays the presence of a non-statistical epistemology. In big data epistemologies, no data is wasted. Big data analytics privilege large sample sizes because they are understood to reveal patterns of correlation, invisible to the naked eye, from the digital evaluation of unrelated data scraps (Comfort et al. 2010). The processing of both appropriate and inappropriate referrals by local authority panels is, in this paradigm, helpful in the *inductive* generation of terrorism-related patterns and profiles.

It is this epistemological paradigm which informs the merging of the primary (population level) and secondary (high risk groups) categories of pre-crime intervention. The national geographical roll-out of Prevent, which has replaced most implementation in residential communities, involves the radical remodelling of British pre-crime around big data epistemology. A probabilistic model could not recommend the application of secondary measures to the entire population, because probability science is used to isolate particular locations/communities as high risk. The geographical shift in Prevent administration is also epistemological: it has moved away from renderings of "likelihood", favouring the nationalised roll-out of Prevent training, surveillance and reporting to all corners of the social care system. The imagination of pre-criminal space is now totalising and all encompassing.

The biopolitics of the prevent duty

In 2008, Michael Dillon and Luis Lobo-Guerrero published an article exploring contemporary biopolitical security, specifically, how security apparatuses have adapted to the molecular age by taking life-itself (rather than species life) as an object to be secured (Dillon and Luis 2008). They introduced modifications to Foucault's conceptions of biopolitics and security, adapting them to twentieth-century understandings of life and biology. The administration and regulation of life through structures of governance addresses population differently than it once did, moving away from the securitisation of behaviours and economic potentials to imagine insecurity through the contingency of the molecular level (Dillon and Luis 2008, 278). Like much of the literature already explored in this article, Dillon and Lobo-Guerrero show how Foucault's biopolitics frames the shift from statistical, economic modelling of stable risks to the objectification of contingency as threat (2008, 283–4). Life rendered by medicine and science as pluripotent, they show, provoked a shift in the operations of security such that it now attempts to regulate and bound life's generative capacity.

This problematisation and securitisation of life-itself is evident in the development of the Prevent Strategy. Counterterrorism has adapted to reconfigured understandings of life and population, moving away from static models of insurgency and rushing to develop to new discourses of radicalisation in the aftermath of the London bombings that could help them to regulate contingency (Kundnani 2015; Sedgwick 2010). That there was felt to be a need for a new counterterrorism discourse to respond to the events is indicative of security's biopolitical shift towards managing contingency in the twenty-first century. The problematisation of the London bombings, and the 9/11 attacks, as ushering in an era of unpredictability and uncertainty (Rumsfeld 2002) – rather than something that could be understood through studying militant groups and their turn towards attacking the "far enemy" (Gerges 2005) – reflects a concern with the contingency and unpredictability of life.

The reorientation of counterterrorism towards regulating contingency and life (where life is understood as adaptive potential, rather than as species life) is demonstrated most clearly in the re-articulation of counter-radicalisation as safeguarding. Safeguarding procedures are established protocols within social care and health care which make practitioners responsible for noticing, and reporting, physical, sexual and financial abuse of vulnerable people (Home Office 2015b; NHS England 2015). The remaking of Prevent as a safeguarding measure implicitly creates a new type of abuse: ideological abuse (Heath-Kelly 2016). At this point, the structures of care and security become blurred beyond distinction – revealing their common biopolitical heritage as structures productive and governing of population (Howell 2014).

Under the Conservative governments, pre-criminal space has been reimagined as a totalising geography. The radical contingency of each life is interpreted as uniquely dangerous, requiring of a population-wide system of monitoring for unauthorised adaptations. I have referred to this elsewhere (Heath-Kelly 2016) as the autoimmune moment in British security policy where the distinction between suspicious and non-suspicious bodies has collapsed; in the absence of traditional immunological security politics, the surveillance of all life, in totality, is now understood as biopolitically necessary and advantageous.

It would befit the future of the Critical Terrorism Studies project to study the intertwining of social care structures with counterterrorism, as well as the blurring of digital and non-digital epistemologies of surveillance and calculation.

Conclusion

This article has explored the shifting geography and epistemology of the Prevent strategy from 2007 until 2017. It has highlighted the de-emphasising of residential communities as sites of intervention during the Coalition and Conservative periods, arguing that this reveals the shift from calculative rationalities of probability towards big data logics of inductive profiling.

In Labour's Prevent Strategy, the tripartite typology of primary, secondary and tertiary crime prevention measures informed the delivery of counter-radicalisation. Local authorities became important players in the deployment of Prevent's secondary-level measures intended to build "resilience" to extremism in "vulnerable" communities. But rather than statistically modelling those communities "most probable" to produce terrorists from available data (a task for which probabilistic science is currently incapable (Sageman 2016)), Labour governments operationalised race as the foundation for their imagination of pre-criminal space. Discourses of radicalisation re-signified British Asian communities as areas of higher extremism risk, and those communities were then targeted with crime prevention measures.

After the change in government, the Prevent review severed the DCLG from Prevent strategy operations and criticised Labour's blurring of integration and counterterrorism. This criticism of Prevent's secondary level of intervention did not end community profiling entirely, however. Some targeted local authorities still deliver some Central Government produced workshops and events, even though the deployment of Prevent through communities is reduced. Instead, the Prevent Duty has now radically altered the geography of counter-radicalisation. Prevent is now nationally deployed across the educational and healthcare sectors. This geographical shift embodies the merging of the primary and secondary levels of prevention: whole-of-population measures have been merged with those identifying more vulnerable groups. The two levels of intervention have merged.

This epidemiological revolution betrays a shift in the epistemology of Prevent. The massive roll-out of Prevent training to all NHS and educational staff does not respond to a population-wide insurgency, nor the likelihood that schools and hospitals are being used as bases for conspiracy. Rather, the educational and health-care sectors have been incorporated into counterterrorism because they have significant access to the public. Home Office documentation lauds the prolific patient contacts experienced by the NHS, arguing that this makes it a valid partner in counterterrorism.

The value accorded to scale betrays a move away from probabilistic science. Algorithmic and big data logics have become prominent within digital surveillance and employ huge data sets in their modalities. The calculative discourse associated with the big data paradigm (more data leads to the identification of previously hidden patterns and detections) appears to have influenced the geographic shift in Prevent's deployment (in addition to the economic austerity drive of the Conservative and Coalition governments). Otherwise, the geographical shift to nationalised Prevent surveillance in all social care facilities would make little sense. Furthermore, the huge rejection rates of Channel referrals by the police would not be tolerated under a probabilistic paradigm.

To conclude, the British government seems to be arriving at the conclusion (qua Marc Sageman) that terrorism cannot be statistically predicted in the style of other crimes. Instead, the fluctuations of the Prevent strategy under varying British governments provide a window onto the biopolitical constitution of pre-criminal geographies, where the contingency of life itself demands regulation, management and intervention. The imagination of pre-criminal space has extended outwards, in a dramatic colonisation of social care by counterterrorism.

Notes

1. Safeguarding is the practice of protecting children and adults (with care needs) from financial, physical and sexual abuse. The duty to note concerns about abuse and escalate them is incumbent upon school and health-care staff. The Prevent Duty has inserted a new category of abuse, "radicalisation", into safeguarding protocol (Home Office 2015b; NHS England 2015).
2. In 2015, it became a legal duty for health-care providers, schools and universities to take part in the suppression of "radicalisation" and report subjects of concern to the police. In schools and health care, this is framed as a safeguarding duty performed for the benefit of the subject concerned.
3. In the decades prior to 9/11, much terrorism research was concerned with the root structural causes of terrorism, or locating the connections between protest cycles and violent offshoot groups, or mapping the pathological mindset which enables terrorist crimes.
4. The Terrorism Prevention and Investigatory Measures Act replaced Control Orders in 2011. They enforce a curfew upon a suspect and limit their use of phones and internet.
5. However, tertiary-level prevention continues through police-led Channel panels in each local authority.

Disclosure statement

No potential conflict of interest was reported by the author.

Funding

This work was supported by the Wellcome Trust [205365/Z/16/Z].

ORCID

Charlotte Heath-Kelly ⓘ http://orcid.org/0000-0002-5237-4691

References

Amoore, L. 2011. "Data Derivatives: On the Emergence of a Security Risk Calculus for Our Times." *Theory, Culture and Society* 28 (6): 24–43. doi:10.1177/0263276411417430.

Amoore, L., and D. G. Marieke. 2005. "Governance, Risk and Dataveillance in the War on Terror." *Crime, Law and Social Change* 43 (2): 149–173. doi:10.1007/s10611-005-1717-8.

Amoore, L., and V. Piotukh, eds. 2016. *Algorithmic Life: Calculative Devices in the Age of Big Data.* Abingdon: Routledge.

Boucek, C. 2008. 'Saudi Arabia's "Soft" Counterterrorism Strategy: Prevention, Rehabilitation, and Aftercare'. *Carnegie Paper: Middle East Program* 97, available from http://carnegieendowment.org/2008/09/22/saudi-arabia-s-soft-counterterrorism-strategy-prevention-rehabilitation-and-aftercare-pub-22155 (last accessed 19 April 2017).

Brantingham, P., and F. Faust. 1976. "A Conceptual Model of Crime Prevention." *Crime and Delinquency* 22 (3): 284–296. doi:10.1177/001112877602200302.

Breen-Smyth, M. 2014. "Theorising the "Suspect Community": Counterterrorism, Security Practices and the Public Imagination." *Critical Studies on Terrorism* 7 (2): 223–240. doi:10.1080/17539153.2013.867714.

Clark, E. 2013. *Control Order House.* London: Here Press.

Coaffee, J. 2004. "'Rings of Steel, Rings of Concrete and Rings of Confidence: Designing Out Terrorism in Central London Pre and Post 9/11'." *International Journal of Urban and Regional Research* 28 (1): 201–211. doi:10.1111/j.0309-1317.2004.00511.x.

Coaffee, J., and P. Rogers. 2007. "Rebordering the City for New Security Challenges: From Counter-Terrorism to Community Resilience." *Space and Polity* 12 (1): 101–118. doi:10.1080/13562570801969556.

Comfort, L., O. Namkyung, G. Ertan, and S. Scheinert. 2010. "Designing Adaptive Systems for Disaster Mitigation and Response: The Role of Structure." In *Designing Resilience: Preparing for Extreme Events*, edited by L. Comfort, A. Boin, and C. Demchak, 33–61. Pittsburgh: University of Pittsburgh Press.

De Goede, M., and S. Simon. 2012. "Governing Future Radicals in Europe." *Antipode* 45 (2): 315–335. doi:10.1111/j.1467-8330.2012.01039.x.

De Goede, Marieke. 2012. *Speculative Security: The Politics of Pursuing Terrorist Money's.* Minneapolis: University of Minnesota.

Department of Communities and Local Government. 2007. *Preventing Violent Extremism Pathfinder Fund 2007/08: Case Studies.* London: HM Government.

Dillon, M., and L.-G. Luis. 2008. "Biopolitics of Security in the Twenty-First Century: An Introduction." *Review of International Studies* 34 (2): 265–292. doi:10.1017/S0260210508008024.

Elshimi, M. 2015. "Prevent 2011 and Counter-Radicalisation: What Is De-Radicalisation?" In *Counter-Radicalisation: Critical Perspectives*, edited by C. Baker-Beall, C. Heath-Kelly, and L. Jarvis, 206–222. Abingdon: Routledge.

England, N. H. S. 2015. *NHS England Prevent Training and Competencies Framework.* London: NHS England Nursing Directorate. Available from https://www.england.nhs.uk/wp-content/uploads/2015/02/train-competnc-frmwrk.pdf (last accessed 09 August 2016).

Gerges, F. 2005. *The Far Enemy: Why Jihad Went Global.* Cambridge: Cambridge University Press.

Goldberg, D., S. Jadhav, and T. Younis. 2016. "'Prevent.' What Is Pre-Criminal Space?' *Bjpsych Bulletin* 41: 2. doi:10.1192/pb.bp.116.054585.

Gutowski, S. 2011. "'Secularism and the Politics of Risk: Britain's Prevent Agenda, 2005-09'." *International Relations* 25 (3): 346–362.

Hacking, Ian. 1990. *The Taming of Chance.* Cambridge: Cambridge University Press.

Heath-Kelly, C. 2013. "Counter-Terrorism and the Counterfactual: Producing the 'Radicalisation' Discourse and the UK Prevent Strategy." *British Journal of Politics and International Relations* 15 (3): 394–415. doi:10.1111/j.1467-856X.2011.00489.x.

Heath-Kelly, C. 2016. "Algorithmic Autoimmunity in the NHS: Radicalisation and the Clinic." *Security Dialogue* 48 (1): 29–45. doi:10.1177/0967010616671642.

Hickman, M., L. Thomas, S. Silvestri, and H. Nickels. 2011. *Suspect Communities'? Counter-Terrorism Policy, the Press, and the Impact on Irish and Muslim Communities in Britain, A Report for Policy Makers and the General Public.* London: London Metropolitan University.

Hillyard, P. 1993. *Suspect Community: People's Experiences of the Prevention of Terrorism Acts in Britain.* London: Pluto.

Home Office. 2009. *CONTEST 2: The Uk's Strategy for Countering Violent Extremism.* London: HM Government.

Home Office. 2011. *Prevent Strategy.* London: HM Government.

Home Office. 2012. *Channel: Protecting Vulnerable People from Being Drawn into Terrorism: A Guide for Local Partnerships.* London: HM Government.

Home Office. 2015a. *Local Delivery Best Practice Catalogue: Prevent Strategy.* London: OSCT: Home Office. last accessed 25 Jan 2017. Available from: http://powerbase.info/index.php/File:OSCT-Prevent_catalogue-March_2015.pdf

Home Office. 2015b. *Revised Prevent Duty Guidance for England and Wales.* London: HM Government.

Howell, A. 2014. "The Global Politics of Medicine: Beyond Global Health, against Securitisation Theory." *Review of International Studies* 40 (5): 961–987. doi:10.1017/S0260210514000369.

Jeory, T., and H. Cockburn. 2016. 'More than 500,000 Public Sector Workers Put through Prevent Counter-Terror Training in Bid to Spot Extremism', *The Independent* 23 July 2016. Available from http://www.independent.co.uk/news/uk/crime/extremism-prevent-counter-terror-training-pub lic-sector-workers-bid-to-spot-a7152466.html (last accessed 27 January 2016).

Kirby, A. 2007. "The London Bombers as 'Self-Starters': A Case Study in Indigenous Radicalisation and the Emergence of Autonomous Cliques." *Studies in Conflict and Terrorism* 30 (5): 415–428. doi:10.1080/10576100701258619.

Klausen, J. 2009. "British Counter-Terrorism after 7/7: Adapting Community Policing to the Fight against Domestic Terrorism." *Journal of Ethnic and Migration Studies* 35 (5): 403–420. doi:10.1080/13691830802704566.

Kundnani, A. 2009. *Spooked! How Not to Prevent Violent Extremism.* London: Institute of Race Relations.

Kundnani, A. 2015. "Radicalisation: The Journey of a Concept." In *Counter-Radicalisation: Critical Perspectives*, edited by C. Baker-Beall, C. Heath-Kelly, and L. Jarvis, 14–35. Abingdon: Routledge.

Lindekilde, L. 2012. "Neoliberal Governing of 'Radicals': Danish Radicalization Prevention Policies and Potential Iatrogenic Effects." *International Journal of Conflict and Violence* 6 (1): 109–125.

Local Government Association. 2008. *Strategic Issues: Preventing Violent Extremism.* Briefing note, 16th April 2008, available from http://lga.moderngov.co.uk/Data/LGA%20Leadership%20Board/20080416/Agenda/$Item%202a%20-%20Violent%20(REV).doc.pdf (last accessed 19 April 2017).

Louise, A., and V. Piotukh. 2015. "Life beyond Big Data: Governing with Little Analytics." *Economy and Society* 44 (3): 341–366. doi:10.1080/03085147.2015.1043793.

McCulloch, J., and D. Wilson. 2016. *Pre-Crime: Pre-Emption, Precaution and the Future.* Abingdon: Routledge.

NPCC (National Police Chiefs' Councils). n.d. Undated. *National Channel Referral Figures.* Available online at http://www.npcc.police.uk/FreedomofInformation/NationalChannelReferralFigures. aspx (last accessed 25 January 2017).

Pantazis, C., and S. Pemberton. 2009. "From the 'Old' to the 'New' Suspect Community: Examining the Impacts of Recent UK Counter-Terrorist Legislation." *British Journal of Criminology* 49 (5): 646–666. doi:10.1093/bjc/azp031.

Ragazzi, F. 2015. "Policed Multiculturalism? the Impact of Counter-Terrorism and Counter-Radicalization and the 'End' of Multiculturalism." In *Counter-Radicalisation: Critical Perspectives*, edited by C. Baker-Beall, C. Heath-Kelly, and L. Jarvis, 156–174. Abingdon: Routledge.

Ragazzi, F. 2016. "Suspect Community or Suspect Category? the Impact of Counter-Terrorism as 'Policed Multiculturalism." *Journal of Ethnic and Migration Studies* 42 (5): 724–741. doi:10.1080/1369183X.2015.1121807.

Ragazzi, F. 2017. 'Countering Terrorism and Radicalisation: Securitising Social Policy?' *Critical Social Policy*. Online first, available from http://journals.sagepub.com/doi/full/10.1177/0261018316683472 (last accessed 25 Jan 2017).

Rumsfeld, D. 2002. *Press Conference by US Secretary of Defence, Donald Rumsfeld*. NATO Headquarters: Brussels. 6 June 2002, Available from: http://www.nato.int/docu/speech/2002/s020606g.htm last accessed 21 April 2017).

Sabir, R. 2017. 'Blurred Lines and False Dichotomies: Integrating Counter-Insurgency into the UK's Domestic 'War on Terror'. *Critical Social Policy*. Online first, available from http://journals.sage pub.com/doi/full/10.1177/0261018316683471 (last accessed 25 Jan 2017).

Sageman, M. 2004. *Understanding Terror Networks*. Philadelphia: University of Pennsylvania Press.

Sageman, M. 2016. *Misunderstanding Terrorism*. Philadelphia: University of Pennsylvania Press.

Sedgwick, M. 2010. "The Concept of Radicalization as a Source of Confusion." *Terrorism and Political Violence* 22 (4): 479–494. doi:10.1080/09546553.2010.491009.

Spalek, B., and A. Imtoual. 2007. "Muslim Communities and Counter-Terror Responses: "Hard" Approaches to Community Engagement in the UK and Australia." *Journal of Muslim Minority Affairs* 27 (2): 185–202. doi:10.1080/13602000701536117.

Therese, O., N. Meer, D. N. DeHanas, S. H. Jones, and T. Modood. 2016. "Governing through Prevent? Regulation and Contested Practice in State–Muslim Engagement." *Sociology* 50 (1): 160–177. doi:10.1177/0038038514564437.

Thomas, P. 2010. "Failed and Friendless: The UK's 'Preventing Violent Extremism' Programme." *British Journal of Politics & International Relations* 12 (3): 442–458. doi:10.1111/j.1467-856X.2010.00422.x.

Thomas, P. 2012. *Responding to the Threat of Violent Extremism: Failing to Prevent*. London: Bloomsbury.

Thomas, P. 2014. "Divorced but Still Co-Habiting? Britain's Prevent/Community Cohesion Policy Tension." *British Politics* 9 (4): 472–493. doi:10.1057/bp.2014.16.

Van Dijk, J. J. M., and D. W. Jaap. 1991. "A Two-Dimensional Typology of Crime Prevention Projects; with A Bibliography." *Criminal Justice Abstracts* 23 (3): 483–503.

Worley, C. 2005. "It's Not about Race. It's about the Community': New Labour and 'Community Cohesion." *Critical Social Policy* 25 (4): 483–496. doi:10.1177/0261018305057026.

Appendix

Priority local authorities which received funding from the Prevent Pathfinder Fund.

Region	Priority local authorities
South West	Bristol City Council
South East	Wycombe District Council; Oxford City Council; Reading Borough Council; Royal Borough of Windsor and Maidenhead; Slough Borough Council; Crawley Borough Council; Woking Borough Council
London	Barking and Dagenham Council; London Borough of Barnet; Brent Council; Camden Council; London Borough of Croydon; Ealing Council; Enfield Council; Greenwich Council; London Borough of Hackney; Hammersmith and Fulham Council; Haringey Council; Harrow Council; London Borough of Hillingdon; Hounslow Council; Islington Council; Royal Borough of Kensington and Chelsea; London Borough of Lambeth; Lewisham Council; London Borough of Merton; London Borough of Newham; London Borough of Redbridge; Southwark Council; Tower Hamlets Council; London Borough of Waltham Forest; Wandsworth Borough Council; City of Westminster City Council
East of England	Bedford Borough Council; Luton Borough Council; Peterborough City Council; Watford Borough Council
East Midlands	Derby City Council; Leicester City Council; Nottingham City Council
West Midlands	Birmingham City Council; Dudley; Metropolitan Borough Council; Sandwell Metropolitan Borough Council; Stoke-on-Trent City Council; Walsall Council
Yorkshire and the Humber	Bradford Metropolitan District Council; Calderdale Council; Kirklees Council; Leeds City Council; Wakefield City Council
North West	Bolton Council; Bury Metropolitan Borough Council; Manchester City Council; Oldham Metropolitan Borough Council; Rochdale Metropolitan Borough Council; Salford City Council; Stockport Metropolitan Borough Council; Tameside Metropolitan Borough Council; Trafford Council; Wigan Council; Blackburn with Darwen Borough Council; Burnley Borough Council; Hyndburn Borough Council; Pendle Borough Council; Preston City Council; Ribble Valley Borough Council; Rossendale Borough Council
North East	Middlesbrough Borough Council; Newcastle City Council

Source: Department of Communities and Local Government 2007 (14–5).

Prevention, knowledge, justice: Robert Nozick and counterterrorism

Matthias Leese

ABSTRACT
This article explores questions of justice and moral permissibility of state action in counterterrorism through Robert Nozick's *Anarchy, State, and Utopia*. Using the case of the Berlin attack in December of 2016 and the ensuing political debate over whether potential terrorists could be put into preventive custody as an illustrative example, it engages Nozick's argument on prevention, knowledge and justice. In Nozick's fierce defence of individual rights, the state comes into being as an aggregate of individuals and their inviolable rights, and thus possesses no moral legitimacy of its own. Individual rights must therefore not be violated for the sake of common goods. In conjunction with his emphasis on free will and the ensuing unpredictability of human decision-making, the article highlights the Nozickian position as a powerful account against the justification of preventive custody, thereby providing a moral "fail-safe" in counterterrorism discourses that build on just war theory and utilitarianism.

Introduction

Individuals have rights, and there are things no person or group may do to them (without violating their rights). So strong and far reaching are these rights that they raise the question of what, if anything, the state and its officials may do. How much room do individual rights leave for the state? (Nozick 1974, ix)

Let us consider the following scenario: a person has been identified by the authorities as a potential terrorist. What should be the morally justified response from the authorities? One might be inclined to say that this person should be put under surveillance (either electronic surveillance that monitors their communication through email, telephone and social media, or actual physical surveillance that monitors their location and behaviour, for instance via an electronic bracelet or via police officers in the streets) in order to enable the authorities to intervene prior to that person unfolding harm. One might be inclined to say that this person should be taken into preventive custody in order to completely cancel out the possibility of the infliction of harm. One might even be inclined to say that this person should, in case they are not a citizen of their country of residence, be expelled from that country, thereby shifting the burden of dealing with a potential terrorist to the authorities of another state.

On the other hand, one might also be inclined to say that for this person – as for every person – persists the presumption of innocence. One might say that surveillance, preventive custody or even expulsion present serious violations of fundamental rights, and that such violations are unbearable in a society that is built on the principles of justice and fairness. One might subsequently be inclined to inquire why this person had been identified as a potential terrorist in the first place. One might be inclined to question the information on which such an evaluation is based, and the degree of certainty that the authorities put into their evaluation. And, it might just as well turn out that such information will be classified and inaccessible, and that one would simply have to believe that the authorities have trustworthy sources and have carefully assessed the stakes.

From a moral point of view, the tension in this scenario stems from the valuation of individual rights vis-à-vis society and security. Might those rights be violated against the backdrop of the potential terrorist attack? And if so, to what extent? Could surveillance be justified? Could preventive custody be justified? Moral philosophical considerations of counterterrorism and justice have for a large part couched their analyses in terms of warfare and exceptionalism, positing that terrorism presents a declaration of (asymmetrical) war on the state, and therefore reasoning that counterterrorism should be judged under the presumption of warfare as well. Theories of just war are in turn largely underpinned by a realist, utilitarian rationale that renders counterterrorism as necessary for the survival of the state, and therefore justifies "collateral damage" of "non-combatants", as long as they would have occurred under principles of prudence. The moral permissibility of the violation of individual rights would thereby be granted through the contribution to a larger social good (i.e. security and the survival of the state).

Conceiving of counterterrorism under the premise of warfare seems, however, empirically inappropriate, given that even though the USA have prominently declared the "war on terror" after 9/11, most states consider counterterrorism measures primarily in terms of policing and criminal justice (Clifford 2016, 9). From this vantage point, questions of justice, fairness, and human rights and civil liberties become much more prevalent, especially against the larger backdrop of critical terrorism studies scholars' calls to deconstruct given assumptions about ontological and normative foundations of terrorism/counterterrorism, and to rather engage their multiple meanings and political, social and economic intertwinings (e.g. Blackbourn et al. 2012; Breen Smyth et al. 2008; Jackson, Breen Smyth, and Gunning 2009).

Opting for a perspective on counterterrorism that is predicated upon notions of normalcy, individual rights and criminal justice, this article engages with Robert Nozick's seminal book *Anarchy, State, and Utopia* (1974). The book, written during Nozick's time as a fellow at the Center for the Advanced Study in Behavioral Sciences in Stanford during the academic year 1971–1972, brings together three separate projects on which Nozick worked at the time and which are reflected in the structure of the argument (Bader and Meadowcroft 2011, 1). Part I ("State-of-Nature Theory, or How to Back into a State without Really Trying") deals with the question of how a state would arise out of the state of nature. Part II ("Beyond the Minimal State?") then goes on to critically engage John Rawls' *A Theory of Justice* (1971), leading Nozick to the development of his own entitlement theory of justice. Part III ("Utopia") eventually lays out why a minimal state would come the closest to a utopian ideal of societal organisation.

The book was awarded the US National Book Award in 1975 and has subsequently received much critical attention. As Schecter (2010, ii) puts it, "Nozick is a seductive writer who expounds his beliefs with confidence and flair. He usually provokes passionate defence or vehement rejection." Wolff (1977, 28) in this vein adds that "Nozick is easily the brightest, most imaginative, most ebullient political philosopher to appear on the American philosophical scene for some time." And yet, as Bader and Meadowcroft (2011, 1) point out, "whilst well respected, widely praised and much discussed, the theory Nozick propounds [in *Anarchy, State, and Utopia*] is almost universally rejected, even by those who agree with many of his substantive conclusions." Critics have thereby, for instance, drawn attention to Nozick's excessive argumentative reliance on market mechanisms and rationality (e.g. Wolff 1977) in conjunction with untenable assumptions about full individual self-ownership (e.g. Papaioannou 2010), as well as to inconsistencies in his derivation of the minimal state (e.g. Holmes 1977; Mack 2011).

Nozick's argument must certainly be read against the larger backdrop of the political and economic situation from which it emerged. The US in the mid-1970s faced racial conflict, increasing military budgets, economic uncertainty, and most notably the experience of the Vietnam War. The libertarian reaction to those problems could be summarised as a general opposition to authority and power, as well as strong advocacy for human rights and negative liberties against state interference (Papaioannou 2010, 6–7). With *Anarchy, State, and Utopia*, Nozick positioned himself both against the revival of individualist anarchism in the US during this time and against the egalitarian position proposed by Rawls. While individualist anarchists would challenge the legitimacy of the state in the first place, Rawls' vision of distributive justice would, in Nozick's view, presuppose too much state regulation. Subsequently, in Parts I and II of *Anarchy, State, and Utopia*, Nozick argues in detail against both positions, i.e. what he considers to be too little (individual anarchism) and too much state (Rawls' egalitarianism), eventually leading him to the conclusion that a minimal state would present the most desirable form of societal organisation. The specific context of the emergence of *Anarchy, State, and Utopia* and the extensive critique that it has sparked raise the question why the book should be read today. And, more particularly, why should it be read in the context of counterterrorism and prevention?

Instead of attempting to defend Nozick against his critics, this article seeks to draw attention to an often overlooked aspect of his argument. In his explorations whether individual rights could be violated and how such violations could possibly be compensated for, Nozick engages questions of knowledge and uncertainty vis-à-vis free will and the essential unpredictability of human action. Moreover, Nozick explicitly ponders the question of whether preventive custody could be justified, given that compensation would be provided. He concludes that free will and major complications in providing compensation for such a wide-ranging interference with individual rights would render preventive custody morally impermissible. Overall, Nozick provides a powerful account of individual rights protection that has so far been under-explored in critical scholarship on counterterrorism. The case of the Berlin attack, presented in the next section, illustrates why Nozick's work, more than 40 years after its original publication, is still relevant and timely.

The case of the Berlin attack

The question of morally permissible state action vis-à-vis the individual and their rights presented at the outset of this article became tangible when on 19 December 2016, Tunisian asylum seeker Anis Amri steered a hijacked truck into a crowded Christmas market in the centre of the German capital Berlin, killing 12 people and injuring more than 50.[1] Responsibility for the attack was later claimed by the "Islamic State" (IS) through the publication of a video in which Amri pledged allegiance to the organisation. The deed was thereby explicitly rendered "terrorist", as it was intended to inflict harm on a Western society considered hostile by IS. In its aftermath, in the light of the failure to prevent the attack, and against the larger backdrop of the quandary of knowledge, uncertainty and prevention in counterterrorism, demands for preventive custody for potential terrorists were publicly put forward.

In fact, Anis Amri had been previously known to the German authorities who had classified him as a so-called "Gefährder". The term translates roughly to "a person likely to threaten public security" and is used particularly in the context of Islamist terrorism. As per a definition provided by the German government in 2004, a person will be classified as a "Gefährder" when specific facts justify the assumption that this person would attempt to commit significant politically motivated offenses, particularly offenses that would justify surveillance of the person's communication (Deutscher Bundestag 2004, 16). Notably, the term does not indicate that the person would yet have committed any offenses, but often relies on statements (made either publicly or within the Islamist milieu) that a person would be willing to commit or contribute to an attack.

German authorities consider such threatening gestures characteristic for a "Gefährder", but at the same time emphasise that utterances of willingness need not be necessarily connected to the actual realisation of an attack. It is the task of the authorities, in turn, to distinguish mere threatening gestures from concrete plans for an attack through their investigations (Landtag Nordrhein-Westfalen 2017, 1). Notably, the classification as a "Gefährder" has no direct implications for enhanced police or intelligence competencies. As such, it is merely a term for internal use within the police and intelligence services that is utilised for information management purposes, allowing the authorities to merge available information and use that information for further investigations concerning the risks or threats which that person would presumably pose (Landtag Nordrhein-Westfalen 2017, 1–2).

Amri was classified as a "Gefährder" in February of 2016 and subsequently put under surveillance (Bundesministerium der Justiz und für Verbraucherschutz 2017). The surveillance was, however, lifted when the authorities had come to the conclusion that it was not likely that Amri would turn from a potential terrorist to an actual terrorist. According to a classified report from the Federal Criminal Police Office (BKA), as reported by the *Süddeutsche Zeitung*, Amri's mobile phone had been wiretapped between March and September of 2016. From this wiretap, authorities had concluded that Amri's willingness to carry out a terrorist attack in the country where he had lodged an asylum application (which had in the meantime been rejected) was diminishing, and that he intended to return to Tunisia instead. Moreover, there were hints that Amri had increasingly turned away from Islamist terrorism and towards petty drug criminality (Leyendecker and Mascolo 2017). Even though he was still classified as a "Gefährder" and his file was discussed at meetings of the German joint counterterrorism centre ("Gemeinsames Terrorismusabwehrzentrum") seven times throughout 2016, authorities agreed upon the fact that, due to available information, no concrete threat emanating from Amri could be assessed (Landtag Nordrhein-Westfalen 2017, 12). The authorities lost touch with Amri after 28 October 2016, when his mobile phone was last located (Bundesministerium der Justiz und für Verbraucherschutz 2017, 19).

The case of the Berlin attack illustrates quite aptly the imponderables that counterterrorism is subjected to. Even though the authorities had been aware of Amri as a potential terrorist early on, even though he had been subjected to extensive surveillance measures, and even though available police and criminal law competencies had been exhausted, formal evaluations of the threat that Amri would pose had come to the conclusion that he was not likely to commit an attack. This assessment, eventually proven to have been incorrect, stirred considerable political discourse after the attack. A parliamentary inquiry claimed an account of responsibilities and possible mistakes made by the authorities from the government (Deutscher Bundestag 2017), and politicians across the party spectrum put forward suggestions to enhance preventive security measures for the sake of counterterrorism, including claims to intensify surveillance and lower data protection standards, and to consider the use of electronic bracelets, as well as preventive custody (Frankfurter Allgemeine Zeitung 2016).

Particularly, the possibility for preventive custody of potential terrorists (i.e. persons classified as "Gefährder") had been publicly discussed earlier, when Minister of the Interior Thomas de Maizière had in August 2016 presented a draft for a legislative package for the "enhancement of security in Germany". Referencing a number of comparatively minor attacks that had happened throughout 2016, the draft document contains a suggestion to implement new police powers that would allow for an arrest of persons based on being assessed as a "threat to public security" (Bundesministerium des Innern 2016, 12). The claim that the authorities would need to be able to take potential terrorists into preventive custody was once again reinforced in October 2016 when a potential Islamist attack with explosive devices was thwarted. Stephan Mayer, spokesperson for domestic affairs for the conservative parliamentary group (CDU/CSU), subsequently put forward that, against the backdrop of the high number of about 500 persons classified as "Gefährder", the authorities had reached their capacitive limits, as it would take up to 30 police officers to ensure non-stop surveillance of potential terrorists. Therefore, preventive custody should be considered as an effective and efficient way to enhance security (Die Zeit 2016).

Counterterrorism and justice

Counterterrorist discourse in fact quite regularly fathoms the boundaries between permissible and non-permissible state action vis-à-vis human rights and civil liberties. For critical scholarship on terrorism/counterterrorism, it is therefore paramount to reflect upon the moral challenges and predicaments that terrorism and the governance thereof pose, and to place them within broader considerations of how we want to live (Jackson

2016, 7). The literature that explicitly engages counterterrorism from such an ethical vantage point can be roughly divided into accounts that evolve around the notion of war and accounts that focus on the criminal justice system. More traditional approaches to the study of terrorism have a tendency to couch counterterrorism and questions of morality in terms of International Relations theory and warfare (e.g. Bellamy 2005; 2008; Coady 2008; Wilson 2005). The justice of counterterrorist measures is thereby often assessed in terms of either realism (i.e. when the survival of the state is at stake, there must be no moral constraints on state behaviour) or pacifism (i.e. killing and damage to innocent "non-combatants" are morally wrong per se). The terminology of the "war on terror" that has dominated debates on counterterrorism after 9/11 thereby resonates with theories of "just war" (e.g. Johnson 1981; Kamm 2004; Walzer 1977) that have their origins in classical inter-state warfare, and that have been adopted to terrorism and other forms of asymmetrical conflict.

Just war theory acknowledges that war in itself is morally wrong, but that it might be justified to prevent even larger moral wrongs. It centres on moral questions inherent in whether it is justified to fight a war in the first place ("jus ad bellum"), thereby considering aspects such as just cause, just intention, proportionality and probabilities of success. Moreover, just war theory engages the morally right conduct within war ("jus in bello"), thereby considering aspects such as the distinction between combatants and non-combatants, the legitimacy and proportionality of military means and strategies, or the treatment of prisoners of war. Bellamy (2005, 291) argues in this vein that for counterterrorism, "the Just War tradition offers a framework that provides both a common moral language and a guide to how political and military leaders should prosecute their war mindful of the need to minimise the damage."

In contrast to just war theory, and refraining from the language of warfare and exceptionalism, scholars from law and criminology suggest to rather study counter-terrorism as a matter of the criminal justice system, thereby exploring questions of procedural justice and fairness (e.g. de Goede and de Graaf 2013; Hasisi and Weisburd 2011; Roach and Trotter 2005), the struggles of criminal justice with uncertainty and temporality (e.g. de Goede 2008; Massumi 2007; McCulloch and Pickering 2009), and the potential infringements of human rights and civil liberties that stem from these strug-gles (e.g. Amoore 2014; de Hert and Papakonstantinou 2014; Ojanen 2010; Breen Smyth 2009; Toivanen 2010; Vermeulen and Bellanova 2012).

It is primarily the latter aspect – individual rights and their possible violation or suspension against the backdrop of threat – that after 9/11 has been subject to a wider debate about whether such violations or suspensions could be morally justified. Ignatieff (2004), for instance, has claimed that exceptional measures could in extraor-dinary situations, given special prudential conditions (such as being only temporary, being publicly justified, being deployed as last resort), be morally justified. His conse-quentialist argument to save the rule through the exception has been widely criticised. Waldron (2010) has in this vein put forward the warning that an ethics of balancing between necessity and dignity presents a slippery slope and is built on a treacherous image of balance in the first place. He therefore calls to carefully consider notions of "the inviolability of the individual, the complexity of security, the abomination of torture, the importance of humanity and dignity in our response to terrorism, and above all the integrity of law" (Waldron 2010, 19).

In the light of these debates on counterterrorism, both philosophically and politically, the relevance of the work of Nozick lies in the fierce rejection of any consequentialist trade-off of a person's rights or liberties for a greater good or for the sake of others. Such a trade-off, from his libertarian perspective, would fundamentally fail to acknowledge the distinctiveness of individuals, as well as the plurality of a society that is made up of distinct individuals. As Waldron (2010, 15) notes, the defence of individual rights put forward by Nozick and others has crucially re-vitalised political philosophy in the 1970s – and yet in contemporary counterterrorism discourses, as has been demonstrated by the example of the Berlin case, interpersonal trade-offs that violate individual liberties are nonetheless considered quite regularly. For Waldron (2010, 15), this subsequently raises the question of whether "no progress had been made in distinguishing consideration of one person's trade-off among various goods that he or she enjoyed, on the one hand, and the pressing issues of justice raised when there was a proposal to trade off one person's well-being for the greater good of others."

Against this backdrop, this article argues that what is needed from an ethical perspective is an account of counterterrorism that is grounded in notions of normalcy and individual rights protection within a framework of criminal justice. A suitable moral angle on counterterrorism must not take side with discourses about the survival of the state, but must stick to arguments of justice that emerge through considerations of the regular treatment of individuals in times without threat. Ethical reflections might at times appear to be abstract, particularly against the backdrop of the actual terrorist attacks that inflict very real harm and thus legitimately produce a desire for effective and efficient counterterrorism. And yet, embarking on consequentialist counterterrorism ethics, as, for instance, proposed by Ignatieff and reiterated in the aftermath of the Berlin attack, can prove to be severely harmful for societies that are built on principles of justice and fairness. The case of the Berlin attack is illustrative here in two dimensions.

First, it demonstrates how easily counterterrorism can actually fail against the backdrop of a complex world that poses threats that are, epistemologically speaking, largely unpredictable and therefore ultimately difficult to prevent – even when intelligence on potential terrorists is available. Think of Donald Rumsfeld's infamous dictum of the "unknown unknowns" (i.e. the double task of identifying previously unknown threats in the first place, before then being able to attempt to cancel them out) that security agencies are struggling to come to terms with. And second, it shows how easily questions about the moral permissibility of state action within counterterrorism can be brushed away in public and political discourse.

The minimal state and moral side constraints

Turning to the work of Robert Nozick, I suggest, provides a viable and so far underexplored way of dealing with questions of moral permissibility within counterterrorism, as his moral philosophical approach specifically explores the nexus between security, state and individual rights, and thereby puts particular emphasis on the relationship between the state and the individual. Arguing against the extension of state power, Nozick, in Part I of *Anarchy, State, and Utopia*, demonstrates how a legitimate state that would not violate any person's rights (the so-called "minimal state") would come into being through a series of steps. For this purpose, he posits "a theory of a state of nature that begins with fundamental general descriptions of morally permissible and impermissible actions" (Nozick 1974, 7).

For a large part building on the political philosophy of John Locke, Nozick (1974, Ch. 2) argues that in the state of nature, individuals possess natural rights that concern their physical and psychological integrity, as well as their private possessions. Such natural rights must not be violated by anyone, and any attempt to do so would be morally impermissible. Since, however, in the state of nature, any restrictions on morally impermissible actions (for example violence, theft, fraud) could not be enforced, Nozick concludes that individuals would inevitably start to cooperate and form so-called "protective associations" which would ensure the non-violation of the individual rights of their members.

Through the effects of market forces, the competition between different protective associations would eventually lead to the emergence of a dominant protective association in a territory, possessing a de facto monopoly of force. This dominant protective association would, so Nozick further argues, have an obligation to compensate non-clients for disadvantages experienced in dealing with the clients of this powerful association. In order to be able to do this, the dominant protective association would have the duty to tax its own clients to provide protection for disadvantaged non-clients. Through this redistribution of resources, according to Nozick, the minimal state would emerge. Notably, this minimal state would come into being without violating anyone's rights, thereby producing security for all without committing morally impermissible boundary-crossings. Therefore, the minimal state would present the best form of societal organisation.

Crucially, for Nozick, it is from the moral primacy of individual rights that the state derives its mandate to legitimately apply force in case the inviolability of those individual rights would be threatened. The detour via the state of nature and the moral imperative of state action is thereby necessary for Nozick's core argument that the state presents itself as an aggregate of its constitutive parts. As he concludes, "the legitimate powers of a protective association are merely the *sum* of the individual rights that its members or clients transfer to the association. No new rights and powers arise; each right of the association is decomposable without residue into those individual rights held by distinct individuals acting alone in a state of nature" (Nozick 1974, 89; original emphasis). Notably, for Nozick, the state is no moral reference object in its own right. From its protective role, no particular additional valuation of the state as such could be derived, and the state could therefore not be regarded as a primary reference object of security.

Following this argument, the claim made by proponents of counterterrorism as warfare (i.e. that not only individuals, but also the state itself would need to be protected from terrorism) must be considered invalid. Nozick argues here explicitly against utilitarian moral philosophy which would posit that for the provision of security for all (and thus the survival of the state), individual sacrifices could be justified. The argument for preventive custody, as has been put forward after the Berlin attack, is in fact an apt example of a utilitarian point of view. According to the logic inherent in preventive custody for counterterrorism, the freedom of some (who are moreover under the suspicion of terrorism in the first place) would be a small price to pay for the enhancement of overall security, from which the vast majority of people would benefit.

Since the preventive custody would contribute to the benefit of the majority, the overall utility of it would outweigh the negative consequences for those taken into preventive custody, and it could thus be considered morally justified.

Against the utilitarian argument that for the sake of a common social good, some persons would at times have to bear costs (i.e. having their individual rights violated) from which others would benefit, Nozick (1974, 32–3), however, holds that

> there is no social entity with a good that undergoes some sacrifice for its own good. There are only individual people, different individual people, with their own individual lives. Using one of these people for the benefit of others, uses him and benefits the others. Nothing more. What happens is that something is done to him for the sake of others. Talk of an overall social good covers this up.

Any *use* of a person, so he infers from this argument, must be morally impermissible, as this would not sufficiently respect the person themselves and their life. This brings Nozick to the conclusion that there must be side constraints not only for actions between individuals, but notably for state action vis-à-vis individuals, and that those side constraints directly follow from the inviolability of individual rights.

As he makes abundantly clear, "the moral side constraints upon what we may do, I claim, reflect the fact of our separate existences" (Nozick 1974, 33) and the state would be, in this view, a poor performer of its original mandate if, in the name of protection, individual rights could be violated. As Nozick (1974, 33; original emphasis) thus clarifies with regard to state power, "no one is entitled to force [a violation of rights] upon [a person] – least of all a state or government that claims his allegiance [...] and that therefore scrupulously must be *neutral* between its citizens." Within Nozick's derivation of state power from the moral integrity of the individual, any attempt to morally justify the results of an action rather than the action itself must be unacceptable. Side constraints on state action thus "reflect the fact that no moral balancing act can take place among us; there is no moral outweighing of one of our lives by others so as to lead to a greater overall *social* good. There is no justified sacrifice of some of us for others" (Nozick 1974, 33; original emphasis).

Compensation, knowledge, prevention

Such a radical position on the inviolability of individual rights would, however, lead to the conclusion that no boundary crossings would be permissible whatsoever. This would mean that in a society built on the unconditional inviolability of individual rights, very few actions would be possible without crossing the boundaries of another person's rights. Moreover, there would be little room for political regulation, notably for the task of protection. As Wolff (1977, 17) points out, this position, "if accepted, [..] would immobilize us all, making us much like a bizarre gathering of morally musclebound rights freaks, lovely to look at, but unable to lift a finger for fear of encroaching on another's moral space." Nozick indeed acknowledges this dilemma and subsequently looks for permissible state action that could delicately manoeuvre between moral constraints and regulatory necessities. He therefore asks, "[a]re others forbidden to perform actions that transgress the boundary [...], or are they permitted to perform such actions provided that they compensate the person whose boundary has been crossed?" (Nozick 1974, 57).

Pondering the possibilities to allow some boundary crossings given that compensation would be provided (notwithstanding the difficulties to define which violations could be compensated for, and to determine the compensation value), Nozick (1974, 67) distinguishes between private wrongs (i.e. boundary crossings where only the injured party would need to be compensated) and public wrongs. Public wrongs, as he argues, "are those people are fearful of, even though they know they will be compensated fully if and when the wrongs occur. Even under the strongest compensation proposal which compensates victims for their fear, some people (the nonvictims) will not be compensated for *their* fear" (Nozick 1974, 67; original emphasis). In the case of public wrongs, Nozick thus in fact argues for clear state regulation (i.e. prohibition) in the form of a criminal justice system that threatens to punish such boundary crossings, thereby compelling individuals not to carry out such actions in the first place. As he concludes, "there is a legitimate public interest in eliminating these border crossing acts, especially because their commission raises everyone's fear of its happening to them" (Nozick 1974, 67).

Whereas private wrongs in Nozick's theory appear to fall mostly into the category of private property protection, public wrongs are, generally speaking, those actions that would intentionally and physically hurt another person. Examples of such actions would, for instance, be violence, assault or murder. Clearly, terrorism falls under the same category, as it seeks to intentionally use people for political purposes by killing or injuring them. Hijacking a truck and driving it into a Christmas market is without a doubt a prohibited action, and therefore, state action is required to either prevent the action in the first place or to punish the offender afterwards. In our case, the possibility to prevent boundary crossings in the first place is pertinent. Nozick for a large part concentrates on "those actions the agent knows will or might well impinge across someone's boundary" (Nozick 1974, 71), as well as on those actions that would only risk to cross another person's boundaries. The latter, as he acknowledges, "pose serious problems for a natural-rights position" (Nozick 1974, 74), as they insert an element of uncertainty into the equation. Put differently, not knowing what consequences certain actions will have makes it hard to determine whether and how to regulate them.

Again, there is a strong parallel to counterterrorism and our example of the Berlin attack. Could it have been known that Anis Amri's actions would inflict major harm on random victims? And if so, how, and with what degree of certainty? Moreover, how would such knowledge relate to actual action and ensuing possible state action? Counterterrorism, as has been shown, suffers from an indissoluble epistemic predicament. Unlike in traditional penal law, counterterrorist measures must seek to prevent the occurrence of the terrorist attack in the first place. This means that there can by definition be no regular sequence of offence-prosecution-conviction. Instead, terrorism requires to be governed through potentials. Knowledge about potential offenders and potential incidents must in turn be created, and upon such knowledge, authorities must intervene before harm can unfold.

Pondering questions of knowledge and the (un-)predictability of human action, Nozick explicitly engages the idea of prevention. Preventive action, for him, includes "all restrictions on individuals in order to lessen the risk that *they* will violate others' rights" (Nozick 1974, 142; original emphasis), for example having to report to the authorities at specific intervals, not being allowed at certain places at specific times, or not being allowed to purchase guns or other weapons. Such restrictions could discourage or even take away the possibilities of a violation of other people's rights and could therefore be considered as appropriate regulatory means by the state. As the most extreme case of such preventive action, Nozick (1974, 142) considers preventive detention, which "would encompass imprisoning someone, not for any crime he has committed, but because it is predicted of him that the probability is significantly higher than normal that he will commit a crime. (His previous crimes may be part of the data on the basis of which the predictions are made.)."

Nozick's reflections here strike at the very core of our case and of counterterrorism epistemology and ethics more generally. The status of knowledge has been one of the most prevalent questions of counterterrorism policy-making (and the critical scholarship thereof), and it has been reinforced and arguably been lifted to an unprecedented level in the global "war on terror" that has unfolded after 9/11. Subsequently, a vast body of critical research into counterterrorism policies has emerged that addresses the question of how knowledge about terrorism is created, and how such knowledge is eventually put into practice. Scholars have addressed the digital practices of surveillance and advanced analytics that are used to extrapolate hints at potential terrorist activities from large amounts of data (e.g. Amoore 2013; Amoore and de Goede 2008; Aradau and van Munster 2007; Bauman et al. 2014); the roles of security professionals, their expertise, and their practices of cooperation and data exchange (e.g. Balzacq 2008; Bigo 2002; Monahan and Regan 2012; Toivanen 2010); as well as the development and implementation of technologies of identification and control (e.g. Aas, Gundhus, and Lomell 2009; Kaufmann 2016; Leese 2015; Salter 2004).

The knowledge produced in such ways is set to assist authorities to come to terms with the complexity of the world and to make choices about who to watch and who to dismiss in their efforts to prevent harm from unfolding. David Lyon (2003, 20) writes in regard to such practices of social sorting based on knowledge production:

> Categorization is endemic and vital to human life, especially to social life. The processes of institutional categorization, however, received a major boost from modernity with its analytical, rationalizing thrust. All modern social institutions, for example, depend upon differentiation, to discover who counts as a citizen, which citizens may vote, who may hold property, which persons may marry, who has graduated from which school, with what qualifications, who is employed by whom, and so on.

On the broadest level possible, sorting the social allows to specifically allocate resources according to where they are presumably needed the most. In counterterrorism, this knowledge-based sorting of the social is usually approached through the category of risk and ensuing practices of profiling that classify persons according to the level of risk that they would arguably pose in terms of inflicting harm. Through the assembling of counterterrorism knowledge, what used to be an undefined "potential" becomes thereby transformed into a specific level of risk. Organisationally, this transformation allows for a legitimate (re-)allocation of resources, as the risk level can be referenced for ensuing (non-)action. In other words, risk assessment yields a reference point that can be used to rationalise decisions.

The problem of free will

These considerations of knowledge and rationalisation became, once more, very tangible in the case of the Berlin attack. The fact that Anis Amri had been known to the authorities and classified as a "Gefährder" mirrors the distinct potentials that are organisationally assigned to individuals in order to subject them to different kinds of state action. Going back to Nozick's account of prevention, this leads us to the question of whether in some cases the violation of individual rights by the state would be morally permissible, even when no offence has been committed by that person yet. In order to explore this question, Nozick (1974, 143) turns to a processual perspective on action and, more specifically, suggests to consider "actions or processes where wrong occurs only if the person later decides to do wrong." The notion of the decision is crucial here, as he ascribes, based on his assumption of full self-ownership, to human beings the capability to decide upon their actions at any given point. This means that a person could decide to either carry out a prohibited action or not, and thereby to either violate others' rights or not.

A mechanistic, path-dependent model of human action would, from Nozick's perspective, have to be rejected, as such a presumed causal chain would deny the capability to decide otherwise. Nozick (1974, 143; original emphasis) argues here that only

> to the extent that some people are viewed as *incapable* of making a future decision and are viewed merely as mechanisms now set into operation which will (or may) perform wrong actions (or to the extent that they are viewed as incapable of deciding against acting wrongly?), then preventive restraint possibly will seem legitimate.

However, since there is free will (and therefore the capacity to decide otherwise), such an argument would have to be considered invalid. Nozick's considerations in this regard are once more pertinent for our case, as he not only rejects utilitarian approaches to justice that would defend the violation of an individuals' right to freedom with reference to the social good of security, but at the same time emphasises the epistemic predicaments of counterterrorism that stem from questions of knowledge and uncertainty. As in the case of Anis Amri, even prior knowledge of potential terrorists might at times not provide a viable way of preventing actual harm. Amri was believed to have decided against carrying out an attack, and yet this rationalised risk assessment was proven wrong, as his decision eventually went in favour of carrying out the attack nonetheless.

In this vein, and assuming that humans do in fact possess free will, Nozick rejects a mechanistic reading of human action and therefore notions of predictability and inevitability. As he argues, "if the evil (it is feared) the person may do really does hinge upon decisions for wrong which he has not yet made, then the earlier principles will rule preventive detention or restraint illegitimate and impermissible" (Nozick 1974, 143). In other words, knowledge about the future would need to be absolute in order to morally justify preventive custody. However, since no knowledge of the future could ever be absolute, no moral permissibility of preventive custody could be posited. In conjunction with the moral imperative of the state that derives from the inviolability of the individual rights of its constitutive elements, Nozick delivers here a powerful argument against moral justifications of "collateral damages" and other utilitarian sacrifices that we find in theories of just war and approaches to counterterrorism that are grounded in warfare and exceptionalism.

Despite this very clear-cut position, Nozick returns once more to the question of compensation and ponders whether preventive custody could not be permissible nonetheless, given that adequate compensation could be provided. The ensuing question for him then becomes what such compensation could look like. Nozick (1974, 143–4) argues that "perhaps only by setting aside a pleasant area for such persons predicted to be highly dangerous, which though fenced and guarded contains resort hotels, recreational facilities, and so forth, can this requirement of compensation for disadvantages imposed be met." However, since such a detention centre would be an attractive place to live in, it could attract people to get deliberately sent into detention. Moreover, as the dangerousness of the place would arguably rise with the number of potential offenders detained in it, Nozick (1974, 144) wonders whether such increased dangerousness would in turn also need to be compensated for. Notably, he makes it clear that he uses the trope of resort detention centres explicitly "*not* to propose them, but to show the sort of things proponents of preventive detention must think about and be willing to countenance *and pay for*" (Nozick 1974, 144; original emphasis). He thus eventually concludes that adequate compensation for taking away a person's liberty based on mere potentials would be ultimately hard to achieve. Nozick (1974, 144) therefore argues that, in combination with his reflections on free will, "this leaves little, if any, scope for legitimate preventive restraint."

Overall, Nozick's argument provides not only an elaborated moral philosophical rejection of preventive custody, but his remarks about mechanistic assumptions of human behaviour also tell us much about contemporary counterterrorism, as they tie in closely with practices of data collection and analytics that seek to render human action predictable through rationalisation and calculation. For advocates of a path-dependency model of human behaviour, counterterrorism must become an enterprise of finding ways to translate the unpredictability of free will into some form of cause–effect relationship. Couched in such terms, terrorism could then be subdued under a calculus of action and reaction that would allow for precise and effective counter-measures. Such a rationale almost seamlessly ties in with utilitarian considerations of what is to be assessed as beneficial or detrimental for the regulatory purpose of security. Through the encoding of populations in numerical terms, statistical methods have enabled contemporary counterterrorism to infer new types of knowledge about populations, and to sort individuals according to criteria of rationalised assumptions about harmlessness/dangerousness. This does not, however, cancel out the possibility that predictions could not still be wrong.

Let us go back to our case of the Berlin attack one final time. Anis Amri was known to the German authorities. He was listed as a "Gefährder" – a potential. He was subsequently put under surveillance in order to determine the level of his potential. Judging from the information gathered through surveillance measures (the wiretap on his phone), the authorities eventually came to the conclusion that the risk that he posed was comparably low, and that the resources used for the surveillance operation on him should be allocated to other potentials (i.e. other persons classified as "Gefährder"), that were assessed to be more risky. As was proven later, the risk level assigned to Amri was sufficiently low for him to lose the attention of the authorities, and to be able to follow through with his attack. Counterterrorism, guided by the belief that Amri had made a decision to return to Tunisia instead of committing an attack in Germany, had failed. In fact, what had failed here was the reliability of behavioural prediction that was based on the knowledge created through surveillance.

How does such a rationale resonate with Nozick's argument about the practical non-predictability of human decision-making? Knowledge created through a presumed rationalisation of free will can, in this vein, never be certain. On the contrary, independent of the ways in which it was generated, it could be easily unhinged by a potential terrorist simply deciding differently. Derrida (1994, 34) notes in this regard that "a decision, if there is such a thing, is never determinable in terms of knowledge" – otherwise there would not have been a decision, but merely an unavoidable consequence from previous intelligence. If we add to this simple, yet powerful distinction the fact that even if decision-making was determinable in terms of knowledge we might never be able to collect all the information to assemble comprehensive knowledge about human intentions, then such a strategy breaks down to the somewhat irritating notion that, as Heath-Kelly et al. (2015, 5) frame it, "contemporary security strategies, and counterterrorism policies in particular, derive their legitimacy from or are based upon forms of knowledge that are structured around uncertainty, ambiguity, imagination and fantasy." In other words, there is simply no way around the non-absolute state of knowledge about the future, and any attempt of a transformation into an absolute state might (or rather: will) eventually fail. In the light of such failure, a violation of individual rights through preventive custody must be, from the angle of Nozick's moral philosophical framework, regarded as impermissible.

Conclusions

How do these reflections resonate with the critical study of terrorism/counterterrorism more generally? As we have shown, counterterrorism policy-making has to carefully manoeuvre between the poles of producing security and at the same time protecting individual rights. This might not always be possible, as the operational logic of terrorist attacks is to distort balancing efforts between those poles. Faced with this predicament, moral questions within counterterrorism too often become couched into notions of warfare, and thereby unhinged from a moral valuation of individual rights. When approaching counterterrorism through notions of normalcy and criminal justice, as must be considered more adequate, utilitarian arguments and the moral justifications provided by just war theory become, however, largely invalid.

On the other hand, it should be kept in mind that Nozick's valuation of individual rights as fundamental constraints for state action might in fact in itself be no less radical than a realist angle on the survival of the state that would justify collateral damages. In practical terms, Nozick's perspective leaves little room for state action vis-à-vis the individual. We should therefore be careful to perceive of it as the ideal typical moral stance that it is, having been developed through a state of nature. Nozick's work has in fact been subjected to a good share of criticism. Nevertheless, so this article has argued, particularly his reflections on prevention, knowledge and justice can offer a fruitful and so-far underexplored perspective for the ethical analysis of current counterterrorism practices and discourses.

As the Berlin case has shown, the problem within contemporary counterterrorism discourse is that, when faced with the options whether to posit the individual or the state as a moral reference object of protection, it shows a tendency to drift decisively into the direction of utilitarian arguments (i.e. justifying the violation of some individual's rights for the sake of the common good of security), thereby running the risk of undermining fundamental principles of justice and fairness. Nozick's argument, as retraced throughout the course of this article and illustrated against the backdrop of the Berlin attack, can, so I suggest, serve as a moral "fail-safe" in these discourses. In times when the pendulum of political arguments tends to swing towards extreme measures such as preventive custody, Nozick's work provides a fierce opposition to arguments of efficiency and effectiveness, and can thus help to challenge counterterrorism policies that potentially violate individual rights.

Thinking about individual rights might at times be easily dismissed politically against the backdrop of the pressure to act and to prevent. And yet, such considerations are important, especially vis-à-vis larger questions of societal organisation. Societies built upon principles of fairness and justice are prone to become unhinged by terrorism – this is what makes it so successful in its own, twisted fashion. At the same time, conceiving counterterrorism in terms of warfare and exceptionalism aggravates the success of terrorism in the first place. Thinking about counterterrorism from the vantage point of normalcy, policing and criminal justice arguably provides a more sensitive way of thinking about the moral permissibility of state action vis-à-vis the individual.

This article has put forward the work of Nozick as an underappreciated perspective on ethics in counterterrorism that can, even more than 40 years after its original publication, provide a fruitful contribution to debates on morally permissible state action. Eventually, for Nozick, the rights that individuals possess in the state of nature are paramount – it is only for the protection of those rights that the state comes into being in the first place. Nozick's proposition is thus to limit state powers to the greatest extent possible, leading him to the conceptualisation of a minimal state which would, so he proposes, be the best state model from the vantage point of individual rights protection. As he concludes *Anarchy, State, and Utopia*,

> The minimal state treats us as inviolate individuals, who may not be used in certain ways by others as means or tools or instruments or resources; it treats us as persons having individual rights with the dignity this constitutes. Treating us with respect by respecting our rights, it allows us, individually or with whom we choose, to choose our life and to realize our ends and our conception of ourselves, insofar we can, aided by the voluntary cooperation of other individuals possessing the same dignity. How *dare* any state or group of individuals do more. Or less. (Nozick 1974, 333–4; original emphasis).

Notes

1. It should be noted that at the time of writing (April of 2017), Amri has not yet been officially convicted for the attack. There are, however, strong indications that he was in fact the attacker. Amri himself, after having fled from the authorities for several days, was shot by the police after having attacked two officers in Milano, Italy, on 23 December 2016.

Acknowledgments

An earlier version of this article was presented at the ISA Annual Convention, Baltimore, 22–25 February 2017. It has largely benefited from critical and constructive feedback provided by Myriam Dunn Cavelty, the editors at *Critical Studies on Terrorism*, as well as two anonymous reviewers.

Disclosure statement

No potential conflict of interest was reported by the author.

References

Aas, K. F., H. O. Gundhus, and H. M. Lomell, eds. 2009. *Technologies of Insecurity: The Surveillance of Everyday Life*. 1 ed. London: Routledge-Cavendish.

Amoore, L. 2013. *The Politics of Possibility: Risk and Security beyond Probability*. Durham/London: Duke University Press.

Amoore, L. 2014. "Security and the Claim to Privacy." *International Political Sociology* 8 (1): 108–112. doi:10.1111/ips.2014.8.issue-1.

Amoore, L., and M. de Goede, eds. 2008. *Risk and the War on Terror*. London/New York: Routledge.

Aradau, C., and R. van Munster. 2007. "Governing Terrorism through Risk: Taking Precautions, (Un) Knowing the Future." *European Journal of International Relations* 13 (1): 89–115. doi:10.1177/1354066107074290.

Bader, R. M., and J. Meadowcroft. 2011. "Introduction." In *The Cambridge Companion to Nozick's Anarchy, State, and Utopia*, edited by R. M. Bader and J. Meadowcroft, 1–11. Cambridge: Cambridge University Press.

Balzacq, T. 2008. "The Policy Tools of Securitization: Information Exchange, EU Foreign and Interior Policies." *Journal of Common Market Studies* 46 (1): 75–100. doi:10.1111/j.1468-5965.2007.00768.x.

Bauman, Z., D. Bigo, P. Esteves, E. Guild, V. Jabri, D. Lyon, and R. B. J. Walker. 2014. "After Snowden: Rethinking the Impact of Surveillance." *International Political Sociology* 8 (2): 121–144. doi:10.1111/ips.2014.8.issue-2.

Bellamy, A. J. 2005. "Is the War on Terror Just?." *International Relations* 19 (3): 275–296. doi:10.1177/0047117805055407.

Bellamy, A. J. 2008. *Fighting Terror: Ethical Dilemmas*. London/New York: Zed Books.

Bigo, D. 2002. "Security and Immigration: Toward a Critique of the Governmentality of Unease." *Alternatives: Global, Local, Political* 27 (1): 63–92. doi:10.1177/03043754020270S105.

Blackbourn, J., H. Dexter, R. Dhanda, and D. Miller. 2012. "Editor's Introduction: A Decade on from 11 September 2001: What Has Critical Terrorism Studies Learned?." *Critical Studies on Terrorism* 5 (1): 1–10. doi:10.1080/17539153.2012.659905.

Breen Smth, M., J. Gunning, R. Jackson, G. Kassimeris, and P. Robinson. 2008. "Critical Terrorism Studies – An Introduction." *Critical Studies on Terrorism* 1 (1): 1–4. doi:10.1080/17539150701868538.

Breen Smyth, M. 2009. "A Human Rights Perspective on the War on Terror: An Interview with Letta Tayler." *Critical Studies on Terrorism* 2 (3): 540–545. doi:10.1080/07393140903338808.

Bundesministerium der Justiz und für Verbraucherschutz. 2017. Behördenhandeln um die Person des Attentäters vom Breitscheidplatz Anis AMRI. January 17. Accessed 22 January 2017. http://www.bmjv.de/SharedDocs/Downloads/DE/Artikel/01162017_chronologie_breitscheidplatz.pdf?__blob=publicationFile&v=4

Bundesministerium des Innern. 2016. *Geplante Maßnahmen zur Erhöhung der Sicherheit in Deutschland*, August 11, Berlin.

Clifford, G. M. 2016. "Just Counterterrorism." *Critical Studies on Terrorism* online first. doi:10.1080/17539153.2016.1254369.

Coady, C. A. J. 2008. *Morality and Political Violence*. Cambridge: Cambridge University Press.

de Goede, M. 2008. "The Politics of Preemption and the War on Terror in Europe." *European Journal of International Relations* 14 (1): 161–185. doi:10.1177/1354066107087764.

de Goede, M., and B. de Graaf. 2013. "Sentencing Risk: Temporality and Precaution in Terrorism Trials." *International Political Sociology* 7 (3): 313–331. doi:10.1111/ips.12025.

de Hert, P., and V. Papakonstantinou. 2014. "The Data Protection Regime Applying to the Inter-Agency Cooperation and Future Architecture of the EU Criminal Justice and Law Enforcement Area." In *Study for the Directorate General for Internal Policies, Policy Department C: Citizens' Rights and Constitutional Affairs*. Brussels: European Union.

Derrida, J. 1994. "Nietzsche and the Machine." *Journal of Nietzsche Studies* 7: 7–66.

Deutscher Bundestag. 2004. Drucksache 15/3284: Schriftliche Fragen mit den in der Woche vom 7. Juni 2004 eingegangenen Antworten der Bundesregierung. 11 June. Accessed 17 January 2017. dip21.bundestag.de/dip21/btd/15/032/1503284.pdf

Deutscher Bundestag. 2017. Drucksache 18/10812, 9 January. Kleine Anfrage der Abgeordneten Irene Mihalic, Konstantin Von Notz, Britta Haßelmann, Volker Beck (Köln), Katja Keul, Renate Künast, Monika Lazar, Özcan Mutlu, Hans-Christian Ströbele Und Der Fraktion BÜNDNIS 90/DIE GRÜNEN: Der Anschlag auf einen Berliner Weihnachtsmarkt am 19. Dezember 2016 und der Fall Anis Amri - Verantwortung und etwaige Fehler der Sicherheitsbehörden. Accessed 22 January 2017. http://dipbt.bundestag.de/doc/btd/18/108/1810812.pdf

Die Zeit. 2016. Unionspolitiker wollen Gefährder präventiv in Haft nehmen. 10 October. Accessed 17 January 2017. http://www.zeit.de/politik/deutschland/2016-10/sicherheit-fluechtlinge-ueberpruefung-union-chemnitz-terrorverdacht

Frankfurter Allgemeine Zeitung. 2016. Fußfessel, Abschiebehaft Und Videoüberwachung gefordert. FAZ, 27 December. Accessed 17 January 2017. http://www.faz.net/aktuell/politik/anschlag-in-berlin/nach-berliner-anschlag-fussfessel-und-videoueberwachung-gefordert-14593011.html

Hasisi, B., and D. Weisburd. 2011. "Going beyond Ascribed Identities: The Importance of Procedural Justice in Airport Security Screening in Israel." *Law & Society Review* 45 (4): 867–892. doi:10.1111/j.1540-5893.2011.00459.x.

Heath-Kelly, C., C. Baker-Beall, and L. Jarvis. 2015. "Editors' Introduction: Neoliberalism And/As Terror." *Critical Studies on Terrorism* 8 (1): 1–14. doi:10.1080/17539153.2015.1009761.

Holmes, R. L. 1977. "Nozick on Anarchism." *Political Theory* 5 (2): 247–256.

Ignatieff, M. 2004. *The Lesser Evil: Political Ethics in an Age of Terror*. Princeton/Oxford: Princeton University Press.

Jackson, R. 2016. "Introduction: A Decade of Critical Terrorism Studies." In *Routledge Handbook of Critical Terrorism Studies*, edited by R. Jackson, 1–13. Milton Park/New York: Routledge.

Jackson, R., M. Breen Smyth, and J. Gunning, eds. 2009. "Critical Terrorism Studies: Framing a New Research Agenda." In *Critical Terrorism Studies: A New Research Agenda*, 216–236. Milton Park/New York: Routledge.

Johnson, J. T. 1981. *Just War Tradition and the Restraint of War: A Moral and Historical Inquiry*. Princeton: Princeton University Press.

Kamm, F. M. 2004. "Failures of Just War Theory: Terror, Harm, and Justice." *Ethics* 114 (4): 650–692. doi:10.1086/383441.

CRITICAL TERRORISM STUDIES AT TEN

Kaufmann, S. 2016. "Security through Technology? Logic, Ambivalence and Paradoxes of Technologised Security." *European Journal for Security Research* 1 (1): 77–95. doi:10.1007/s41125-016-0005-1.

Landtag Nordrhein-Westfalen. 2017. Sondersitzung des Innenausschusses: Mündlicher Bericht Landeskriminaldirektor Dieter Schürmann. 5 January. Accessed 17 January 2017. http://www.mik.nrw.de/fileadmin/user_upload/Redakteure/Dokumente/Startseite/170105iaberlin_schuermann.pdf

Leese, M. 2015. "'We Were Taken by Surprise': Body Scanners, Technology Adjustment, and the Eradication of Failure." *Critical Studies on Security* 3 (3): 269–282. doi:10.1080/21624887.2015.1124743.

Leyendecker, H., and G. Mascolo. 2017. Union fordert Ausschuss im Fall Amri. Süddeutsche Zeitung, 15 January. Accessed 17 January 2017. http://www.sueddeutsche.de/politik/berlin-attentat-union-fordert-ausschuss-im-fall-amri-1.3333572

Lyon, D. 2003. "Surveillance as Social Sorting: Computer Codes and Mobile Bodies." In *Surveillance as Social Sorting: Privacy, Risk, and Digital Discrimination*, edited by D. Lyon, 13–30. London/New York: Routledge.

Mack, E. 2011. "Nozickian Arguments for the More-Than-Minimal State." In *The Cambridge Companion to Nozick's Anarchy, State, and Utopia*, edited by R. M. Bader and J. Meadowcroft, 89–115. Cambridge: Cambridge University Press.

Massumi, B. 2007. "Potential Politics and the Primacy of Preemption." *Theory & Event* 10 (2).

McCulloch, J., and S. Pickering. 2009. "Pre-Crime and Counter-Terrorism: Imagining Future Crime in the 'War on Terror'." *The British Journal of Criminology* 49 (5): 628–645. doi:10.1093/bjc/azp023.

Monahan, T., and P. M. Regan. 2012. "Zones of Opacity: Data Fusion in Post-9/11 Security Organizations." *Canadian Journal of Law and Society* 27 (3): 301–317. doi:10.1017/S0829320100010528.

Nozick, R. 1974. *Anarchy, State, and Utopia*. Oxford/Cambridge: Blackwell.

Ojanen, T. 2010. "Terrorist Profiling: Human Rights Concerns." *Critical Studies on Terrorism* 3 (2): 295–312. doi:10.1080/17539153.2010.491343.

Papaioannou, T. 2010. *Robert Nozick's Moral and Political Theory: A Philosophical Critique of Libertarianism*. Lewiston/Queenston/Lampeter: The Edwin Mellen Press.

Rawls, J. 1971. *A Theory of Justice*. Cambridge: Harvard University Press.

Roach, K., and G. Trotter. 2005. "Miscarriages of Justice in the War against Terror." *Penn State Law Review* 109 (4): 967–1042.

Salter, M. B. 2004. "Passports, Mobility, and Security: How Smart Can the Border Be?." *International Studies Perspectives* 5 (1): 71–91. doi:10.1111/j.1528-3577.2004.00158.x.

Schecter, D. 2010. "Foreword." In *Robert Nozick's Moral and Political Theory: A Philosophical Critique of Libertarianism*, T. Papaioannou. Lewiston/Queenston/Lampeter: The Edwin Mellen Press.

Toivanen, R. 2010. "Counterterrorism and Expert Regimes: Some Human Rights Concerns." *Critical Studies on Terrorism* 3 (2): 277–294. doi:10.1080/17539153.2010.491341.

Vermeulen, M., and R. Bellanova. 2012. "European 'Smart' Surveillance: What's at Stake for Data Protection, Privacy and Non-Discrimination?" *Security & Human Rights* 23 (4): 297–311. doi:10.1163/18750230-99900034.

Waldron, J. 2010. *Torture, Terror, and Trade-Offs: Philosophy for the White House*. Oxford: Oxford University Press.

Walzer, M. 1977. *Just and Unjust Wars: A Philosophical Argument with Historical Illustrations*. New York: Basic Books.

Wilson, R. A., ed. 2005. *Human Rights in the 'War on Terror'*. Cambridge: Cambridge University Press.

Wolff, R. P. 1977. "Robert Nozick's Derivation of the Minimal State." *Arizona Law Review* 45: 7–30.

How terrorism ends – and does not end: the Basque case

Joseba Zulaika and Imanol Murua

ABSTRACT

This article examines the end of ETA (Euskadi ta Askatasuna "Euskadi and Freedom") in the light of the literature on "how terrorism ends". Was it the result of police repression, defeat, negotiation, elimination, tactical success? Was it the result of military failure but not defeat? What role did the rebellion of its own social base play? Was it, in the end, a case of political transformation? The discourse of "unilateralism" developed by the Basque Nationalist Left is examined. The role of international actors and the so-called "virtual diplomacy" is situated in the context of the State and the global order. But did ETA really end? Four years after ETA declared its unconditional ceasefire, and after the international media considered it finished, the Spanish government does not think so. In conclusion, the article considers the lessons that derive from the Basque case regarding the issues of how terrorist groups end.

Introduction

The case of the Basque armed group ETA (Euskadi ta Askatasuna "Euskadi and Freedom") became in the work of many scholars a classical example to study how terrorist organisations operate. However, its cessation of violence in 2011 has not received much attention. When Jones and Libicky (2008) produced their book on the end of terrorist groups, ETA was still active, and they made no reference to the Basque case. Leonard Weinberg published a book devoted to the end of terrorist groups in 2012, when ETA was still in its final days, and thus he did not consider it as a base for his theories, except for a brief mention of its internal struggles between those in favour and those against armed struggle (2012). Neither does Audrey K. Cronin (2009) study in any depth the Basque case. At the same time, academic and journalistic analyses of ETA's ending of violence have been published in Spanish and in non-academic venues by, among others, Domínguez (2012), Escrivá (2012), Batista (2012), Aizpeolea (2013), López Adán (2012) and Zabalo and Saratxo (2015).

The one outstanding exception to the absence of interest in ETA's disappearance is Teresa Whitfield's *Endgame for ETA*. She has weaved in great detail a convincing narrative of the various perspectives and actors that took part in the process, with an emphasis on the participation of international agents in the final stages of the ending of

ETA. Murua's book *Ending ETA's Armed Campaign* (2017) provides a substantive complement to Whitfield's work. Having followed Basque politics as a journalist for decades and having interviewed extensively the main protagonists in the peace process, Murua brings the perspective internal to the Basque political actors. While comparing and expanding on Whitfield's work, this article sums up and elaborates on Murua (2016, 2017). The final argument is that ETA presents a distinctive case on "how terrorism ends".

How terrorism ends

Terrorist organisations can be so unstructured and improvisational that, almost by definition, no loss or challenge can be decisive enough to determine their "end" as long as there is one combatant willing to continue the fight. No matter how weakened the group or how anachronistic their armed struggle, the underground militant does not have to emerge from the shadows to sign a surrender. If the "exit strategy" is a key problem in any type of war, in the case or terrorism, due to the very informality and invisibility of its structures and tactics, there is simply no established exit strategy unless the underground group submits to one. The militants might consider after a while that the value of their continuation should not be measured mainly in military terms but in sheer resistance – "resisting is winning".

Cronin (2009) identified six patterns to explain the end of terrorism: decapitation, negotiation, success, failure, elimination by repression and reorientation into other forms of violence. Jones and Libicky (2008) distinguish five causes of the end of terrorist groups: joining the political process, defeat by police and intelligence agencies, defeat by military forces, goals achieved and splintering. Marta Crenshaw (2005) does not propose a single set of patterns, but different levels of analysis. First, she relates the decline of terrorism to the interplay of three factors: the government response, which could lead to a defeat of armed organisations; the strategic choices of the groups, which could lead to a decision to abandon violent means; and the lack of resources of the groups, which could lead them to organisational disintegration. Having distinguished three main factors, she focuses on the analysis of the choices made by the groups. She found three general sets of reasons for abandoning violent means: success in achieving the goals; decline of the utility of using violence for obtaining the goals and the availability of new alternatives preferable to violence. In an earlier work, Crenshaw foresaw a factor that proved pivotal for the Basque case examined here: terrorist group that decided to end the fight because of the withdrawal of support by its own base (1996, 264–268).

Weinberg (2012) proposes three general patterns: success, defeat and transformation. These three patterns sum up the main typologies concerning the end of armed groups. The other patterns proposed by the rest of the authors, such as decapitation, military repression, police repression, negotiation or reorientation, can be analysed as variables within these three general patterns. Defeat, success and transformation are not mutually exclusive. Both Cronin and Weinberg specify that these patterns are not necessarily separate and distinct, because more than one dynamic may provoke the demise of these groups. An awareness of imminent defeat, for instance, can provoke the transformation of a group, and a transformation can provoke some negotiations whose result can be considered a success by the rebel group.

The definitive end of ETA's campaign has produced diverse kinds of narratives. No narrative claims a total success or a total defeat. Most of the narratives are a combination of the three patterns; the success factor is dominant is some of them; the defeat factor clearly prevails in others; transformation is considered the key element in yet others.

"Are we winning or losing the Global War on Terror?" Donald Rumsfeld asked in a leaked memo in October of 2003. "Today we lack metrics to know", he replied to himself: "Are we capturing, killing or deterring and dissuading more terrorists every day than the madrassas and the radical clerics are recruiting, training and deploying against us?" (*USA Today*, 16 October 2003). The very framing of such victory or loss in merely quantitative terms is most problematic if we consider the metrics that really matter to the way terrorist groups think and operate. One only has to look at the Basque group ETA to realise that the continuation or end of terrorism depends on complex political and historical realities. Despite the fact that the Basque Country enjoys a high standard of living and substantive autonomy, and despite the overwhelming rejection of their violent tactics by Basques, ETA managed to endure for over half a century. It presents a singular case of what it means to end terrorism and allows for different readings. We should take into account what ETA's unilateral ceasefire means for Spain and for the international community, but also for the political movement to which ETA belongs, the Basque Nationalist Left, the perspective from which we begin.

Self-defeat and transformation

On 22 May 2007, having just attended the collapse of the peace process in Geneva, Arnaldo Otegi and Rufi Etxeberria were travelling back home by train. They could still see Paris in the distance, when Etxeberria commented to his colleague: "This model of negotiation and strategy is finished" (quoted in Munarriz 2012, 70). There had been a long history of negotiations between various Spanish governments, most notably in Algiers (1989) and during the Lizarra-Garazi ceasefire of 1998–1999, which had gone nowhere (Clark 1990; Azurmendi 2014). The failure of the latest negotiations during the years 2005–2007 with the Zapatero government, after ETA's bomb in Madrid's airport while the ceasefire was still on, seemed to put an end to any further negotiating hopes. The political leadership of the Basque Nationalist Left knew that they had reached a dead end. During the 2005–2007 years of negotiations, there had been a debate about whether to have "first peace and then politics" (the Spanish government and the Basque Nationalist Party (PNV)), or "first politics and then peace" (ETA and the Nationalist Left). But now there would be no negotiations, no politics or no peace to talk about.

ETA's endgame is not one of success. Many people who had identified with the armed group in their youths came to experience it as "gravestone" (Elzo 2014). But neither is it strictly one of military defeat, as the organisation had the means and the will to continue the armed struggle. Following Murua (2017), it can be best described as one of "failure" in achieving the military and strategic goals, while at the same time "transforming" itself into a new political entity. But what type of failure and transformation do we see in this endgame?

The dominant narrative in the Spanish media is clearly one of ETA's defeat at the hands of police repression and judicial intervention. There is much truth to this view, but it is by no means the full story. For this we must also listen to ETA's political arm's own narrative according to which the final decisive blow is the rebellion of its own social base. This article's thesis is that it is this view "internal" to ETA's political movement that makes the Basque case interesting for the literature on how terrorist groups end. That is, it is a case of transformation of a political base that results not from any negotiation (there was none) but from a unilateral decision by ETA and the Nationalist Left in the broader context of an ambiguous process in which international actors played a pivotal role.

ETA not only failed to achieve its overall strategic goals of Basque independence and socialism, but even the more "technical" issues such as settling the fate of the exiles and militants and prisoners in exchange for a permanent ceasefire and laying down the arms are still unsolved. Throughout its history, the Spanish police proclaimed countless times that ETA was in its final throes. In their structural and temporal indeterminacy, however, terrorist groups can never be "ended" as long as there is a splinter group with a minimal will to continue; no military or police blow can end the idea of resistance and the desire for the fight. ETA's own history provides examples of such a process of splintering with a weakened group carrying the name and the torch of the organisation. The only valid ending is contingent on the rebellious group's unanimous will to stop. In the case of ETA, that decision was dependent on the will of its social base. By ending the armed struggle without having achieved any of its goals or even securing the fate of its prisoners, ETA enacted a purposeful self-defeat facilitated and made visible by the Nationalist Left. But such a reflexive act after half a century of armed struggle, with hundreds of dead people on both sides and thousands of exiles and tortured victims, could only be the result of a deep transformation in their ways of thinking and acting.

Opaque organisational structure and the ultimate taboo

How was ETA brought to an end by its own political base? One essential tool was reshaping the organisational model of the Nationalist Left's power structure. This model consisted basically of a coordinating body controlling the entire movement, which included representatives from Batasuna (the main entity, a political party) as well as LAB (the movement's workers union), Askatasuna (a collective seeking amnesty for the prisoners), Segi (representing the nationalist youths) and Ekin ("a structure of political dynamization", the liaison between ETA and the Nationalist Left according to a ruling by the Spanish court for terrorism issues) (Murua 2017, 57, 80). And then there was ETA. In actual operational and subjective terms, ETA had been the deciding actor historically. As the underground armed organisation whose members were deemed "terrorists" by the State, and who had surrendered themselves to a life most likely resulting in torture, exile or death, ETA was since its inception the Nationalist Left's guiding reference. ETA de facto imposed its will in the overall strategy of the movement's military and political activities, including peace negotiations.

Critical to ETA's influence over the Nationalist Left was the very opaque structure of its decision-making bodies, about whose workings little was known. The reassessment of the relationship between ETA and its political base became the key power struggle within the entire movement after the collapse of the 2005–2007 negotiation process. When Batasuna called for a debate within the rank and file, a protracted struggle ensued between the leadership of Batasuna and other organisations of the Nationalist Left, each side producing its own document regarding what had to be done in the current circumstances.

ETA disagreed with the model of the debate and requested that it be cancelled, a petition that was contested by Batasuna leaders in defiance of ETA. "Where are the decisions made? Is someone developing a [strategic] line outside of the leadership?" a letter by ETA asked while rebuking Batasuna, which was determined to carry on with the debate regardless of ETA's will. Batasuna later produced an internal report stating that Batasuna "is the main organ of discussion and decision of the Nationalist Left social base", and that "it is wrong to believe that what is decided in a certain closed organ has to be accepted by all organizations and structures [of the movement]" (Murua 2010, 176–77). In the past, ETA had de facto resolved internal debates through military actions, but this time Batasuna let ETA know that nothing would stop their going forward with the debate and its consequences.

Batasuna called for a debate among its followers town by town. There were 274 meetings and over 7600 activists gave their opinion. A big majority of the social base supported the change of strategy proposed by the political leadership. Actual voting was rare in these meetings, but some authors estimated that about 80% backed the proposal (Letamendia 2013, 57–58). Everything had to be discussed. An unprecedented slogan was added as a prelude to the debate – "people should think without any taboo". One did not have to think much to realise where the taboos had been in the past. Being called to think for yourself meant that you could put into question ETA's modus operandi, which was the key element in "the politico-military strategy" of the entire movement. Batasuna's leadership was proposing that a pivotal change should be considered: the use of a strategy based on "politics alone" on the basis of "efficacy" – in short, a pragmatic perspective. The bases had to ask themselves the question: what serves best our long-term political interests? At a later stage, the Batasuna leadership proposed a document that included the need to adopt "the Mitchell principles" that guided the Irish peace process, which meant that only political means were acceptable. This was a way of saying the unsayable and without using the actual words – that the violence of the armed struggle had to be rejected.

A document drafted by Batasuna's leadership at the time, known as *Argitzen* ("Clarifying"), did not openly mention that what it proposed was the end of the armed struggle. The document mentioned a "democratic process", "the accumulation of strength", "the change of the balance of forces" and so on, but no mention of the elephant in the room: ETA and the armed struggle. The very topic of the value of the armed struggle was a taboo simply because it amounted to question the validity of half a century of sacrifice by thousands of militants who had been ready to give it all for the cause. The issue could be so explosive as to create a split within the movement – as it did in the past when members of ETA had questioned the priority of the armed struggle over the organisation of the working class. The document to be debated could not mention "armed struggle", but the members of Batasuna were called to *think* anything without any taboo. The Nationalist Left was getting into uncharted waters.

The end of the armed struggle was for all purposes the end of ETA. In the post-war history of the Nationalist Left battling Francoism and rejecting a Spanish democracy, ETA had been simply the origin and the militant organisation that anchored the entire movement. Could the struggle continue without ETA? In 1968, Txabi Etxebarrieta had marked the beginning of a tragic subject marked by the readiness to kill and die for the homeland as the exceptional request of a revolutionary moment. Since then, many thousands of Basques had been willing to give up everything for the Cause; now they were required to give up the war for the sake of a truly modern political subjectivity. Had their previous sacrifices been useless? The Batasuna leaders were confronting the end of ETA in order to save its historic legacy. They had to sacrifice their big Other in order to save its political truth.

The transformation required from the Nationalist Left went well beyond a tactical and even a strategic change. What was needed in the end was to leave behind a type of structure, politics and even persona that is typical of underground groups, and which can be described as characterised by informality and the polluting "formlessness" of taboo (see Zulaika and Douglass 1996, 151–152). It all had to be replaced with the explicit and regulated structure of normal politics in organisational, legal and social terms. Given the invisible and illegal nature of revolutionary/terrorist action, abrogation of form is quintessential to it – as expressed in its logic of chance, its disregard for any stable rule, the bluff of ritual threat, the contagiousness of taboo and the charismatic nature of the activist. This kind of politics is by its very nature underground, informal, disorderly, ritualistic in the sense that it makes good use of the cultural premise that "ritual recognizes the potency of disorder" (Douglas 1996, 94). The militant subject formed in this type of action ultimately relies not on parliamentarian or representative politics but on the charisma of revolutionary martyrdom. After the failure of the 2005–2007 negotiations, Batasuna had to change all of this. In short, it had to create a post-ETA type of politics and give form to a new political subject able to carry it out.

Why now?

But why now the call to think anything without any taboo? Why not 10 or 20 or 30 years ago?

Avoiding a split was a priority. The entire movement should follow it in unison for the reason that there could be no clear change of direction and no sense of closure if a splinter group continued in the name of ETA. If anything, it had been the convenience or not of the armed struggle that provoked various dissensions and splits in the past. A constant in the history of ETA had been the difficult coexistence between nationalism (justifying armed struggle) and socialism (insisting on the primacy of working class struggle); this had created major splits in the history of the organisation (Clark 1984; Jauregui 1981; Sullivan 1988; Woodworth 2001; Watson 2007).

After the post-Franco Spanish democracy in the late 1970s, the debate on the need of armed violence reached a crescendo. In 2001, a faction from the Nationalist Left openly critical of ETA's violence decided to split from the movement and form its own party, Aralar. Batasuna was outlawed in 2003; the banning of the party and the failure of 2005–2007 peace process clearly hurt the Nationalist Left's electoral chances. By 2011, the IRA and other armed groups had vanished in Europe; the post-9/11 international discourse on the "war on terror" had taken hold (its Spanish version being the Madrid bombings of 11 March 2004, mendaciously attributed to ETA by Aznar's government). All these facts were arguments for Batasuna to convince its base that it was time for an historic change.

It had to be everyone or no one – even if this required a unilateral decision; it had to be taken in unison and by unanimity. Or else it would not be a change of direction of the "transatlantic ship", but simply one more split in which a new branch might carry with it ETA's name and movement. There were segments of the Nationalist Left who clearly wanted ETA to continue no matter who left the boat, cognizant that what had maintained the torch up to now had not been political expediency but a blind determination, an amor fati, to affirm what seemed impossible – Basque independence from Spain and France's military oppression.

Everything is ETA

As the Batasuna leaders were about to distribute the report *Argitzen* advocating an exclusively political strategy, judge Baltasar Garzon ordered the arrest of the entire leadership, including Otegi, in October 2009. They were accused of reconstituting a post-Batasuna political party under ETA's orders. The obvious question was: why they should be arrested now, the very people who were trying to move away from violence, at the very moment they were forcing ETA to change course? There is always recourse to the independence of the judiciary as an explanation, but in issues having to do with ETA, most Basques are sceptical as to the impartiality of the Spanish judiciary; there was not much doubt among Basque political leaders of various parties that the Spanish Home Minister Alfredo Perez Rubalcaba was behind the arrests. The principle under which much of the Spanish media and judiciary had gotten used to operating was that in the Nationalist Left "everything is ETA".

Already during the 2006 ceasefire, an unexpected pattern took over Spanish politics: "a series of judicial actions that appeared to be deliberately sabotaging the peace process. Old cases were resurrected from the archives and new ones pursued in what was the highest rate of prosecution of cases related to Basque terrorism (some eighty during the ceasefire) during Spanish democracy" (Whitfield 2014, 167). The pattern continued after the collapse of the ceasefire in 2007, when judge Garzon ordered the detention of most of the leadership of the Nationalist Left. In December, the Audiencia Nacional[1] charged another 47 members of civil organisations for their alleged ties to ETA. But the judicial overreach would reach new heights in 2009 during the process in which Batasuna's leaders were moving their base away from ETA's armed struggle, and were rewarded with jail terms of 10 years under allegations that they were acting under ETA's instructions. It had to be either a fundamental intelligence failure or a sabotage against the possibility to achieve the end of ETA. Otegi had been the main interlocutor with the socialist José Luis Zapatero's government through the mediation of Jesús Egiguren, as well as with the international actors in the process. The socialist Eguiguren would go visit Otegi in prison; he even went to Otegi's trial and shook hands with him as a sign of his respect for his political antagonist. But the Spanish right had a vested interest in continuing to define him, even after he had brought ETA to end its armed struggle, as a "pure and simple terrorist" (ABC editorial, 18 September 2011).

Years after ETA definitively ended violence, Otegi and various other Batasuna leaders remained imprisoned, leading many Basques to wonder whether they are in prison *because* they forced ETA to stop. A pattern emerged by which each step by the Nationalist Left towards a change of course would be met with scepticism and downright hostility by the government and the Spanish mainstream media. On 14 April 2010, as the collective of ETA's prisoners was discussing the new political strategy, 10 people were arrested and accused of liaising between ETA and its prisoners, three of them lawyers. On 14 September 2010, nine alleged members of the leadership of Ekin were jailed. On 11 January 2011, ETA declared a permanent and verifiable ceasefire, and a week later, 10 members of Nationalist Left's leadership were arrested by the Spanish police. Some of them claimed to have been tortured. The question could not be avoided: Was the government unhappy that ETA had announced a permanent ceasefire? The Nationalist Left had little doubt as to what the aim of Zapatero's government was with Rubalcaba as its Home Minister: to provoke a split within the movement by arresting the leaders. The end result of such a split, if it were to happen, was clear: the continuation of the armed struggle by an irreducible core of ETA's supporters and the endless perpetuation of "terrorism".

Unilateralism regarding ETA and the state: "a revolution in thought and politics"

Every Spanish prime minister since the transition had always vowed no negotiation with ETA only to later end up trying to negotiate. As the campaign for general elections of March 2008 began, both leaders of the main Spanish parties, the Socialist Zapatero and the opposition leader Mariano Rajoy, vowed once again there was no place for dialogue with ETA, even if 84% of the Basques thought the opposite. The Basque moderate nationalists of the PNV, despite their anger at ETA's intransigence, could not take an attitude of doing nothing; their president, Ibarretxe, had proposed a consultation in the summer of 2007 to ask whether there would be support for a solution through dialogue after ETA's unequivocal intention to end violence, and whether Basque political parties should start negotiations for an agreement on the right to decide. The proposal would pass the Basque Parliament in June 2008, but was turned down as unconstitutional by the Constitutional Court.

During the years 2009 and 2010, the government's firm position was voiced repeatedly through the Spanish Home minister, Rubalcaba: there would be no negotiations. The State reduced ETA to its weakest position and Batasuna had been illegalised by the Spanish judiciary and its work seriously hampered. The last blow, one of great political and symbolic significance, took place in June of 2009 when the European Court of Human Rights ratified the banning of Batasuna, alleging its complicity with ETA. The State was safe in resorting to the old mantra that there was no reason that it should engage in any negotiation with a terrorist group.

But a move unanticipated by the State was about to happen. Suddenly, the Nationalist Left decided a new strategy it called *unilateralism*. Otegi, the leader and spokesperson for the movement, added that unilateralism would give way to a true "revolution in thought and politics" (quoted in Munarriz 2012, 146). How so? What the new axiom pretended was the transformation of the Nationalist Left's devastating failure into a new historic opportunity.

If anything, the long struggle for Basque "freedom" (ETA's acronym stands for "Euskadi and Freedom") translated in political terms into Basque "independence" has been a dogged fight against the State's various military, police, legal, media and educational branches. The fight created casualties in the form of victims, prisoners, exiles and so on, and the handling of this long chain of suffering created more antagonism against the State. What did it mean that "unilateralism" was a strategic solution now? Wasn't this alleged solution simply the result of age, Otegi wondered, "the biological factor" (quoted in Munarriz 2012, 146) telling them that they had fought enough and it was now time to give up without actually having achieved much of anything? Add to this the experience of those in jail, whose basic perception is "that everything continues to be the same" and it is hard not to avoid the feeling that "unilateralism is taking us nowhere" (Jokin Urain quoted in Murua 2017, 124).

ETA seriously weakened, Batasuna illegalised, the entire Nationalist Left isolated internationally, it might seem only natural that there was no other way out but unilateralism. But it had looked like that for decades, at least since Bidart 1992, when the entire leadership of ETA had been arrested, and it had resisted and resisted against all odds. In such moments of crisis, ETA had shown that its strength should not be measured primarily in terms of military power but rather as an idea and blind determination. ETA cadres were ready and willing to continue, to the chagrin of the Batasuna's leaders.

The challenge in such a situation was not only the adoption of unilateralism by a Batasuna leadership that saw their political capital evaporating – that seemed the easy part. The real challenge was convincing their base that they were all in the same boat and that it had to be unilateralism with unanimity, or else the boat was about to sink. It was the transformation of their base's thinking that was the hardest. Confronting a future without ETA required a new political subject willing to believe in politics alone without the narcissism of identifying with an armed group who seemingly would always be there to save them from their weakness. Now it all would depend on something as ephemeral and unstable as citizens' ballots. What if the electorate did not understand that what was at stake here is a Cause that is more than an ordinary political cause? And here was the final demand for the sake of a truly modern political subject: even the Cause might have to be sacrificed for the sake of its truth. This was the hardest *transformation* – its toughness only comparable to the willingness to give it all for the Cause.

After half a century of armed struggle, ETA was finally ending in complete failure, all its military and strategic goals unachieved. ETA was being defeated by the will of its own political base demanding that the group quit unilaterally. Generations of ETA followers, who had identified with the underground organisation and dreamt of Basque independence and socialism, suddenly had to come to terms with the prospect that their political messiah had never been as revolutionary as when it ceased to be. These same generations, so willing until recently to combat the Spanish State, were now becoming aware that their declaration of unilateral politics meant that the real enemy was not some all-controlling State power but the lack of unity and purpose in their own nationalist community.

But such a historic move carried with it an implicit next logical step: if ETA had to abandon its armed struggle unilaterally and without conditions, if the Nationalist Left could give up ETA, why not do something similar with the Spanish State? If they did not need an armed branch to fight militarily the State, why did they need dependence on the State's reactions to a struggle that was no longer directed against it? ETA and the Spanish State: these had been the two big Others in the Basque military and political imaginary of the post-war resistance, battling each other since the 1960s, despite their very uneven forms. Suddenly, ETA had been forced to dissolve; what if its political movement, the Nationalist Left, were to resort to "unilateralism" regarding the Spanish State – namely, a conscious attitude not to remain "waiting for anyone or anything" (Otegi quoted in Munarriz 2012, 99), not to depend on the State's reactions to carry out the disarmament and the adjustment to the new political conditions? The founder of Aralar, Patxi Zabaleta, had anticipated such a "Copernican change" of unilaterally giving up armed struggle when he advocated that it had to be done in exchange for nothing, "without any concrete achievement" (quoted in Whitfield 2014, 228).

It was to be taken for granted that the State would do anything in its power to obstruct the reconstitution of the Nationalist Left by turning ETA's loss into a political victory. Thus, let there be a unilateral surrender by ETA, let everyone know that there will be no "terrorism" contagion in the future. But also, let the State know that we are no longer interested in fighting some quixotic battle against the windmills of the Spanish military. ETA's failure would force a radical transformation of committing themselves to "politics alone". In the very space left vacant by the de facto disappearance of ETA and the State, "a revolution in thought and politics" was taking place. Let the State believe they have scored a "victory" by forcing the end of the armed struggle in exchange for nothing; let the Nationalist Left be empowered by the unique symbolism of their willing determination to enact a historic "failure" – sacrificing a militant revolution for the sake of transforming it into its next stage.

International actors and virtual diplomacy

The Nationalist Left's adoption of a unilateral strategy was prompted in good part by the State's unwillingness to engage in any negotiation process. The strategy had two recipients: Basque society and the international community. Several international agencies had participated in the failed negotiations of 2005–2007, the Center Henri Dunant for Humanitarian Dialogue in Geneva in particular, but also the Norwegian and British governments and the Irish Sinn Fein. Whitfield has chronicled in a balanced narrative the participation of the international actors. One of her subheadings in the search for a way out of the Basque crisis is entitled, tellingly, "the great taboo" – namely, "the involvement of an external third party" in the process (2014, 122). Third parties have been common and instrumental in Ireland, Colombia, Indonesia, Sri Lanka and other many situations of political violence. Spain championed in 1991 the Madrid Conference on the Palestinian problem when Felipe González was prime minister and for many years it appealed successfully to the international community in the fight against ETA's terrorism, but the prospect that an international agency might help facilitate the end of the conflict became "taboo".

The fear was that it would be an infringement on Spanish sovereignty. As José Luis Barbería put it in *El País*, Spain was becoming a "pole of attraction for international experts in conflict resolution – the well-known 'mediation industry'" (1 June 2008). The mere prospect that ETA might want an international verification commission similar to the one they had in Northern Ireland led by John de Chastelain was hardly acceptable. As the same paper put it in an editorial, Spain could "under no circumstances delegate functions which affect the security of threatened citizens to international personalities or organizations, however respectable they might be" (quoted in Whitfield 2014, 233). When the international actors were going to launch the so-called "Brussels Declaration" to fuel a peace process, several news media considered the international negotiators naïve people manipulated by ETA. The declaration demanded a ceasefire from ETA but this in itself was most questionable because, as critics of the peace process pointed out, reinforcing the narrative of conflict was already framing the issue in terms favourable to the terrorists (Uriarte 2013; Arregi Aranburu 2015). The international signatories were intruding on Spanish sovereignty primarily by calling a "conflict" what should be called, according to those critics, squarely and exclusively "terrorism".

Among the international facilitators involved in the Basque case, the South African lawyer Brian Currin became a pivotal actor during the final years leading to the end of ETA. He had been involved in his country's Truth and Reconciliation Commission as well as in Northern Ireland's peace process. Two months after the collapse of the ceasefire in May of 2007, Currin was in San Sebastián to meet with Batasuna representatives. He trusted the Batasuna leadership at a time when almost nobody trusted them; he believed they were genuine in their commitment for a renunciation of violence, and he decided to help them in the transition.

One would think that Currin's efforts of promoting Batasuna's radical change of direction would be welcomed by everyone. Nothing was further from reality. His efforts became disquieting to the Spanish government, which requested other governments not to meet with him nor to fund him. The efforts by Currin and his group were a major support for Batasuna's leaders in their internal struggle to steer the Nationalist Left away from violence; the international cover was key in convincing their social base of the radical change that was needed in order not to lose all the political capital accumulated during half a century of political resistance. With the support of the local negotiation group, Lokarri, Currin increasingly became a vocal proponent of the Nationalist Left's efforts. He proposed the declaration of Brussels endorsed by 20 signatories, including four Nobel Prize laureates, the former president and former prime minister of Ireland and the Nelson Mandela Foundation.

The Brussels statement of March 2010 affirmed the Nationalist Left's commitment to a "total absence of violence" and to "exclusively political and democratic" means. The signatories appealed for the support of the statement to ETA "by declaring a permanent, fully verified ceasefire" (Murua 2017, 96–97) and to the Spanish Government by requesting an appropriate response. The statement provided ETA with the coverage it needed to give a ceasefire without appearing to cede to Madrid´s demands. In November 2010, Currin created an International Contact Group to assist "political normalisation". All of this brought Currin much criticism from those non-aligned with the Nationalist Left who believed that the only way to move forward was by not helping them and forcing them to accept defeat and nothing else; Rubalcaba dismissed him as being nothing but a mediator between Batasuna and ETA; an association of victims even demanded that he should be investigated for providing "material support" to terrorism.

"We did the campaign for them"

Having unilaterally called for a ceasefire, and still debating a radical change of direction in their movement, all that mattered now to the Nationalist Left was participation in the upcoming elections of May 2011. Batasuna had been illegalised in 2003 for its ties to ETA (a measure *The Economist* thought was a mistake), thus disenfranchising about 15% of the Basque electorate at the time. With a few exceptions, each umbrella party into which Batasuna had morphed to contest elections had been banned. *Sortu*, the post-ceasefire reformulation of Batasuna, with a clear renunciation of violence as requested by the law of political parties, had also been banned. This time the Nationalist Left looked for alliances with other parties whose legality had never been questioned; it found them in two parties that agreed to create an electoral coalition with pro-independent actors who were not "contaminated" by former political activism filling in for Batasuna, representatives who had previously signed a commitment to reject any use of violence (some 40,000 people loyal to Batasuna were dismissed as potential representatives). They named the coalition *Bildu* ("To Join"). But even Bildu was banned by the Supreme Court, a ban that was disapproved by a substantive majority of Basques.

Election after election, the legal fate of the party that represented the Nationalist Left became a political issue. For the Basque public, it was a given that the Supreme Court or the Constitutional Court would rule according to what the government in turn wanted.[2] In the Zapatero government, there were members sceptical about the possibilities of a resolution and opposed to granting the Nationalist Left any electoral opportunity, but it was also under much pressure from key allies such as the PNV to grant permission for Bildu to contest elections. In the end, the Zapatero government's will to allow the legalisation of Bildu prevailed narrowly in the Constitutional Court, provoking the ire of the Spanish right.

The Basque nationalist media had received the news of ETA's September 2010 ceasefire positively. The mainstream Spanish and Basque media pointed out the insufficiency of the step forward, while the Spanish right-wing presented it in entirely negative terms, as if the cessation of the armed struggle were in fact bad news – a portrayal that would be repeated even after the October 2011 ETA declaration of complete and definitive ceasefire. Was the end of ETA actually bad news for Spain? The Spanish ambivalence became glaring: on the one hand, ETA was "an illegal band guilty of the perpetration" of many crimes; on the other hand, it prevented Basque nationalists' broad alliances and allowed successive Spanish governments to dismiss nationalist claims "with a tacit understanding that the continuation of ETA's violence at a manageably low level was the least bad option available" (Whitfield 2014, 301). The perception that Spain preferred the continuation of ETA became widely shared among Basques. Elections would be the way to measure Basque public's reaction.

When election day finally arrived, the electorate knew what was at stake. In coalition with other forces under the umbrella coalition Bildu, the Nationalist Left collected its best results ever: 313,000 ballots or 26% of the electorate. They obtained the mayoralty of 113 towns, including San Sebastián, as well as Gipuzkoa's Provincial Hall. This was the same movement that used to receive around 250,000 votes at the peak of their electoral successes of the 1980s and 270,000 during the 1998–1999 peace process (a whopping 15%-18%). Later, embattled by repression and illegalisation, its electoral support went significantly down, although their actual support was difficult to measure because their votes were usually counted as non-valid: in the Basque parliament elections (non-including Navarre), their electorate had gone down to 150,000 in 2005 and 100,000 in 2009. The trend was a gradual and continuous decrease of electoral support, before it emerged as the great winner in 2011. Alluding to the politicisation of the judiciary and the anti-terrorism hysteria, Odon Elorza, the San Sebastián Socialist mayor who had lost to Bildu, concluded: "We did the campaign for them".

The electorate knew that it was the sheer need for political survival that had pushed the Nationalist Left into giving up the armed struggle and developing their new discourse around unilateralism – and that their "conversion" might be instrumental rather than a deep rejection of their support, until just yesterday, of ETA's violent means. And yet for an entire generation of Basques, this was the greatest political news in a very long time. There was the immediate reason that, in the internal struggle between the forces advocating politics alone and those still favouring the continuation of ETA, casting a ballot for Bildu/the Nationalist Left was a reinforcement of the first option. The electoral results confirmed the validity of the political option and ended definitively the debate with ETA.

But there were other implications of the "end of ETA" for a generation that, even if lately opposed to it, had in the past deeply identified with the armed group and supported it. ETA's submission to the decision taken by its base could be taken by this generation as a proof that, beyond terrorism, its goals had been ultimately political in nature. The people casting the ballot for Bildu were doing so in part because they wanted a *political* end to the shame and drama of a generation, rather than the criminal end of senseless terrorism (Elejabarrieta 2015). The electorate had to agree and make the transformation happen. We could say that the Basque electorate was faced with a self-fulfilling double bind: if we consider them terrorists and do not vote for them, then terrorism will continue; if we vote for them as a sign that their struggle is political and not terroristic, then terrorism will end. How ETA's terrorism ended can be summarised thus: it ended by its Basque political base telling ETA that they were *not* terrorists, while at the same time demanding from them *not* to practice terrorism in their name.

Theatre, the state and the global order

Many within the Popular Party, the Spanish right-wing party that replaced Zapatero's government by the end of 2011, would never forgive the Socialists the one capital sin they had committed while in power: allowing Bildu to contest the May 2011 elections. The result was there for everyone to see: as the Nationalist Left came out as the great victor, it was its participation in democratic elections that turned into a political disaster for the Spanish democracy. The victims' associations reacted vociferously. During Zapatero's eight years in power, ETA had killed eight people; the conservative writer Luis María Ansón compared ETA to a small ulcer which might bleed but does not kill. Now there would not be the yearly one or two average killings by ETA, but instead you had a political coalition (that for the Spanish right was ETA itself) governing over 100 towns and one of the three provinces in the Basque autonomous community. What could have been more calamitous politically? It was not surprising that once in power, the Popular Party would be in no hurry to produce the steps necessary to bring ETA's end to its final conclusion.

The position of the Spanish right towards the resolution of the conflict was best expressed by the hardliner former Home Minister Jaime Mayor Oreja. He interpreted the end of ETA and Bildu's electoral success squarely in terms of ETA's triumph (Murua 2017, 114–115). From this perspective, not only is ETA and the Nationalist Left the same thing, but there is hardly any difference between obtaining their pro-independence goals through the bullet or the ballot. This is a reflection of the ultimate political antagonism between Basque and Spanish nationalisms.

But this was not the case with the Spanish Socialists, who never discarded dialogue as a tool to facilitate the end of ETA, and regarded the reintegration of the Nationalist Left in electoral politics as a key element. The Socialists would not only allow Bildu to contest elections, but also to have secret contacts with the international actors which would lead to the hastily arranged but momentous October 2011 peace conference of Aiete in San Sebastián. There had been communication between the international actors and the government, but never direct talks; it was all *virtual peacemaking*. As a result, the international facilitators managed to agree on a confidential road map with both ETA and the Spanish government, never confirmed by the latter. Only the existence of such a map would explain the series of events that preceded the definitive end of ETA's campaign – such as the subscription of the prisoners' collective to the new political line, the formation of the International Verification Commission and the peace conference of Aiete.

Distinguished international leaders, headed by the former UN Secretary-General Kofi Annan, attended the Aiete conference.[3] They read a document calling upon ETA to end armed activities, asking the Spanish and French governments to talk with ETA in order to deal with the consequences of the conflict, such as disarmament and prisoners, and advising the Basque political parties to initiate a political dialogue to address the roots of the conflict. Three days later, ETA declared a permanent and definitive ceasefire, thus ending four decades of violence.

Critics scorned the Aiete conference as nothing but theatre. Yet it was a much needed theatre to counter the theatre of the State's sovereign power. The government did not organise the Aiete conference, but it allowed it, as this was what Batasuna needed to reassure its base. An international conference shaping the issue as a political conflict was what ETA needed to save face while ending. There was also the risk of what it might do to Spain's international reputation if people such as Kofi Annan were not allowed to come on a peace mission, later to be backed by Tony Blair (who published his support in the *New York Times*), Jimmy Carter and George Mitchell. Rubalcaba, the man in Madrid in charge of counterterrorist policy at the time, commented sarcastically: "if the price to pay for ETA to abandon its violence is that Kofi Annan comes to San Sebastián, I would buy the ticket myself" (Whitfield 2014, 262).

In short, it was a parody of a peace conference for Spain, and yet ETA and the Nationalist Left were smart enough to turn the parody into the real thing. Their seriousness was de facto implicitly telling Spain: in order to get by with the unilateral approach to disarmament, this is the only "parody" that is needed, the one recognised by international actors and not the one based on Spanish constitutional legitimacy. There was no formal peace agreement or anything, and yet the act itself, witnessed by international signatories, was enough for ETA and the Nationalist Left to make a decision that changed the course of action 180 degrees – it was as historic as ETA's decision during the late 1960s to engage in a politico-military strategy of armed struggle. Aiete allowed the replacement of the Spanish State with the representation of an international community. It could be said that the consequences of Aiete's theatrical tolerance were historically transformative for the Nationalist Left in that it turned the presence of the Spanish State into a sideshow, while it was the international community that acted as the ultimate witness – the only political big Other that was taken as such.

The parody in which the Nationalist Left, the Spanish State and the international actors were involved consisted in that, at the end of the day, one cannot write that in the Basque case, strictly speaking, there were "negotiations", or a "peace process", or a "conference", or a "mediation" by any foreign institution, or an "end" for that matter of the conflict – indeed, even calling it a "conflict" is a misnomer and an anathema for much of the Spanish elites and media. And yet there was all of it as well.

In the end, the debates about negotiations that are not negotiations, and peace conferences that are not peace conferences, and ending of terrorist groups that are not endings, as well as transformative changes by adopting "unilateralism" and the like, are intimately related to the changing status of the sovereignty of a nation state which is increasingly being transferred to the new global society ruled by what Michael Hardt and Antonio Negri called *Empire* (2001). It is not that sovereignty has evaporated with the decline of the nation states, but that it has taken new national or supranational forms, ruled by a new capitalist order that brings together economic and political powers. As illustrated by the Irish or Colombian cases, even the successful resolution of terrorism conflicts calls in this new order for the involvement of what Castells calls a *network state* (1999, 30) – Great Britain, Ireland and the U.S. in the Irish case, several South American countries in the Colombian case.

Something similar was bound to happen in the Basque case as well. Unlike Great Britain in the Irish case, Spain failed to accept the normalcy of such transference of sovereignty to the network of international organisations and actors, and this despite the close collaboration between Zapatero and Blair. Zapatero's government realised that the end of terrorism required international actors, and allowed for them while keeping a distance from them. This added the sense of "theatre" and "comedy" to the entire dialogue process that was officially denied while it was taking place.

But beyond Spain and the international community, what kind of negotiation and peace process did or did not happen for the Nationalist Left? Here it is where the issue of "unilateralism" gets its full relevance. Political unilateralism in the Spanish context goes here hand in hand with implanting the international community as witness. It is as if the Basque Nationalist Left had been driven by Spanish intransigence into the realisation that, in order to turn their political project into *reality*, they first had to turn the State into *theatre* and transfer true sovereignty to the international order.

How terrorism does not end

On 21 October 2011, Tony Blair published an op-ed piece in the *New York Times* entitled "A Basque Peace" in which he commended Zapatero and Rubalcaba for their "firmness", but then added that a lesson to be learned from the Basque case is that "governments must also recognize the need to 'talk to their enemies'" and that beside security pressure they must provide a "way out" to the militants. Drawing a comparison with Ireland, he wrote that what is left now is dealing with the "consequences" of the conflict, which are "necessary to assure the dissolution of ETA as a military force". This final stage had been drafted in the confidential road map outlined by international facilitators and was publicly demanded by the signatories of the final declaration of the Aiete Conference. But this is what Rajoy's new government would refuse to do.

To put an end to any violent process, one expects concessions from both parts. "Peace for prisoners" had been the last hope for Basque prisoners when the real political goals of the right to self-determination and territoriality were already beyond any reach. But now, with ETA weakened and its movement clearly looking for an end to violence, the Spanish government felt emboldened to deny the most minimal concessions, including a more humane treatment of ETA's hundreds of prisoners within the existing laws.

The organisations of ETA victims took a leading role in opposing any negotiation with ETA; they undermined the efforts of the Zapatero government and constrained Rajoy from showing more flexibility towards the prisoners. In the name of justice and morality, they were given a pivotal voice in deciding political issues in counterterrorist terms. As a result,

> Spain refuses any forgiveness or partial amnesty for ETA's crimes and killings. Yet Spain fully amnestied all the killers and torturers of the Franco regime and – even years later – refused all appeals by victims of the dictatorship and their family members for recognition and some form of justice. Spain, almost uniquely in the world – much less Europe – has even been unwilling to fully identify and uncover graves of leftist forces and victims of Franco during the Civil War. (Whitfield 2014, 310)

It was not enough that all the steps had been taken unilaterally by ETA and the Nationalist Left without any political concessions from the government. Still, the peace process could not be accepted as an achievement. The nationalist movement wanted now to move forward towards ETA's disarmament and dissolution – but disarm to whom?

The dominant discourse in Spain regarding the end of ETA, including the more liberal opinion such as *El País*, was that it should be "an end without a process" – namely, as the result of police and judicial work. But soon people began to have second thoughts about even the very idea of "an end", for "as the likelihood of ETA's end began to approach, a kind of collective vertigo affected the Spanish right and the media it controlled" (Whitfield 2014, 214). The Socialists might indeed benefit from such ending for electoral purposes, the Popular Party feared. As so often before in Spanish politics, the two main parties were dealing with the end or continuation of "the Basque problem" through the terms of what was more advantageous for their own next electoral politics. Bildu's historic victory was de facto what "an end without a process" had produced.

Did the government ever accept the very fact that ETA's violence had ended? Before going to the October 2011 Aiete conference in San Sebastián, Zapatero had reassured Kofi Annan that this really was the end of ETA. It would soon be obvious to everyone that ETA had ended its military campaign for good. But did ETA as such and ETA's *terrorism* in particular really end for the Spanish government? The answer is no.

The State might be theatrical in its acting and non-acting, but it holds the power to keep jailed hundreds of ETA prisoners. The international actors thought that conditions existed to permit discussions to begin to disband ETA forever. According to a Basque government's survey, 72% of the citizens were in favour of the reinsertion of prisoners who renounced violence (Sociometro vasco 48, March 2012). Instead, under the pressure of right-wing sectors close to Aznar and Major Oreja and victims' associations, the government "refused to assume the flexibility in penitentiary policy advocated by the PSOE and PNV ... and rejected all offers of international assistance to facilitated it while pursuing ETA with the full force of the police and law" (Whitfield 2014, 267). One of the ETA leaders who read the declaration to end the violence was arrested. Lawyers of ETA prisoners and numbers of activists involved in prisoners' issues were arrested in the post-ETA period: 18 activists in September 2013, two lawyers and six activists in January 2014, and 12 lawyers and four activists in January 2015. Most of them were released on bail, and some of them held in preventive detention. What was presented as a principled stance of justice for past crimes appeared to international mediators as "an almost inexplicable rejection of all that experience elsewhere – and indeed common sense – suggested about the value of building confidence in the shift of violent actors towards peace" (Whitfield 2014, 267). After the Aiete Conference and at the request of the Socialist government, Norway had agreed to shelter the political leadership of ETA to facilitate contacts with the international verifiers, but the new Popular Party government refused to attend the meetings, and Norway ended up expelling ETA's delegation.

The international actors treated the Basque issue as "a conflict". This in itself was intolerable to the Spanish politicians who saw no political conflict but only a case of "terrorism". The difference in discourse became a major stumbling block for reaching an end of ETA. The politicians and the public would continue to be hostages of the terrorism discourse. About 69% of citizens of the Basque Autonomous Community favoured moving their prisoners to the Basque Country (Sociometro vasco 48, March 2012), but 60% of Spaniards were opposed to it and 66% were against granting them the benefits equal to other prisoners (CIS barómetro, November 2011) – ETA prisoners were "terrorists" and worse than ordinary criminals.

Rubalcaba, the victor in ETA's surrender, summed up best the entire conundrum: "After winning the war, what we cannot allow is that they [ETA] win the peace" (quoted in Barbería 2011). The democratic State had been victorious in winning the war, but amazingly the "terrorists" appeared victorious in winning the peace. But how could that be? While terrorists were willing to end the fight, counterterrorists were unprepared to accept the new status quo outside of the coordinates of terrorism discourse and legality. In short, peace meant "victory" for terrorists and "defeat" for counterterrorists. This provides the classical ground for counterterrorism aiming at terrorism perpetuating itself by becoming a self-fulfilling prophecy (Zulaika 2009).

Conclusion

In conclusion, we propose that the changes in the basic coordinates of the Basque political situation reveal the following pivotal lessons behind ETA's ending *and* non-ending. Terrorist groups end not only as the result of police repression and military defeat, or else by having succeeded in achieving the intended goals, but also when (a) prompted by failure, their political base compels them to cease the violence; (b) thus they deny the State its grip on the discourse of terrorism; (c) "a revolution in thought and politics" makes them take unilateral positions irrespective of their antagonist's reactions; (d) allow for mediating "third parties" as witnesses to the definitive disarmament and (e) define the "ending" from the perspective of their political base and the international community.

Alternatively, terrorist groups are prevented from ending when (a) terrorism or counterterrorism obtain political benefits from the status quo (as when terrorism has been reduced into an inconvenient "ulcer"); (b) the discourse of terrorism invalidates the political goals of the enemy; (c) one party in the struggle does not recognise unilateral moves by the other; (d) no mediating "third party" is allowed to intervene or (e) one of the contending parties does not want to determine an "ending" to the conflict.

Disclosure statement

No potential conflict of interest was reported by the authors.

Notes

1. A court created in 1977 to address terrorism issues.
2. Among other many instances, egregious cases such as arbitrary closing of the only Basque newspaper *Egunkaria*, on the specious argument that "everything is ETA", and years later proven to be entirely baseless, made Basques lose all respect for the Spanish judicial system.
3. Besides Annan, other participants included Bertie Ahern, the former prime minister of Ireland; Gro Harlem Bruntland, the former prime minister of Norway; Jonathan Powell, Tony Blair's former chief of staff; Pierre Joxe, former French interior minister and Gerry Adams of Sinn Fein.

References

Aizpeolea, L. R. 2013. *Los entresijos del final ETA: Un intento de recuperar una historia manipulada*. Madrid: Los Libros de la Catarata.

Arregi Aranburu, J. 2015. *El terror de ETA. La narrativa de las víctimas*. Madrid: Tecnos.

Azurmendi, J. F. 2014. *ETA de principio a fin. Crónica documentada de un relato*. Donostia: Ttarttalo.

Barbería, J. L. 2008. "Las ´embajadas´ de ETA." *El País*, June 1.

Barbería, J. L. 2011. "Listo para el gran ´spring´." *El País*, July 3.

Batista, A. 2012. *Adiós a las armas: Una crónica del final de ETA*. Barcelona: Debate.

Castells, M. 1999. "Globalization, Identity, and the Basque Question." In *Basque Politics and Nationalism on the Eve of the Millennium*, edited by W. A. Douglass. Reno: Basque Studies Program, UNR.

CIS (Centro de Investigaciones Sociológicas), barómetro, Nov. 2011. http://datos.cis.es/pdf/Es2917mar_A.pdf[datos.cis.es]

Clark, R. P. 1984. *The Basque Insurgents: ETA, 1952-1980*. Madison: University of Wisconsin Press.

Clark, R. P. 1990. *Negotiating with ETA: Obstacles to Peace in the Basque Country, 1975-1988*. Reno: University of Nevada Press.

Crenshaw, M. 1996. "Why Violence Is Renounced or Rejected: A Case Study of Oppositional Terrorism." In *A Natural History of Peace*, edited by T. Gregor, 249–272. Nashville: Vanderbilt University Press.

Crenshaw, M. 2005. "Pathways Out of Terrorism: A Conceptual Framework." In *Pathways Out of Terrorism and Insurgency. the Dynamics of Terrorist Violence and the Peace Processes*, edited by S. Germani and D. R. Kaarthikeyan, 3–11. Elgin: New Dawn Press.

Cronin, A. K. 2009. *How Terrorism Ends: Understanding the Decline and Demise of Terrorist Campaigns*. Princeton: Princeton University Press.

Domínguez, F. 2012. *La agonía de ETA: Una investigación inédita sobre los últimos días de la banda*. Madrid: La Esfera de los Libros.

Douglas, M. 1996. *Purity and Danger*. London: Routledge and Kegan Paul.

Elejabarrieta, G. 2015. "From Freedom Fighters to Terrorists and Back Again." In *Researching Terrorism, Peace and Conflict Studies: Interaction, Synthesis and Opposition*, edited by I. Tellidis and H. Toros. New York: Routledge.

Elzo, J. 2014. *La losa de ETA. Por una sociedad vasca justa y reconciliada*. Madrid: PPC.

Escrivá, A. 2012. *Maldito el país que necesita héroes: Cómo los demócratas acabaron con ETA*. Madrid: Temas de Hoy.

Hardt, M., and A. Negri. 2001. *Empire*. Cambridge: Harvard University Press.

Jauregui, G. 1981. *Ideología y estrategia política de ETA: análisis de su evolución entre 1959 y 1968*. Madrid: Siglo XXI.

Jones, S. G., and M. C. Libicky. 2008. *How Terrorist Groups End: Lessons for Countering Al Qa'ida*. Santa Monica, CA: Rand.

Letamendia, F. 2013. *Dos ensayos vascos*. Madrid: Fundamentos.

López Adán, E. 2012. *ETAren estrategia armatuaren historiaz*. Baiona: Maiatz.

Munarriz, F. 2012. *El tiempo de las luces. Entrevista con Arnaldo Otegi*. Donostia: Gara.

Murua, I. 2010. *El triángulo de Loiola*. San Sebastián: Ttarttalo.

Murua, I. 2016. "No More Bullets for ETA: The Loss of Internal Support as a Key Factor in the End of the Basque Group's Campaign." *Critical Studies in Terrorism, Online*, August 8. 1–22. doi:10.1080/17539153.2016.1215628

Murua, I. 2017. *Ending ETA's Armed Campaing: How and Why the Basque Armed Group Abandoned Violence*. London and New York: Routledge.

Sociometro Vasco 48, March 2012. http://www.euskadi.eus/sociometros-vascos/web01-s1lehike/es/[euskadi.eus]

Sullivan, J. 1988. *ETA and Basque Nationalism: The Fight for Euskadi, 1890-1986*. New York: Routledge.

Uriarte, E. 2013. *Tiempo de Canallas. La democracia ante el fin de ETA*. Vitoria-Gasteiz: Ikusager.

Watson, C. 2007. *Basque Nationalism and Political Violence: The Ideological and Intellectual Origins of ETA*. Reno: Center for Basque Studies, UNR.

Weinberg, L. 2012. *The End of Terrorism?* London: Routledge.

Whitfield, T. 2014. *Endgame for ETA: Elusive: Peacein the Basque Country*. London: Hurst & Company.

Woodworth, P. 2001. *Dirty War, Clean Hands: ETA, the Gal and Spanish Democracy*. Crosses Green Cork: Cork University Press.

Zabalo, J., and M. Saratxo. 2015. "ETA Ceasefire: Armed Struggle Vs. Political Practice in Basque Nationalism." *Ethnicities* 15 (3): 362–384. doi:10.1177/1468796814566477.

Zulaika, J. 2009. *Terrorism: The Self-Fulfilling Prophecy*. Chicago: The University of Chicago Press.

Zulaika, J., and W. A. Douglass. 1996. *Terror and Taboo: The Follies, Fables, and Faces of Terrorism*. New York: Routledge.

CTS, counterterrorism and non-violence

Richard Jackson

Introduction

Notwithstanding the potential dangers of using 9/11 as a temporal marker (see Toros, this issue), it has been a little over 15 years since the start of the current phase of the war on terror, and not much more than a decade since critical terrorism studies (CTS) first began to coalesce in its analytical and normative critique of the dominant, mostly Western and quite violent, approaches to counterterrorism. The current juncture afforded by this special issue therefore presents an opportune moment to reflect on the nature and outcomes of the CTS critique of the war on terror and aspects of contemporary counterterrorism, and to explore future avenues for research and activism.

In this commentary, I want to suggest that while CTS has developed an impressive body of scholarship which exposes and deconstructs the violence, negative effects and disturbing consequences of a great many aspects of counterterrorism over the past decade (for a summary, see Jackson 2016), it has not fully developed the normative and analytical foundations of the critique, nor has it adequately expounded any real alternatives to current counterterrorism approaches and models (for an initial exception, see Lindahl 2017). In particular, it has for the most part shied away from confronting a key dimension of the problem with a major feature of contemporary counterterrorism – the frequently overriding reliance on physical violence to eliminate and deter terrorists and protect society. That is, while CTS scholars have been incisive in their criticisms of the epistemic, cultural and structural violence that are inherent to some forms of counter-terrorism, such as counter- and de-radicalisation programmes, mass surveillance, border controls, and the like, and while there have been powerful criticisms of war, drone killings and torture from a human rights perspective, the normative basis of these critiques nonetheless remains a little opaque, and the critique of the use of physical violence in counterterrorism as a whole is underdeveloped. In other words, it is not yet clear exactly why and on what basis CTS opposes violent forms of counterterrorism, particularly in relation to the question of the legitimacy or not of the use of physical violence.

I want to briefly suggest here that there are pragmatic, material and political-normative reasons for rejecting the use of all forms of direct physical violence (along with other forms of epistemic, cultural and structural violence) in counterterrorism, and that CTS ought to adopt an openly, and principled, non-violent standpoint, and begin to articulate non-violent responses to the security threat posed by terrorism. (Of course, the same logic applies to the use of terrorism itself: there are good reasons why state and nonstate actors pursuing any political project ought to reject the use of violence, including terrorist violence.) This suggestion, in part, comes out of a larger research project I am currently engaged in on the subjugation of pacifism and non-violence in international relations (IR) and politics (see Jackson 2017, forthcoming). My findings thus far show that as forms of theory and political practice, pacifism and non-violence have a great deal to offer in relation to normative theory about the use of force, theories of power, understandings of agency, an approach to political epistemology and peacebuilding theory, among others. More importantly, they have a great deal to offer Security Studies, and within that Terrorism Studies, by way of a more realistic understanding of the nature and effects of the use of physical violence in political conflict, the potential of functional alternatives to the use of violence for change, security and protection, and an approach to political theory which could potentially break the cycle of violent politics of which terrorism is frequently a part.

It is on this foundation – that pacifism and non-violence offers analytical, normative and pragmatic alternatives to direct political violence, and the assessment that the current critique of counterterrorism has probably not gone quite far enough – that I want to suggest that CTS, as a similar kind of subjugated knowledge within IR (see Jackson 2012), and as a form of insurrectional, outsider knowledge, ought to openly adopt a radically non-violent approach to counterterrorism and politics, and begin to articulate how it could work in practice. In what follows, I present a number of key reasons for adopting such a standpoint, before finally reflecting on some obstacles and opportunities to the adoption of such a radical position.

The empirical failure of violence

The first and simplest reason for rejecting forms of counterterrorism which rely on physical violence, and for adopting non-violent approaches to counterterrorism instead, is that there is little evidence that political violence actually works very well in practice, either strategically or normatively. In fact, as Dustin Howes (2013, 433) has noted, there is "gathering evidence for the ineffectiveness of violence in a variety of empirical literatures." This includes, among others, studies which show that states with greater material capabilities are no more likely to win wars than those with weaker capabilities (Biddle 2004), and are winning wars less often despite their superior firepower (Arreguin-Toft 2005); studies which question the effectiveness of torture (Rejali 2009) and drone killings (Calhoun 2015) to reduce or prevent terrorism and insurgent violence; studies which show how infrequently armed insurgencies or terrorist groups achieve their stated goals (Chenoweth and Stephan 2011; Abrahms 2006); studies which show how rarely violent forms of counterterrorism succeed in ending terrorist groups or reducing levels of terrorist attacks (Argomaniz and Vidal-Diez 2015; Jones and Libicki 2008); studies which show that violent state repression (Anisin 2016) is ineffective in suppressing or resolving popular protest; studies which show the relative failure of employing violence as a means of protecting civilians by armed groups in situations of war or repression (Wallace 2016); and studies which show how previous political violence is a predictor of future bouts of political violence rather than of peace (Anderton and Ryan 2016; Walter 2004).

From another perspective, we only have to contemplate the recent historical record of the use of military violence – in cases such as Korea, Vietnam, Lebanon, Somalia, Afghanistan, Iraq, Syria, Libya and many others – to see how rarely large-scale political violence works, how unpredictable are its consequences, and how the application of increasing force and the achievement of political or strategic success bears no direct or clear-cut relation to one another. The reality is that even in those rare instances when actors won a clear-cut military victory on the battlefield, such as defeating a regime's military or killing the leader of a terrorist group, they frequently failed to achieve the broader political aims for which the war was waged in the first place (see English 2013).

This is no more so the case than with the "war on terror", which has resulted in over a million deaths so far (see PSR 2015), the widespread use of torture, rendition, and extensive human rights violations, all without any discernable increase in security or success in preventing future terrorist attacks. In fact, the number of terrorist fatalities recorded by the major terrorism databases shows an increase over the period of the war on terror, and the number of groups affiliated with al Qaeda and latterly, Islamic State (IS), has increased since the military campaign began. A realistic assessment of the war on terror would conclude that it has been a self-fulfilling prophesy which has increased global insecurity, destabilised regions such as the Middle East and the Horn of Africa, proliferated the number of terrorists and terrorist groups, and entrenched a whole number of cycles of violence, such as in Pakistan, Iraq, Syria, Yemen, Somalia and elsewhere (see Jackson 2015).

Certainly, it is hard to argue that violent forms of counterterrorism can resolve the political conflicts at the root of terrorism or prevent its future recurrence. In some specific contexts, violent counterterrorism operations temporarily slow down the number of terrorist attacks, or make it more difficult for terrorist groups to operate, but, for reasons outlined later, counterterrorist violence cannot resolve the issues or conflicts which motivate terrorist violence in the first instance, nor can they be relied upon to even minimally deter terrorists from acting. Considering the empirical record, Howes suggests that in believing that violence can be an effective policy tool (including in terms of responding to terrorism, as well as for terrorists themselves), "[t]he weight of extensive empirical evidence demonstrates that the practitioners of violence are more often the tragic idealists than are pacifists" (2013, 438).

Importantly, there are strong theoretical reasons for this commonly observed failure of violence. Most basically, it can be argued that violence fails because proponents of violence misunderstand and confuse the critical relationship between violence and power, and between brute force and coercion – and how the effectiveness of violence to deter or compel depends entirely on how people respond to the violence, not the violence itself. That is, the capacity to kill and destroy bears no direct relationship to the ability to coerce; in the real world, the application of violence can provoke either deterrence or retaliation, intimidation or rage, submission or resistance, and crucially, the desired response can never be assured. This explains why proponents of violence, including those who argue that counter-violence is a necessary response to terrorism, often mistake the reliability of violence as a political tool. To quote Dustin Howes (2013, 436) again,

Arendt's theory of action demonstrates that violence is not as reliable as is often assumed. Killing people does not have predictable political results because it operates in the 'somewhat intangible' '"web" of human relations' which makes it difficult to know what meanings people will assign to it or what actions they will take in response to it.

Related to this, Stellan Vinthagen (2015) explains how power and violence are analytically distinct, given that violence involves unilateral action, whereas power is by definition relational and operates through the approval of the subordinate. Even in the most authoritarian and repressive contexts, individuals consent to subordination. He suggests that as a consequence, "the most extreme result of violence – the killing of a human being – is something that ensures that there will never again be subordination within that relationship. Killing results in an absolute absence of power. In fact, violence is a … failure of power" (2015, 193–94). In other words, it is an analytical error to assume that power and coercion comes in the form of a capacity for violence and that violence can therefore be rationally applied as a policy instrument to deter, coerce, secure and protect – or, indeed that terrorist violence itself can be a rational instrument of political change.

More generally, pacifist theory points to the often misunderstood performative, message-sending aspect of violence – how it requires a broader political-normative discourse to make it both possible in the first place and meaningful to its perpetrators and its audience (see Jackson and Dexter 2014). In part, this is because violence, in its material aspect, is a dehumanising, world-shattering experience requiring tremendous discursive effort to legitimise, obscure or aestheticise its brutal characteristics and highlight its positive, redemptive features (see Wallace 2016; Scarry 1985). This explains in part why acts of violence can be experienced and interpreted in completely different ways, leading to very different (and often unpredictable) responses.

Importantly, from this perspective, the use of violence as a political instrument (re)constructs the discursive context which makes violence possible in the first place. In other words, employing violence in the name of countering violence primarily functions to reinforce the initial reasons for which violence is legitimately employed as a tool for politics: violence constitutes the conditions for its own practice. Thus, when the counterterrorist employs violence (or force, as it will often be called) against terrorists, they are reinforcing the claim that "it is legitimate to use violence ("force") against those who use violence against you". This clearly contributes to the social construction of further violence. In conflict resolution terms, it is a recipe for constructing cycles of violence.

Related to this point, we can also highlight the psychological dimensions of violence in terms of its inherent escalatory and mimetic processes – as a great deal of research in social psychology, not to mention the war theorist, Clausewitz, makes clear. The important point is, in keeping with basic social theory, violence is never purely instrumental, but rather is *constitutive* of identities, ethics, practices and, consequently, politics. At the very least, it constitutes society through the institutionalisation and normalisation of the war system (or counterterrorism system), and the normalisation of violence as a political instrument and as central to political life. As Frazer and Hutchings (2008, 104) put it, the idea that violence can be employed instrumentally as a tool "misses the link between violence as doing and violence as being", especially "when we take into account that our bodies themselves are prime instruments of violence." They conclude that "violence is not actually very much like a tool at all." More prosaically, the use of violence, particularly in its justificatory dimension, is constitutive of identities of friend and enemy, citizen and extremist, victim and perpetrator, and grievable and ungrievable lives (see Butler 2004) – which in turn are constitutive of, and necessary for, organised political violence (Jackson and Dexter 2014).

As a result, as we have seen in the current war on terror, counterterrorist violence functions primarily to constitute or construct a securitised and militarised context in which further violence is always possible, and indeed, highly likely. This is one of the reasons why CTS should seek to avoid legitimising or advocating the use of forms of counterterrorism which rely on physical violence: it reifies the social practice of political violence and helps to constitute and perpetuate a violent world and violent forms of politics.

CTS and emancipation

In addition to the empirical evidence and the theoretical arguments for the failure of violent counterterrorism, there are also political-normative reasons for rejecting violent forms of counterterrorism. In our first major attempt to outline the key commitments of CTS, my colleagues and I stated that CTS ought to have a core commitment to *emancipation*, and that such a commitment implied, among other things:

> a commitment to praxis [and] … a continuous process of "immanent critique" of existing power structures and practices in society; *the moral and intellectual questioning of the instrumental rationality paradigm of political violence* …; the prioritising of human security over national security and working towards *minimising all forms of physical, structural, and cultural violence* …; and *the serious scholarly and practical exploration of non-violence*, conflict transformation, and reconciliation *as practical alternatives to terrorist and counter-terrorist violence*. (Jackson, Breen Smyth, and Gunning 2009, 225; emphasis added)

Although we did not spell it out at the time, the reality is that adopting such an emancipatory approach demands a radical commitment to non-violence, or pacifism. In part, this is because of the nature of violence – which can never be an emancipatory means (or end), given its world-shattering and dominatory character, its use of people as means to an end, its self-justifying and constitutive nature, and its inherent incapacity for creating positive peace and security. The ethical character of violent political action is incompatible with, and indeed, antithetical to, the notion of emancipation. Obviously, this applies to terrorist groups as well, who may be pursuing an emancipatory project with violent means.

In addition, it is also because principled (as opposed to pragmatic) non-violent political action offers an alternative emancipatory ethics based on a series of key values, including the dignity and equality of others, humility and the recognition of human fallibility, and the principle of treating people as means not ends (May 2015). That is, rooted in Kant's second formulation of the categorical imperative – "[a]ct so that you treat humanity, whether in your own person or in that of another, always as an end and never as a means only" (quoted in Holmes 2013, 113) – and recognising that "[t]o kill others to promote your own ends is to use the others as means" (194), pacifist ethics entails the search for realistic and functional alternatives to violence.

Similarly, recognising human limitations, the potential for mistakes (and the consequent need to reverse course and experiment in political life), and that human understanding of the truth will always be partial, pacifist ethics (and, I would argue, the kind of emancipatory ethics we gestured towards at the beginning of CTS) recognises the problematic nature of violence which requires certainty of purpose and outcome. As Holmes puts it (2013, 197), "[v]iolence is for the morally infallible," in large part because it is inherently irreversible. On this point, and considering the uncountable (and uncounted) lives lost or irrevocably damaged to invasion, drone strikes, institutional torture, shoot-to-kill policies and the global violence of the war on terror, we are bound to heed Howes' (2013, 437) warning: "[p]racticing violence makes it difficult to reverse course or admit one's mistakes, and even when temporarily effective, it ensures that domination becomes the marker of legitimate authority. This inclines more people to use it, creating a competitive and violent atmosphere of escalation."

Perhaps most importantly, pacifist ethics, and the emancipatory ethics we outlined for CTS, is rooted in a commitment to maintaining means-ends consistency. This is the recognition of the fundamentally *constitutive* nature of social action, as noted, and the understanding that the outcomes of political actions are always prefigured in the means. For example, grounded in the lived reality of human beings, the pacifist conception of means-ends consistency starts with Duane Cady's (2010, 51) observation that "[i]n our ordinary lives we do not regard means and ends as separate, independent, and distinct from one another. In fact we work toward an integrated life in which our activities are compatible with and appropriate to our goals." Similarly, in political life, "[h]owever hard we try to separate means and ends, the results we achieve are extensions of the policies we live ... Means and ends are aspects of one and the same event" (Cady 2010, 54).

From this perspective, it is implausible that peaceful ends can be achieved by violent means, particularly given the dominatory, world-destroying nature of violence, just as it is implausible that trust can be built by deception, that equality can be constructed through selfishness, or indeed that a world free from terrorism – a form of organised killing – can be achieved through force-based counterterrorism – another form of organised killing. In other words, the ultimate ends of counterterrorism – a society free from political violence – cannot be constructed on the foundations of violent political action in the form of counterterrorism; counterterrorist action has to prefigure the kind of politics and society it wants to create in its actions now.

Added to this, in broader political terms, as Molly Wallace (2016) explains it, the fact that violence ends the otherness that is another human life radically abrogates our responsibility to that other, and prevents them from challenging the truth or justice of our political project – or indeed, our one-dimensional characterisation of them as terrorists, fanatics, barbarians, or whatever label we have used to dehumanise and demonise them. The use of violence, in other words, is incompatible with an emancipatory political project rooted in the recognition of irreducible difference and radical disagreement (see Shinko 2008; Ramsbotham 2010), and the concurrent impossibility of certainty or absolute truth.

In contrast, non-violent forms of political action (including non-violent forms of counterterrorism) remains open to revision in a way that violent action can never be, and revision, experimentation, humility and acknowledging mistakes are inherent to a normative, dialogic, emancipatory (and peaceful) form of politics. That is, "[n] onviolence offers a self-limiting, pragmatic, and realistic approach that accounts for the manifold difficulties of politics" (Howes 2013, 428). Or, as Stanley Hauerwas (2002, 425–26) expresses it, "nonviolence is the necessary condition for a politics not based on death."

In sum, given the nature of direct physical violence, particularly its horrific material, psychological and political effects, its irreversibility, and its constitutive nature, it can be argued that pacifism and non-violence provide an ethical approach which is consistent with emancipation and the kind of ethics and politics we set out for CTS when we began several years ago. Such a radically emancipatory commitment, and such a critical standpoint on the failure of violence, needs to be at the foundational heart of the CTS critique of the war on terror and contemporary counterterrorism.

Functional alternatives to violence and the possibilities of peaceful politics

For the ethical and theoretical reasons touched on above and elsewhere (see Jackson 2017, forthcoming), it can be argued that in practice, anything that violence purports to be able to do, non-violence can also do – whether that is deterring, coercing, securing or protecting people, or engendering major political transformation (see also, May 2015). In particular, violence does not have a monopoly on security provision or civilian protection (see Wallace 2016). In theory, it is perfectly possible to create security and respond effectively to acts of terrorism without the employment of counter-violence. More concretely, there are a number of bodies of literature and research which gesture towards the potential of non-violence to deal effectively with security threats and violent political conflicts which involve acts of terrorism. These literatures are the mirror image of the literatures which demonstrate the failure of violence, and they strongly support the assessment well known by activists around the world that non-violence works effectively in a great many situations, including those characterised by endemic or intense political violence.

For example, there is a growing literature on the success of non-violent movements in overthrowing authoritarian regimes, changing state policies, repelling military occupations and winning independence for subnational groups (see, among many others, Bartkowski 2013; Celestino and Gleditsch 2013; Nepstad 2011; Schock 2011; Roberts and Ash 2009). This body of research is based on, and inspired by, Erica Chenoweth and Maria Stephan's groundbreaking (2011) study on the comparative success of violent and non-violent political movements. In part, the significance of this literature is that it demonstrates that state terrorism and repression can be effectively responded to with non-violent strategies, and that responses to violent attack do not necessitate violent responses, but that there are a large number of creative, non-violent options.

I would also suggest that this data could be further examined with a view to thinking about its application to cases where lqcal communities seek to secure themselves from armed actors (state or nonstate) employing non-violent strategies. There is an emerging literature on cases in Colombia, Somalia, Syria and elsewhere where forms of non-violent community action have proved to be effective in resisting violent incursions by armed groups (see Stephan 2015; Juan Masullo 2015; Anderson and Wallace 2013; Kemp and Fry 2003). While these cases are often small-scale, sometimes only partially effective, and nascent and relatively unknown, they nonetheless gesture towards the ethical and practical potential of non-violent counterterrorism approaches.

Related to this, there is a growing literature detailing and examining the successes of unarmed peacekeeping and non-violent accompaniment in situations of violent conflict, including in situations like Colombia and South Sudan (see Wallace 2016; Julian and Schweitzer 2015; Schirch 2006). This literature includes cases where UN troops chose to be unarmed, as well as non-violent peace-forces such as Peace Brigades International. This literature gestures towards the potential of replacing armed military or police forces with unarmed peacekeepers who can fulfil the same functions and provide the same kinds of protection, but without the use of lethal or injurious force.

More broadly, there is a long-standing literature which examines the successes of dialogue and negotiation in resolving violent conflicts, including conflicts which have involved acts of terrorism (see Goerzig 2010; Zartman 2003; Sederberg 1995). Such approaches make perfect theoretical sense when we recognise that acts of political violence (such as acts of terrorism) are a symptom of political conflict, and not the conflict itself. That is, even if violent forms of counterterrorism are successful in destroying the ability of armed groups to operate effectively (such as occurred in Sri Lanka when government forces overran the LTTE), such violence leaves unresolved the political conflict which gave rise to the terrorist acts in the first instance. Only dialogue and negotiation, and the reforms and adjustments which flow from it, can deal with the long-term roots of the violent political conflict.

It is also important here to note the long-standing literature on the possibilities of civilian-based forms of national defence (see Bartkowski 2015; Burrowes 1996; Miniotaite 1996; Martin 1993; Sharp 1990; Salmon 1988). Rooted in both the realistic recognition that most small or medium states in the world would be unable to defend themselves from invasion by the most powerful states using military force (and such resistance would be very costly in terms of life and destruction), and that there are actual cases of successful non-violent resistance to powerful invaders (such as India against the British, and Lithuania against the Soviets), such approaches provide strategies for broad civil non-cooperation and raising the costs of occupation.

Finally, there is an important literature on the political philosophical basis for new forms of politics based on a radical commitment to non-violence. In particular, a growing number of recent publications (see Wallace 2016; Atak 2012; Mantena 2012; Howes 2009, 2016; Godrej 2006) have gone some way towards articulating a Gandhian theory and practice of political action which offers a "more realistic" approach for dealing with the current imperfect world in which there is both a plurality of perspectives and continuous deep-rooted conflict. Describing a new kind of politics rooted in non-violence and agonism, such theory gestures towards the possibilities of devising forms of politics which makes violence – state and non-state – unnecessary and unlikely, thereby breaking existing cycles of violent escalation and preventing the emergence of future political violence.

It is important to note that these literatures do not suggest that non-violence works every time or in every case; there is no silver bullet for dealing with intense political conflict or security threats, and certainly, we know that violence does not work every time and in every case. But, knowing that non-violence works well in a great many documented cases and different areas (including in peacefully resisting state and non-state terrorism) opens up our imagination and intellectual horizon to new possibilities, and demands of us that we seriously explore non-violent alternatives to the ineffective and destructive counterterrorism approaches which currently dominate policy and practice.

Looking at this from another perspective, it can be argued that we cannot know for sure whether non-violent approaches to terrorism will really work effectively until we put the same level of resources and efforts into them as we currently put into the war on terror and contemporary counterterrorism (see Holmes 2013, 167). That is, only when we have spent 4–5 trillion dollars, and employed millions of people in coordinated forms of non-violent counterterrorism (comparable to what we have done in the war on terror) will we know for sure whether it works as well or better than all the military and hard security measures have thus far.

Concluding remarks

In conclusion, I want to briefly reflect on both the obstacles and the opportunities which currently face the CTS community in thinking about openly adopting a non-violent approach to counterterrorism. To reiterate, I have been discussing the adoption of a radically non-violent approach towards those forms of counterterrorism which rely primarily on direct physical violence; CTS scholars have already advanced a powerful critique of forms of counterterrorism which are epistemically, culturally and structurally violent. However, among others, I see two main objections, and two main obstacles to adopting a radically non-violent approach to counterterrorism.

The first objection will be that it is idealistic and unrealistic to think that non-violence can be used against terrorists who are violent, evil fanatics. Most likely, the current example of Islamic State will be mentioned here. Rather, it will be argued that, following Max Weber's assertion in "Politics as a vocation", the "decisive means for politics is violence", "the quite different tasks of politics can only be solved by violence", and "[a]nyone who fails to see this is, indeed, a political infant" (cited in Howes 2013, 427). However, given the accumulated empirical evidence (including the evidence relating to the use of violence in the attempt to defeat al Qaeda and IS), the historical record, and the theoretical reasons given earlier, the opposite assessment is probably more accurate: believing that physical violence can be an effective policy tool, including in counterterrorism, is naïve and tragically idealistic.

A second objection will be that responding to terrorism non-violently is potentially dangerous because it will encourage more terrorism. In fact, apart from the empirical evidence which contradicts such an assertion (see Goerzig 2010), it can be reasonably argued that it is the use of violence which encourages terrorism because it generates further grievances, provokes anger and resistance, and, more importantly, reinforces and legitimises the commonsense belief that political violence is an effective and legitimate tool of political contention, and thus constitutes more violence. Additionally, in its material practice and relational dimensions, violence is inherently mimetic and prone to escalation spirals. The problem of terrorism today (and historically, such as in the case of Northern Ireland, Spain, Israel and elsewhere) is not the result of non-violence; it is the result of the primacy and ubiquity of violence as a mode of political action; it is the direct result of violent counterterrorism.

More serious than these rather facile objections however, the first main obstacle to adopting an avowedly non-violent standpoint in CTS is the dominant discourse of our culture and our primary discipline. Within the truth regime of Western society and IR, pacifism is a subjugated knowledge which is suppressed through a series of processes including silencing and shaming, as well as a whole series of narratives and analogies designed to prove that pacifism should be shunned as a theory or approach to politics and security (see Jackson, forthcoming). The experience of Jeremy Corbyn when he opposed the renewal of trident and the bombing of Syria illustrates how the term "pacifist" can be used as a term of insult and a mode of subjugation (Jackson, forthcoming). In other words, declaring oneself pacifist, like declaring oneself a CTS scholar, means going against the grain and being willing to be considered an outsider.

A second serious obstacle is the immense political and material interests invested in violent forms and practices of counterterrorism. At the very least, this includes, among others, the expanding power of the military-industrial complex, growing security sector employment and profits (see Boukalas 2015), and the ongoing and proven institutional and political benefits which accrue to counterterrorist actors (see Jackson and Tsui 2016; Jackson 2013). All of these actors and vested interests are likely to resist and oppose any proposed suspension of violent counterterrorism and a refocus on non-violent approaches.

However, notwithstanding these obstacles, I sense two main opportunities inherent in the current historical moment. First, the spectacular failures of the war on terror, and counterterrorism more generally (following a lull, the wars in Afghanistan and Iraq are once again drawing in foreign involvement, and the bombing campaigns against IS are having little effect on the number of terrorist attacks in Europe and elsewhere), along with a palpable sense of war weariness, make this an ideal moment to propose radical alternatives to the status quo and to the patently ineffective strategies which appear to produce the same self-fulfilling results over and over (see Jackson 2015). Abandoning physically violent forms of counterterrorism will not necessarily see an end to other forms of counterterrorism which are epistemically or culturally violent, such as many counter-radicalisation programmes, but it would be a major step in the direction of ridding counterterrorism of all the different forms of violence it embodies.

Second, as I have noted earlier, there is a growing body of research and practice by different communities around the world which illustrates how community-based non-violent strategies can help to construct security against terrorism and state violence. Moreover, the adoption of a non-violent, pacifist approach to counterterrorism is not as big a step as might be imagined; it certainly does not leave us with the option of "doing nothing" in the face of terrorist violence. For the most part, it requires refusing to employ military force, extra-judicial killing, or torture in counterterrorism efforts, and instead, focus on intelligence-led operations, community policing, criminal justice, reconciliation, dialogue and reform-based efforts, among others. At the same time, adopting an avowedly non-violent standpoint for the critique of counterterrorism would strengthen the current CTS critique of the kinds of counterterrorism practices which may not be physically violent but which are structurally or culturally violent.

In short, now is the ideal moment to be researching and advocating for the serious consideration of non-violent models and approaches to counterterrorism and political violence. Certainly, given the inherent weaknesses and failures of violence as a political instrument, the ethics and successes of non-violent political action, and the prior commitment of CTS to a means/ends consistent model of emancipation, now is the

CRITICAL TERRORISM STUDIES AT TEN

opportune time for critical scholars to adopt an openly, radically non-violent approach to the current challenges of counterterrorism.

Acknowledgements

I acknowledge the support of the New Zealand Marsden Fund in the preparation of this Commentary, the research for which was conducted under the Marsden Fund proposal, 14-UOO -075, "A new politics of peace? Investigations in contemporary Pacifism and Nonviolence". I am also grateful to the Global Insecurities Centre in the School of Sociology, Politics and International Studies (SPAIS), University of Bristol, for the award of a Benjamin Meaker Visiting Professorship which enabled a period of study leave at in July-August 2016 where I wrote the first draft of this Commentary. Thanks to my fellow editors of the special issue for comments on an earlier draft of this Commentary which have improved it a great deal.

Disclosure statement

No potential conflict of interest was reported by the author.

Funding

I acknowledge the support of The Royal Society of New Zealand Marsden Fund in the preparation of this Commentary, the research for which was conducted under the Marsden Fund proposal, 14-UOO-075, "A new politics of peace? Investigations in contemporary Pacifism and Nonviolence".

References

Abrahms, M. 2006. "Why Terrorism Does Not Work." *International Security* 31 (2): 42–78. doi:10.1162/isec.2006.31.2.42.

Anderson, M., and M. Wallace. 2013. *Opting Out of War*. Boulder, CO: Lynne Reinner.

Anderton, C., and E. Ryan. 2016. "Habituation to Atrocity: Low-Level Violence against Civilians as a Predictor of High-Level Attacks." *Journal of Genocide Research* 18: 539–562. doi:10.1080/14623528.2016.1216109.

Anisin, A. 2016. "Violence Begets Violence: Why States Should Not Lethally Repress Popular Protest." *The International Journal of Human Rights* 20 (7): 893–913. doi:10.1080/13642987.2016.1192536.

Argomaniz, J., and A. Vidal-Diez. 2015. "Examining Deterrence and Backlash Effects in Counter-Terrorism: The Case of ETA." *Terrorism and Political Violence* 27 (1): 160–181. doi:10.1080/09546553.2014.975648.

Arreguin-Toft, I. 2005. *How the Weak Win Wars: A Theory of Asymmetric Conflict*. New York: Cambridge University Press.

Atak, I. 2012. *Nonviolence in Political Theory*. Edinburgh: Edinburgh University Press.

Bartkowski, M., ed. 2013. *Recovering Nonviolent History: Civil Resistance in Liberation Struggles.* Boulder, CO: Lynne Rienner.

Bartkowski, M. 2015. "Nonviolent Civilian Defense to Counter Russian Hybrid Warfare." White Paper, The John Hopkins University Center for Advanced Governmental Studies. Accessed 4 September 2015. http://advanced.jhu.edu/academics/graduate-degree-programs/global-security-studies/program-resources/publications/white-paper-maciej-bartkowski/

Biddle, S. 2004. *Military Power: Explaining Victory and Defeat in Modern Battle.* Princeton, NJ: Princeton University Press.

Boukalas, C. 2015. "Class War-On-Terror: Counterterrorism, Accumulation, Crisis." *Critical Studies On Terrorism* 8 (1): 55–71. doi:10.1080/17539153.2015.1005932.

Burrowes, R. 1996. *The Strategy of Nonviolent Defense: A Gandhian Approach.* New York: State University of New York Press.

Butler, J. 2004. *Precarious Life: The Powers of Mourning and Violence.* London: Verso.

Cady, D. 2010. *From Warism to Pacifism: A Moral Continuum.* 2nd ed. Philadelphia, PA: Temple University Press.

Calhoun, L. 2015. *We Kill because We Can: From Soldiering to Assassination in the Drone Age.* London: Zed Books.

Celestino, M., and K. Gleditsch. 2013. "Fresh Carnations or All Thorn, No Rose? Nonviolent Campaigns and Transitions in Autocracies." *Journal of Peace Research* 50 (3): 385–400. doi:10.1177/0022343312469979.

Chenoweth, E., and M. Stephan. 2011. *Why Civil Resistance Works: The Strategic Logic of Nonviolent Conflict.* New York: Columbia University Press.

English, R. 2013. *Modern War: A Very Short Introduction.* Oxford: Oxford University Press.

Frazer, E., and K. Hutchings. 2008. "On Politics and Violence: Arendt Contra Fanon." *Contemporary Political Theory* 7: 90–108.

Godrej, F. 2006. "Nonviolence and Gandhi's Truth: A Method for Moral and Political Arbitration." *Review of Politics* 68 (2): 287–317.

Goerzig, C. 2010. *Talking to Terrorists: Concessions and the Renunciation of Violence.* Abingdon: Routledge.

Hauerwas, S. 2002. "September 11, 2001: A Pacifist Response." *The South Atlantic Quarterly* 101 (2): 425–426. doi:10.1215/00382876-101-2-425.

Holmes, R. 2013. *The Ethics of Nonviolence: Essays by Robert L. Holmes,* edited by P. Cicovacki. New York, NY: Bloomsbury.

Howes, D. 2009. *Toward a Credible Pacifism: Violence and the Possibilities of Politics.* Albany, NY: SUNY Press.

Howes, D. 2013. "The Failure of Pacifism and the Success of Nonviolence." *Perspectives on Politics* 11 (2): 427–466. doi:10.1017/S1537592713001059.

Howes, D. 2016. *Freedom without Violence: Resisting the Western Political Tradition.* Oxford: Oxford University Press.

Jackson, R. 2012. "Unknown Knowns: The Subjugated Knowledge of Terrorism Studies." *Critical Studies on Terrorism* 5 (1): 11–29. doi:10.1080/17539153.2012.659907.

Jackson, R. 2015. "Commentary: Groundhog Day and the Repetitive Failure of Western Counterterrorism Policy in the Middle East." *Insight Turkey* 17 (3): 35–44.

Jackson, R., ed. 2016. *Routledge Handbook on Critical Terrorism Studies.* Abingdon: Routledge.

Jackson, R. 2017. "Post-Liberal Peacebuilding and the Pacifist State." *Peacebuilding* 1–16. doi:10.1080/21647259.2017.1303871.

Jackson, R. Forthcoming. "Pacifism: The Anatomy of a Subjugated Knowledge." *Critical Studies on Security.*

Jackson, R., and C. Tsui. 2016. "War on Terror II: Obama and the Adaptive Evolution of US Counter-Terrorism." In *The Obama Doctrine: Legacy and Continuity in US Foreign Policy,* edited by M. Bentley and J. Holland, 70–83. Abingdon: Routledge.

Jackson, R., and H. Dexter. 2014. "The Social Construction of Organised Political Violence: An Analytical Framework." *Civil Wars* 16 (1): 1–23. doi:10.1080/13698249.2014.904982.

Jackson, R., M. Breen Smyth, and J. Gunning, eds. 2009. *Critical Terrorism Studies: A New Research Agenda*. Abingdon: Routledge.

Jackson, R. 2013. "The Politics of Terrorism Fear." In *The Political Psychology of Terrorism Fears*, edited by S. Sinclair, 267–282. Cambridge: Cambridge University Press.

Jones, S., and M. Libicki. 2008. *How Terrorist Groups End: Lessons from Countering al Qa'ida*. Santa Monica, CA: RAND.

Juan Masullo, J. 2015. *The Power of Staying Put: Nonviolent Resistance against Armed Groups in Colombia*. ICNC Monograph Series. Washington, DC: International Center on Nonviolent Conflict. https://www.nonviolent-conflict.org/wp-content/uploads/2016/01/The-Power-of-Staying-Put.pdf

Julian, R., and C. Schweitzer. 2015. "The Origins and Development of Unarmed Civilian Peacekeeping." *Peace Review: A Journal of Social Justice* 27 (1): 1–8. doi:10.1080/10402659.2015.1000181.

Kemp, G., and D. Fry. 2003. *Keeping the Peace: Conflict Resolution and Peaceful Societies around the World*. London: Routledge.

Lindahl, S. 2017. "A CTS Model of Counterterrorism." *Critical Studies on Terrorism*.

Mantena, K. 2012. "Another Realism: The Politics of Gandhian Nonviolence." *American Political Science Review* 106 (2): 455–470. doi:10.1017/S000305541200010X.

Martin, B. 1993. *Social Defence, Social Change*. London: Freedom Press.

May, T. 2015. *Nonviolent Resistance: A Philosophical Introduction*. Cambridge, UK: Polity.

Miniotaite, G. 1996. "Lithuania: From Non-Violent Liberation Towards Non-Violent Defence?" *Peace Research: The Canadian Journal of Peace Studies* 48 (4): 19–36.

Nepstad, S. 2011. *Nonviolent Revolutions: Civil Resistance in the Late 20th Century*. New York: Oxford University Press.

PSR (Physicians for Social Responsibility). 2015. "Body Count: Casualty Figures after 10 Years of the "War on Terror"." *IPPNW Germany*. Accessed 22 May 2017. http://www.psr.org/assets/pdfs/body-count.pdf

Ramsbotham, O. 2010. *Transforming Violent Conflict: Radical Disagreement, Dialogue and Survival*. Abingdon: Routledge.

Rejali, D. 2009. *Torture and Democracy*. Princeton, NJ: Princeton University Press.

Roberts, A., and T. Ash, eds. 2009. *Civil Resistance and Power Politics: The Experience of Non-Violent Action from Gandhi to the Present*. Oxford: Oxford University Press.

Salmon, J. 1988. "Can Non-Violence Be Combined with Military Means for National Defence." *Journal of Peace Research* 25 (1): 69–80. doi:10.1177/002234338802500107.

Scarry, E. 1985. "Injury and the Structure of War." *Representations* 10 (Spring): 1–51. doi:10.1525/rep.1985.10.1.99p0402z.

Schirch, L. 2006. *Civilian Peacekeeping: Preventing Violence and Making Space for Democracy*. Uppsala: Life and Peace Institute. http://www.life-peace.org/wp-content/uploads/Civilian-Peacekeeping-Preventing-Violence-and-Making-Space-for-Democracy-Lisa-Schirch.pdf

Schock, K. 2011. *Unarmed Insurrections: People Power Movements in Nondemocracies*. Minneapolis: University of Minnesota Press.

Sederberg, P. 1995. "Conciliation as Counter-Terrorist Strategy." *Journal of Peace Research* 32: 295–312. doi:10.1177/0022343395032003004.

Sharp, G. 1990. *Civilian-Based Defence: A Post-Military Weapons System*. Princeton: Princeton University Press.

Shinko, R. 2008. "Agonistic Peace: A Postmodern Reading." *Millennium: Journal of International Studies* 36 (3): 473–491. doi:10.1177/03058298080360030501.

Stephan, M. 2015. "Civil Resistance Vs. ISIS." *Journal of Resistance Studies* 1 (2): 127–150.

Vinthagen, S. 2015. *A Theory of Nonviolent Action: How Civil Resistance Works*. London: Zed Books.

Wallace, M. 2016. *Security without Weapons: Rethinking Violence, Violent Action, and Civilian Protection*. Abingdon, UK: Routledge.

Walter, B. 2004. "Does Conflict Beget Conflict? Explaining Recurring Civil War." *Journal of Peace Research* 41 (3): 371–388. doi:10.1177/0022343304043775.

Zartman, I. W. 2003. "Negotiating with Terrorists." *International Negotiation* 8 (3): 443–450. doi:10.1163/1571806031310815.

Index

9/11 2, 7–23, 50, 108, 111, 117; and Basque case 147; and causal analysis 27, 32; forgetting 9/11 8, 19–20; and non-violence 161; and Nozick 125, 129, 134; and reflexive narratives 16–19; and reproducing narrative 11–16; and temporal rupture 9–11

Aachen Prize 92
academic freedom 87–90, 92–3, 96
Academics for Peace 78–100
Academics Solidarity Platform 88
Academics for Turkey 91
activism 58, 60, 71–2, 81, 83, 147, 153, 158, 161, 167
actuarial model 114–16
Afghanistan 48, 50, 163, 170
Africa 10–11, 163
African National Congress (ANC) 86
Afrikaners 86
Agamben, G. 82
agency 32, 38, 62–4, 72, 113, 162
agonism 168
ahistoricism 15–16, 19, 25–6, 28, 30–2, 34, 36, 38–9
Aiete Conference 155–8
Aizpeolea, L.R. 142
Akdeniz University 89
Akdeniz, Y. 82, 95
Akgönül, S. 78–100
Akkoyunlu, K. 81
Aktar, C. 87
Alevis 94
Algeria 85
alienation 4
Altıparmak, K. 82, 95
American Creed 52
Amnesty International 13
Amoore, L. 115
Amri, A. 127–8, 133, 135–7
Anarchy, State and Utopia 125–6, 130, 138
Anglo-American traditions 4
Annan, K. 155, 158
Ansón, L.M. 154
apartheid 86

Arab Spring 68
Arabs 48, 52, 68
Aralar 147, 151
Area Studies 57
Arendt, H. 164
Aristotle 9, 33–4, 36
armed struggle 142–51, 153–6, 162, 167–8
Armenians 79, 87
Ashley, R. 44
Asia 10–11
Askatasuna 145
Associated Press (AP) 17
Association of Chief Police Officers 111
asylum seekers 127
Atlantic divide 4
austerity 102, 105, 115, 118
Australia 14
authoritarianism 80–2, 87, 96, 164, 167
autocracy 82, 88
autoethnography 16, 36
autonomy 82, 88, 93, 144
Aydinlar Dilekcesi manifesto 86
Aznar, J.M. 148

Bader, R.M. 126
Balkans 80
Barbados 11
barbarism 45–52, 166
Barbería, J.L. 152
Barkawi, T. 69
Baser, B. 78–100
Basham, V. 63, 68
Basque case 142–60
Basque Nationalist Left 144–57
Basque Nationalist Party (PNV) 144, 149, 153, 158
Batasuna 145–50, 152–3, 155
Batista, A. 142
Bayramoğlu, A. 87
behaviourism 28
Belkin, A. 63
Bell Pottinger 112
Bellamy, A.J. 129

INDEX

Berlin attack 126–8, 130–1, 133, 135–6, 138
Berlin Wall 11
Bhaskar, R. 33–5
bias 29, 81, 85, 91
big data 103, 105, 115–16, 118, 134, 136
Bildu 153–5, 157
Bilgi University 92–3
Bin Laden, O. 48
binaries 32, 34, 46, 53, 57–77, 110
biopolitics 114, 116–17, 119
Bjørgo, T. 27–8, 36
Blair, T. 103–4, 155–7
Botha, P.W. 86
boundaries 36, 44, 57, 59, 61, 70, 80, 110, 128, 131–3
Bourdieu, P. 8, 13–14, 16
bourgeoisie 46, 49–50
Brantingham, P. 111
Breakthrough Media Network 112
Breytanbach, W. 86
British Asians 103–5, 108–10, 112, 118
British International Studies Association Conferences 13
British Transport Police 107
Brussels Declaration 152
Brym, R.J. 61
Bulmer, S. 60–1, 65, 70
bureaucracy 93–4
Bush, G.W. 8–9, 13, 15, 18, 48
Butler, J. 15, 17

Cady, D. 166
Call to Unite for Academic Freedoms 89
Camcı, M. 92
Cameron, D. 114
Canada 48
Cantle Report 108
capitalism 156
Carter, J. 155
Castells, M. 156
causal analysis 2, 24–43, 107
ceasefires 79, 84, 86, 144–5, 149, 152–3, 155
censorship 63, 81, 88
Center for the Advanced Study in Behavioral Sciences 125
Centre Henri Dunant for Humanitarian Dialogue 151
Çetin, H. 86
Channel Programme 111, 113–16, 118
Chastelain, J. de 152
chauvinism 65
Cheney, R. 9
Chenoweth, E. 167
Cherney, A. 14
China 11
Chisholm, A. 70
Chomsky, N. 78, 85
Christianity 10, 46, 49–50
chronology 8, 10–11, 15–16, 19–20

citizenship 52, 59, 91, 93
civil disobedience 80, 168
civil liberties 81, 125, 128–9
civil rights 14
civil society 81, 87, 89, 92, 94
civil wars 26, 80, 82–3
civilisational barbarism 45–52
Clancy, T. 48
Clark, E. 111
class 17, 59–60, 146–7
Clausewitz, C. von 164
Clini, C. 12
Coaffee, J. 107
coercion 81, 163–4, 167
Cohn, C. 17
Cold War 80
collateral damage 125, 136–7
Colombia 151, 156, 167–8
colonialism 44, 53, 90
community policing 102, 104, 109–11, 170
compensation 126, 132–6
conflict resolution 18, 152, 155–9, 163–5, 168
conscientious objectors 85
conscription 65
consequentialism 129–30
CONTEST strategy 10
Control Order House 111
Corbyn, J. 170
corporations 48, 87, 95
Council of Higher Education (YÖK) 79, 88, 90, 93, 95
counter-insurgency studies 26
counter-narratives 8, 17
counter-radicalisation 2, 16, 101–4, 106, 108, 112, 114, 117–18, 170
counter-terrorism 2–4, 9–11, 13–15, 18–19, 25, 28–9; and Basque case 155, 157–9; and causal analysis 37, 40; and non-violence 161–73; and Nozick 124–41; and state violence 68; and Turkey 78–100; and UK 102–3, 105–7, 109–19
Counter-Terrorism Committee 11
Counter-Terrorism Law 92
coups 80, 86, 88, 94–5
covering law 31
Cox, R. 29–30
Crenshaw, M. 26, 143
crime prevention 102, 104–14, 118
criminal justice 102, 107, 125, 129–30, 133, 137–8, 170
criminalisation 78–100
criminology 129
Critical Realism (CR) 2, 25, 33–5, 39
Critical Studies on Terrorism (CST) 1–23, 59
Critical Studies on Terrorism Working Group (CSTWG) 3, 5
critical terrorism studies (CTS) 1–6, 137, 161; and 9/11 narrative 7–23; and Academics for Peace 78–100; and Basque case 142–60; and causal analysis 24–43; and emancipation

INDEX

165–7; end of terrorism 142–60; and non-violence 161–73; and Nozick 124–41; and radicalisation risk 101–23; and reproducing narrative 11–16; and state violence 57–77
critical theory 2, 29–30, 36, 126, 128, 134; critical race studies 44; critical security studies 4, 29, 57–77; and immanent critique 165; and non-violence 167, 169, 171
Cronin, A.K. 142–3
Cuba 49, 52
curfews 78–9, 84, 111
Currin, B. 152
Czechia 96

Daphna-Tekoah, S. 2, 57–77
death 17–18, 96, 145, 147, 163, 167
death threats 87, 90–1
decontextualisation 25, 31–2, 34, 36, 38–9
dehistoricism *see* ahistoricism
democracy 12, 31, 59, 70, 80–2, 86–7, 95, 146–7, 152, 154, 158
Democracy Index 81
demography 3, 27, 104, 106–8
deprivation 27–8
Derrida, J. 137
detentions 79, 86, 92, 111, 134–6, 148, 158
deterrence 144, 161, 163–4, 167
deviance 50, 103, 105, 107, 109–11
DeVotta, N. 80, 82
dialogue 4, 7, 11, 18, 24–43, 72; and Basque case 149, 151, 155–6; and non-violence 166, 168, 170; and UK 104
diasporas 52–3
Dillon, M. 116–17
diplomacy 93, 151–3
dissent 9, 11, 78–100
division of labour 61
dominant discourse/narratives 8–10, 13–14, 16, 19, 145, 157, 169
Domínguez, F. 142
drones 161–2, 166
Düzce University 91

e-borders programme 115
earthquakes 18
effective history 8, 16
egalitarianism 126
Egiguren, J. 148
Ekin 145
elections 80–2, 84, 147, 149–50, 153–5, 157
elites 57, 59–60, 68, 81, 86, 156
Elorza, O. 154
Elshtain, J.B. 58
emancipation 2, 4, 11, 58–9, 61, 71–2, 165–7, 170
empathy 66, 71
empiricism 28
England 102
Enlightenment 107

Enloe, C. 72
epidemiology 101, 106–23
epistemology 4, 12, 26, 28–9, 32–4, 36; and causal analysis 38–9; epistemic communities 31, 37–8, 169; and non-violence 162; and Nozick 130, 133–5; and UK 105, 112–18
Erdoğan, R.T. 79–82, 87, 90–4, 96
Ersanli, B. 88
Ersoy, K. 92
eschatology 47–8, 51
Escrivá, A. 142
Esen, B. 81
Esterhuyse, W. 86
ethics 2, 26, 29–30, 37, 52, 59; and non-violence 164–8, 170; and Nozick 129, 134, 138; and state violence 63, 66, 72; and Turkey 89
ethnicity 3, 60, 83, 105, 110, 112–14
ethnography 69–70, 72
Etxeberria, R. 144
Eurocentrism 69
Europe 4, 103, 113, 147, 157, 170
European Court of Human Rights 83, 95, 149
European Union (EU) 81, 83
Euskadi ta Askatasuna (ETA) 2, 142–60
exceptionalism 82, 94, 110, 125, 129, 136, 138
exclusion 58–64, 86
Extebarrieta, T. 147
extremism 101–3, 105, 107–9, 111–16, 118, 165

fanaticism 14, 27, 46–7, 49–51, 166, 169
Faust, F. 111
Federal Criminal Police Office (BKA) 127
feminism 15, 19, 44, 57–8, 62, 66, 68, 70–2
fertility rates 45
Feynman, R. 35
fifth columnists 85, 90
Fimreite, A. 12
First-Worldism 15, 17
Flader, U. 79, 92
foreign policy 10, 44, 82
Foucault, M. 8, 13, 16, 49–50, 117
Foundation University Workers' Solidarity Network 88
France 10, 85, 88, 90, 96, 148, 155
Franco, F. 147, 157
Frankfurt School 29
Frazer, E. 164
free speech 79–80, 82–4, 86–90, 92–3, 95–6
free will 126, 135–7
freedom fighters 62
Freedom House 82
Freud, S. 50
fundamentalism 47
funding 123
further research 2–5, 33, 38–40, 44–5, 57–8, 60–2, 67–9, 71–2, 142, 161–2, 167, 169–70

Gandhi, M.K. 168
Garzon, B. 148

INDEX

Gaza Strip 61, 63–6, 68, 86
Gefährder classification 127–8, 135–7
gender/gender studies 2–4, 44, 59, 61, 67, 71, 73
genocide 11, 79, 87
geography 14, 48, 57, 60–1, 101–23
geopolitics 45, 47, 52–3, 57
Germany 48, 88, 91–2, 96, 127–8, 136–7
Gifkins, J. 63
Giroux, H. 87, 96
Gleichschaltung 92
globalisation 27, 31
Gocek, F.M. 88
González, F. 151
governance 109, 117, 128
governments 10–11, 48, 60, 64–5, 70, 168; and
 Basque case 148–9, 151–8; and end of
 terrorism 143; and Nozick 128, 132; and Turkey
 79–87, 90–1, 93–4; and UK 101–5, 107, 118–19
Grand National Assembly of Turkey (TBMM) 86
Gregorian calendar 10
Grioux, H.A. 87
Grossman, M. 14
Groupe international de travail (GIT) 88–9
Guantánamo Bay 49, 52
Gülen Movement (GM) 94–5
Gümüşcü, S. 81
Gunning, J. 30–2
Gurr, T. 26

habitus 8, 11, 13, 16, 19
Hamas 66
Harari, Y.N. 64
Hardt, M. 156
Harel-Shalev, A. 2, 57–77
Hauerwas, S. 167
Heath-Kelly, C. 1–6, 101–23, 137
hegemony 8, 10–11, 15, 19–20, 26, 40, 59, 63, 67,
 80–1, 94
hermeneutics 24, 26, 33–43
Hidek, M. 14
Hijjra 10
Hispanics 45
historians 35
historical materialism 3
historical narrative 34–6, 38–9
historiography 10, 35
Hoffman, B. 10
Holland, J. 7, 9, 12
Hollywood 47
Holmes, R. 166
Home Office 101, 104, 109, 111–14, 118
homeland 45–6, 48–53, 147
homosexuality 44–56
Horkheimer, M. 29
Howes, D. 162–4, 166
Hozat, B. 91
human rights 13–14, 44, 59–60, 79, 83–5, 149;
 and non-violence 161, 163; and Nozick 125–6,
 128–9; and Turkey 93, 95

Human Rights Foundation of Turkey 84
Human Rights Watch 84, 91
Hume, D. 25–6, 28, 33–5, 39
Huntingdon, S. 45, 47, 52
Hutchings, K. 164

Ibarretxe, J.J. 149
identity 45, 57, 67, 83, 90, 110, 112, 164–5
ideology 47, 88, 101, 104, 108–9, 117
Ignatieff, M. 129–30
imagination 101–23, 137, 168, 170
Imperial War Museum 111
imperialism 59
Imtoual, A. 110
India 12, 19, 168
individual anarchism 126
individual rights 124–7, 129–32, 135–8
Indonesia 151
inequality 27–8, 71–2
initiation rites 64
Insel, A. 87
instrumentalism/instrumentalisation 25, 80–2,
 151, 154, 164–5
insurgency 16, 26, 117–18, 162
intellectual role 85–94, 96
intelligence/intelligence services 10, 15, 67–8,
 84, 102, 110, 127, 130, 143, 170
interdisciplinarity 38
internalisation 8–9, 11, 13–16, 19, 67
international community 144, 151–2, 155–9
International Contact Group 152
International Relations (IR) 2, 4, 8, 10, 15–16,
 25–6; and causal analysis 30, 33–5, 38–9; and
 non-violence 162, 170; and Nozick 129; and
 state violence 57–9, 68; and terrorist figures
 44–56
International Studies Association Annual
 Conventions 13
International Verification Commission 155
International Working Group on Academic
 Liberty and Freedom of Research in Turkey 88
interpretation 24–43
interventions 39, 85, 94, 101–16, 118–19, 133,
 145, 159
Iran 10, 68
Iraq 15–16, 163, 170
Irish Republic 151–2, 156
Irish Republican Army (IRA) 104, 107, 147
ISIS 44
Islam 8, 46–7, 49–51, 53, 103–5, 110
Islamaphobia 103, 114
Islamic State (IS) 16, 127, 163, 169–70
Islamism 12, 127–8
Israel 2–3, 58, 61–4, 66, 68–70, 72, 86, 169
Israel Defense Forces (IDF) 58, 63

Jaap, D.W. 110
Jackson, D. 60–1, 65, 70
Jackson, R. 1–7, 9, 12, 59, 161–73

INDEX

Jarvis, L. 1–7, 9, 12
jihad 12, 46, 50–1, 113
Jones, S.G. 142–3
Joseph, J. 32
Journal of Narrative Politics 16
journalists 81, 83, 85–6, 91–2, 94, 142–3
judgement 24–43
judiciary 60, 79–82, 93–4, 107, 145, 149, 154, 157
just war theory 125, 129, 136–7
justice 102, 107, 124–5, 128–41, 157–8, 166, 170
Justice and Development Party (AKP) 80–4, 88, 91, 93–4

Kant, I. 165
Kaya, M. 92
Kemalists 94
Kerrigan, D. 87
Klausen, J. 110
knowledge 124, 132–41
Kocaeli University 91
Korean War 163
Kosovo 17
Küçük, Y. 86
Kurdistan Workers' Party (PKK) 79, 82–4, 89–92, 95
Kurds 78–9, 82–4, 86–90, 93–5
Kurki, M. 33–4

LAB 145
labelling 1, 12, 29–30, 32, 90, 166
Laegreid, P. 12
Latin America 45, 80
law enforcement 60, 109
Lawton, K. 17
lawyers 149, 152, 158
leadership 48, 66, 81–2, 84, 91–2, 94; and Basque case 144, 148–9, 152, 155, 158; and end of terrorism 146–7; and non-violence 163; and Nozick 129; and UK 111
Lebanon 163
Leese, M. 124–41
legislation 1, 11, 14–15, 81, 83, 92, 113, 128
legitimacy/legitimisation 3, 9, 11, 37, 50, 61, 81, 85, 92, 94, 110, 126, 129–31, 133–7
liberal democracy 81, 87; and Basque case 156; and non-violence 161, 164–6, 169; Nozick 126, 129–31, 133–7; and UK 110
libertarianism 126, 130
Libicky, M.C. 142–3
Libya 163
Lithuania 168
lived experience 8
Lobo-Guerrero, L. 116–17
local authorities 104–5, 108–9, 111–14, 116, 118, 123
Locke, J. 131
Lokarri 152
London bombings 102, 104, 108, 117

López Adán, E. 142
Lund University 89
Lyon, D. 134

Mac Ginty, R. 12
McCulloch, J. 102
Macedonia 17
McGowan, W. 14
MacKenzie, M.H. 69
MacKinnon, C. 71
Madrid bombings 148
mafia 91
Maizière, T. de 128
Major Oreja, J. 155, 158
mancraft 44–6, 49, 53
Mandela, N. 152
Manifesto of the 121 85, 90
Maoz-Shai, Y. 61
market forces 131
Marmara University 89
martial law 86
Martial Law Command 86
martyrdom 147
Mayer, S. 128
Mazrui, A. 10
Mead, M. 45, 52
Meadowcroft, J. 126
means-ends consistency 166, 170
media 27, 81–2, 86, 90, 93–4, 96, 103, 108, 114, 145, 149–50, 152–3, 156–7
mediation industry 152–3, 156, 158–9
memory studies 2, 4, 20
Mexico 45
Michigan University 85
Middle East 9–10, 68, 163
Middle East Association's Academic Freedom Award 92
Migdal, J.S. 60
migrants 16, 44–6, 52–3
militants 104, 117, 143, 145, 147, 151, 157
militarisation 69–72, 165
militarism 60–1, 68, 71
military 12, 15, 70, 79, 83, 85–6; and Basque case 148, 150–1, 157–9; and end of terrorism 143–6; and non-violence 163, 167–70; and Nozick 126, 129; and state violence 59–68; and Turkey 88, 91, 94
military-industrial complex 15, 170
Milton-Edwards, B. 12
minimal state 126, 130–2, 138
mistakes 128, 153, 163, 166
Mitchell, G. 155
Mitchell principles 146
moral panics 1, 14
morality 1, 9, 14, 36–7, 39, 49; and Basque case 157; and non-violence 166; and Nozick 124–5, 127–8, 135–8; and side constraints 130–2
multiculturalism 110
Mumcu, U. 86

INDEX

Mungan, E. 92
Murphy, K. 14
Murua, I. 142–60
Muslims 10, 12, 14–15, 19, 48, 52, 103–5, 108, 110, 112–14

National Book Award 126
National Health Service (NHS) 102, 115–16, 118
National Intelligence Agency (MIT) 84
National Security Council (MGK) 86
nationalism 18, 51–3, 82–4, 94, 108, 147, 149–50, 153, 155, 157
nationality 3
Nazis 92
negotiation 7–9, 11, 13–16, 19, 30, 79; and Basque case 143–7, 149, 151–2, 156–7; and end of terrorism 143–7; and non-violence 168; and Turkey 83–4, 86, 89, 95
Negri, A. 156
Nehring, D. 87
Nelson Mandela Foundation 152
neoliberalism 47–8, 51, 87, 96
Nesin, A. 86
network states 156
neutrality 85
New York City 8, 18
Nobel Prize 152
non-governmental organisations (NGOs) 89
non-state actors 16, 30, 162, 168
non-violence 9, 11, 161–73
normalcy 125, 130, 137–8, 152, 156, 164
normativity 50–1, 53, 60, 67, 71–2, 87, 125, 161, 164, 166
North 1, 3, 32, 46, 48–9, 51–2
North America 4, 88
Northern Ireland 11, 146, 151–2, 156–7, 169
Norway 151, 158
Nozick, R. 124–41

Observations and Requests about the State of Democracy in Turkey 86
Occupied Territories 61, 63–4
Office of the Public Prosecutor 87
Office for Security and Counterterrorism (OSCT) 102, 105, 112
Office of the United Nations High Commissioner for Human Rights (OHCHR) 79, 84
Öktem, K. 81
ontology 4, 26, 32–4, 52–3, 125
Oran, B. 87, 96
Oriola, T. 12, 14
Ortbals, C.D. 64
orthodox terrorism studies (OTS) 2, 4, 24–30, 32, 35–40, 94
Otegi, A. 144, 148–51
Ottoman Empire 83, 87
Ozbank, M. 92
Özturk, A.E. 78–100
Özür Diliyorum campaign 87

pacifism 71, 129, 162–7, 170
Pakistan 12, 15, 163
Palestinians 64, 66–7, 69, 151
Palm Prize 92
Pape, R. 27
patriarchy 49, 59–60, 63–4, 67, 71
Patriotic Revolutionary Youth Movement (YDG-H) 79, 84
patriotism 9, 18, 53
Peace Brigades International 168
peace processes 80–4, 86–7, 89, 94–5, 143–4, 146–8, 152, 154–8, 162, 167–9
Peace Studies 57
performativities 53, 110, 164
personal narratives 8, 13, 15–16, 18–19
Peterson, V. 45
petitions 78–80, 85–93, 95
Pew Research Centre 20
phenomenology 36
philosophy 2, 25, 28, 32–4, 39, 125–6, 130–1, 136–7, 168
pluralism/plurality 2–4, 26, 31–2, 34, 38, 130, 168
police/policing 61, 79–80, 86, 90–1, 93, 103; and Basque case 149–50, 157–9; community policing 102, 104, 109–11, 170; and end of terrorism 143, 145; and non-violence 168, 170; and Nozick 124–5, 127–8; and UK 107, 113, 116, 118
policy-makers 2, 9, 11, 13, 64, 69; and non-violence 164, 166, 169; and Nozick 134, 137; and Turkey 78–100; and UK 105, 108, 110
political philosophy 2, 126, 130–1, 168
political science 66
Political Studies Association (PSA) 13
political theory 162
political violence 19, 24–7, 30–2, 35–7, 101, 151; and non-violence 162–3, 165–70; and state violence 57–77
politicians 65–6, 81, 83, 86, 91–2, 94–5, 128, 158
Poloni-Staudinger, L. 64
polygamy 49–50
Porpora, D.V. 34
positionality 65, 67
positivism 28, 32, 34, 36, 39
post-colonialism 3, 47, 53
post-modernism 32, 34
post-positivism 33, 38–9
post-traumatic stress disorder (PTSD) 64
poverty 27–8, 31, 107
power 9–11, 81–3, 85, 87–8, 102, 110; and Basque case 150–1, 155–6, 158; and end of terrorism 145; and non-violence 162–5, 168; and Nozick 130–2; power relations 30, 66; and state violence 58–77
pragmatism 146, 161–2, 165, 167
praxis 4, 70, 72, 165
pre-criminal space 101–23
pre-emption 102–3, 105–6, 112

INDEX

predictive turn 102
Prevent Duty 103–4, 112–18
Prevent Pathfinder Fund 104–5, 108–9, 112–13, 123
Prevent Pathfinder Programme 102, 104
Prevent Review 102, 105, 112, 118
Prevent Strategy 101–23
Prevent Training and Competencies Framework 102
Prevent Workshops 114
prevention/preventive custody 124–8, 131–41, 158
prisoners of war 129
prisoners/prisons 79, 86, 92, 103, 107, 110–11, 134, 145, 148–50, 155, 157–8
private wrongs 133
privilege 31, 51, 59, 64, 86, 110, 116
probability science 107, 116, 118, 134
professional status 3, 13–16, 19, 27
profiling 103, 112, 115–16, 118, 134
profit 65, 170
propaganda 79, 83, 85, 88–92, 112
protest movements 2, 30, 59, 92, 108, 162
prudence 125, 129
psychoanalysis 50
psychology 26–7, 34, 49, 57, 96, 112, 131, 164, 167
Puar, J. 49–50
public opinion 10
public wrongs 133
purges 80, 92, 94–6

al-Qaeda 10, 16, 44–8, 50–3, 163, 169
Queer International Relations 44–5
queer studies 2, 44–5, 51–2

race 44, 59, 108, 112, 118
racialisation 44, 47, 49, 111–12
racism 44, 49, 51, 59, 126
radicalisation 8, 27, 46, 88, 101–23, 170
Ragazzi, F. 110, 113
Rai, A. 49–50
Rajoy, M. 149, 157
Rapoport, D. 26
rationalism 28
Rawls, J. 126
realism 125, 129, 137, 168
recidivism 107
rectors 79, 93, 95
reflexivity 2, 4, 16–19, 29–30, 36–7, 39; and end of terrorism 145; and non-violence 162, 169; and Nozick 128, 130, 137–8; and state violence 59, 69–73
refugees 16
rehabilitation 101, 103, 106–7, 110–11, 113, 116
relativism 38
religion 10, 27, 31, 46–7, 50, 60, 83, 103, 111
rendition 163
repression 2–3, 19, 89, 143, 145, 154, 159, 162, 164, 167

reproductivity 51–3, 59
Research Information and Communications Unit (RICU) 112–13
resilience 104, 107, 109, 112, 118
resistance/resistance studies 2, 59, 62–3, 66, 69, 71; and Basque case 143, 150–2; and end of terrorism 145; and non-violence 163, 167–70; and Turkey 82–3, 95–6; and UK 109
Resolution 1373 11
responsibilisation 107, 114
returnees 16
Richardson, L. 27–8
risk/risk assessment 3–4, 15–16, 19, 46, 48–9, 51–2; and Basque case 155; and causal analysis 25–7, 30, 32; and Nozick 127, 133–5, 137–8; and state violence 69; and UK 101–23
Rogers, P. 107
Ron, J. 61
Rowlandson, W. 8
Rubalcaba, A.P. 148–9, 152, 155, 157–8
Rule of Law Index 82
Rumsfeld, D. 130, 144
Russia 80
Rwanda 11
Rykkya, L. 12

Sabir, R. 112
Sageman, M. 108, 119
Saratxo, M. 142
Sartre, J.-P. 85
Sato, M. 10
Saudi Arabia 10, 103, 110
Schalk, D.L. 85
Schecter, D. 126
Scholar Rescue Fund 96
Scholars at Risk 96
securitisation 46, 80, 102–3, 109, 113–14, 117, 165
Security Council 11
security studies 4, 8, 10, 13–16, 18–19, 53, 57–77, 162, 170
Segi 145
separatism 82
September 11 2001 9–10, 12, 15–20, 32, 107, *see also* 9/11
sexism 59, 65
sexual barbarism 45–6, 49, 51–2
sexual harassment 61–2, 71
sexualised organisations 44, 46, 53
sexuality 44–5, 49
Sikhs 52
Sinn Fein 151
Sjoberg, L. 64
Sluka, J. 13
social construction 2, 10, 26, 32, 37, 114, 164–7
social media 27, 82, 90, 93, 95, 124
social movements 59, 96
social relations 14, 30, 32, 35–6, 39, 50

social sciences 12, 28, 30, 37, 39
social work 57, 116
socialisation 108
socialism 145, 147–50, 154–5, 157–8
sociology 91
solidarity 79, 88, 92–3, 96
Somalia 163, 167
Sortu 153
South 3, 32, 46–7, 49
South Africa 86, 152
South America 156
sovereignty 8–11, 44, 48, 52–3, 152, 155–6
Soviet Union 168
Sozeri, E.K. 79
Spain 144–5, 147–58, 169
Spalek, B. 110
Spanish Civil War 157
sponsorship 27
Sri Lanka 82, 151, 168
Stanford University 125
state terrorism 2–3, 13, 27, 167–8
state violence 13–16, 18, 29, 57–100, 162, 167, 170
statecraft 44–6, 49, 53
states of emergency 78, 83–4, 94–6
statistical analysis 11–13, 102–9, 112, 114–19, 136
Stellenbosch '85 Discussion Group 86
Stellenbosch University 86
Stephan, M. 167
Stephenson, C. 92–3
Sternberg, M. 7, 9, 11
stigmatisation 79, 90–1, 93, 95, 103, 105
Stoics 16–19
Sudan 168
Suganami, H. 35–8
surveillance 4, 14, 93, 103–5, 109–10, 112–18, 124–5, 127–8, 134, 136–7, 161
Sweden 89
Switzerland 88
symbolism 9–10, 17, 53, 149, 151
symptomatology 106, 108–9, 115–16
Syria 163, 167, 170

taboos 145–7, 151
Taliban 48
Tamil Tigers 82, 168
targeting 89–92, 105–7, 112, 118
Tatham, S. 112
temporality 7–20, 47–8, 50–1, 106, 129, 145, 161
Terreblanche, S. 86
terrorism 1–6; and 9/11 narrative 7–23; and Academics for Peace 78–100; and Basque case 142–60; and causal analysis 24–43; definitions of 8, 27, 29–30, 37, 80, 83, 92, 102, 114, 127, 143; end of terrorism 2, 142–60; mono-causal explanations of 31–2; new terrorism 27; and non-violence 161–73; and Nozick 124–41; and radicalisation risk 101–23;

and reproducing narrative 11–16; and state violence 57–77; terrorism discourse 2, 36, 39; terrorism studies 8, 10, 13–15, 18–19, 24–5, 29, 33, 36, 38–9, 108, 162; terrorist figures 44–56, 62; terrorist propaganda 79, 83, 85, 88–92
theology 104, 110
A Theory of Justice 126
Thomas, P. 108
thought crimes 86
Tilly, C. 26
Toros, H. 1–23, 30, 32, 44, 65
torture 3, 84–6, 129, 145, 149, 157, 161–3, 166, 170
totalitarianism 92, 95
transformation 1, 13–14, 16, 19, 47, 52; and Basque case 143–5, 147, 150–1, 154, 156; and causal analysis 25, 37–8; and non-violence 165, 167; and Nozick 134, 137; and state violence 61, 70; and Turkey 81; and UK 115
trauma studies 58–77
treason 79, 85
triggers 28
trolls 93
Trump, D. 20
Truth and Reconciliation Commission 152
Tunisia 127–8, 137
Turkey 18, 78–100

Uludağ University 91
unilateralism 144–5, 148–51, 153–7, 159, 164
United Kingdom (UK) 10–11, 48, 86, 101–23, 151, 156, 168
United Nations (UN) 11, 79, 92, 155, 168
United States (US) 8–11, 15, 17–19, 45, 48, 50, 85, 96, 102–3, 106, 125–6, 156
universalisation 10–11, 15, 46, 49, 88, 126
utilitarianism 125, 131–2, 135–6, 138

Valls, M. 10
Van Dijk, J.J.M. 110
Van Milders, L. 24–43
Van Yüzüncü Yıl University 91
Vérité-Liberté 85
Vietnam War 85, 126, 163
Vinthagen, S. 164
violence 2–3, 7–9, 11, 13–15, 19–20, 161–73; alternatives to violence 165, 167–70; and Basque case 142, 147, 149, 151–5, 157–9; cycles of violence 163–4, 168; and end of terrorism 143, 146; escalation of violence 13, 164, 166, 168–9; failure of violence 162–3, 165, 167; and Nozick 131, 133; and queer IR 47, 49, 51–2; state violence 57–77
voice 58–9, 62–5, 70–1
vulnerable people 102–4, 109, 111–15, 117–18

Waldron, J. 129–30
Wall Street Journal 17

INDEX

Wallace, M. 166
war on terror 1, 3, 7, 9, 12, 15–18; and Basque
case 148; and causal analysis 27; and end of
terrorism 144; and non-violence 161, 163,
165–7, 169–70; and Nozick 129, 134; and
queer IR 48, 50, 52; and UK 102, 113
warfare 57–77, 85, 125, 129, 131, 136–8; and
Basque case 158; and end of terrorism 2, 104,
117, 143–5, 147, 151, 157; and non-violence
161–2, 164, 170; war veterans 61, 63–8, 70–1
watersheds 9
weapons of reason 13–14
Weber, C. 44–56
Weber, M. 169
Weinberg, L. 142–3
West 3, 8, 10, 12, 14–16, 27, 44–53, 80, 93, 127,
161, 170
West Bank 61, 63–4, 67–8
Western Europe 113
whites 46–7, 49–50, 105

Whitfield, T. 142–3, 151
Wibben, A.T.R. 72
Wilkinson, P. 10
Wilson, D. 102
Wolff, R.P. 126, 132
women 2, 57–77, 84, 89, 113
World Justice Project 82
World Trade Center 17
World War II 52
WRAP 114

Yemen 163
Yesilada, B. 81
Youngs, G. 12

Zabaleta, P. 151
Zabalo, J. 142
Zapatero, J.L. 144, 148–9, 153–4, 156–8
Zeyfuss, M. 8–9, 13, 19
Zulaika, J. 142–60